Aspects of Evan

The Last
Viscount Tredegar

ISBN 10 1-905914-15-6
ISBN 13 978-1-905914-15-9

Published by
William P. Cross
Book Midden Publishing
58 Sutton Road
Newport
Gwent
NP19 7JF
United Kingdom

Evan Frederic Morgan
1893-1949
The Last Viscount Tredegar

Evan Morgan
" poet, painter, musician, aristocrat and millionaire…"

Aspects of Evan

The Last
Viscount Tredegar

With a transcript of his Court Martial
for offences against the
Official Secrets Acts

Aspects of Evan
A personal glance at Evan Morgan, the last Viscount Tredegar of Tredegar House

by William Cross, FSA Scot

Evan Tredegar [the last descendant of soldiers, great land-owners, and industrial magnates who built up the family fortunes on the wealth of coal that lay beneath the soil [1]]..... looked like a Prince of the Renaissance, wore huge rings and dressed in picturesque flowing capes and coloured waistcoats. [2]

Evan: An Eccentric and a Fantasist

Evan Morgan was one of the *Bright Young People.*

In the years between the two world wars of the last century he rejoiced in being a part of that irreverent faction of well-off, immoral pleasure seekers who sought unlimited thrills, with little care for the consequences of their own actions.

Stephen Fry's film *Bright Young Things*[3] captures the high spirits and high jinxes of the toffs, like Evan, with nothing better to do with their lives than to indulge themselves and each other.

Evan is seen by one historian as just an *"onlooker"* [4], but he cherished being dubbed by another scribe *"a leader and inspiration of the Bright Young People."* [5] He was always on *"bowing terms"* [6]with all the *"fatuous, smirking male-flowers"* [7] of that *"gin-soaked, jazz-syncopated, frivolous time."* [8]

Evan surely remains one of *the* fabulous aristocratic eccentrics of that bygone age of the hedonistic 1920s and 1930s, when he was best known as the Hon. Evan Morgan or Evan Tredegar.

His own creation, he was a seemingly unstoppable fantasist whose antics are captured in anecdotes, references and footnotes in a galaxy of memoirs and diaries of his often more acclaimed and better achieved contemporaries.

But for anyone who desires a novel-size glimpse of the incomparable Evan, he is caricatured in several books, for instance in comical terms as Ivor Lombard in Aldous Huxley's *Crome Yellow* and more extraordinarily and farcically as the Hon. Eddy Monteith in Ronald Firbank's biting satire *The Flower Beneath the Foot.* [9]

For the first forty-one years of his life Evan was an heir in waiting. From 1934, he became the second Viscount, the Fourth Baron Tredegar, a peer and baronet of the realm of the United Kingdom. A descendant of an ancient, wealthy Welsh family, who claim their ancestry from 11th century warlords. [10]

The writer Aldous Huxley describes Evan in his diaries as a *" poet, painter, musician, aristocrat and millionaire..."* [11] The author of the futurist novel *Brave New World* adds in greater glory that his friend Evan was nothing less than *" the unique fairy prince of modern life".* [12] . A more elaborate depiction of the Evan is in a profile defining *"the peer who is everything."* [13] and this amazing CV takes in Evan's triumphs as *" a Knight of Malta; former Welsh Guards officer; fellow of the Royal Society of Literature; world authority on the poet John Donne;*

gourmet; collector of objet d'arts; menagerie owner; Conservative Parliamentary candidate; member of the Rhododendron Society; yachtsman; life governor of three hospitals; landlord of most of Bow and Bromley; housing and unemployment expert; Royalist; .....actor; bird tamer; coal magnate; musician and traveller...." [14]

Although Evan is only ever recalled to life nowadays by the National Trust guides during public tours of the old Morgan homesteading of Tredegar House, Newport, South Wales[15], at one time *everyone* in London and Paris' upper crust Society between the world wars, in swanky literary circles across continents knew or knew of the Hon. Evan Morgan.

Ogling dowagers indulged him, everyone had an opinion about him and his latest fads and daring exploits. Others mocked him, for instance Lady Ettie Desborough, the celebrated hostess thought him *"quite mad"* [16] : whilst Bloomsbury's more *femme fatale* Virginia Woolf describes him, somewhat dismissively as *"so foolish that it didn't seem to matter"*. [17]

Incurably vain Evan was loved by men and by woman – but he never found any real love or true happiness with either, his misfortune, said another friend, the literary critic Alan Pryce-Jones, *"was to have been born with too much money, too little health and no practical sense at all..."*[18]

Evan's death, in 1949, from acute broncho pneumonia and cancer of the pancreas[19] at the age of just 55, at Honeywood House, near Dorking, in Surrey, brought his colourful, scandalous but altogether unaccomplished life to a sad and bitter end.

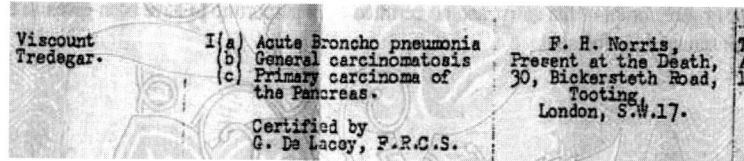

9

Evan's Two Wives - Lois Sturt (left) and Princess Olga

Evan was twice married, each time to a beautiful woman. His first matrimonial excursion was in 1928 to the film and stage actress Hon. Lois Sturt, [20] who was *"well known at the bohemian end of the beau monde"* [21] This was followed later by marriage to a Russian Princess, Olga Dolgorouky, who as a child had escaped the Bolsheviks, in the famous dash from the Balkans in 1919 by the British warship *HMS Marlborough* which also brought the Tsar's mother into exile and safety. [22]

Although separated from Evan, when Lois died of heart failure in 1937, in Budapest, aged only 37, she remained Viscountess Tredegar. Olga married Evan when she was aged 24, in 1939, divorced him in 1943 but survived him by almost 50 years, she died in 1998. [23]

Both of Evan's wives confronted in different ways the fact that he was a homosexual, a situation for actresses and Princesses before them who had still often gone on to produce the family heir!

But Evan died childless and Tredegar House with its elegant contents were sold off in 1951 and later years. [24] In her last decades Princess Olga lived quietly in retirement on the Island of Guernsey, Channel Isles. She was a god-send to the staff of Tredegar House when in 1973 Newport Council took up ownership of the building from St Joseph's Roman Catholic Convent School.

During the late 1970s the Princess's personal testimony was sought by the House's Curators David Freeman and David Beevers. Olga proved a most valuable source (with others besides who also knew Evan) in providing unique, insider knowledge. This assisted the plan to recreate the times gone by at Tredegar House, including efforts to bring back many of the family artefacts and recoup an identikit picture of the house's interiors when Olga and Evan had lived there.

Olga was immensely respectful towards Morgan history and also to Evan's memory. But she was crystal clear too about her husband's warped nature and the flaws in his character.

"I wish I could remember more of the historical facts about the family, but I was very young at the time and not, I must confess, terribly interested. Also at times my husband, who was an eccentric, used to have 'great flights of fancy' at times and I never knew what was fact or fiction!" [25]

This book and other attempts to write Evan's biography

THE LIFE STORY OF LORD TREDEGAR

THIS autumn a friend is writing the biography of Viscount Tredegar, and it is understood that in the story will be included a discussion of his poetry, and there will be a section devoted to his love of animals. Newport folk know more about Viscount Tredegar's love of animals, for many have had the opportunity of visiting the private zoo at Tredegar House. They are not so familiar with his lordship's poetry, but competent judges aver that much of it has great lyric power.

Viscount Tredegar.

Viscount Tredegar has taken Sir Geoffrey Archer's villa outside Tunis, and he will entertain a holiday party there for a few weeks.

He will shortly join the ranks of the few men who can say that their life story has been written while they are still alive.

* * * *

The original basis of this book was to deal with Evan's Court Martial in 1943 for breaches of the Official Secrets Act, but the opportunity provides a chance to add a considered review (from personal, archival, newspaper and book sources) relating to Evan Morgan.

Virtually nothing is to be found anywhere of real essence indicating the highs and lows of Evan's life from cradle to grave, despite a number of people declaring an intention (which runs over many decades) to write and publish Evan's whole life story. [26]

An early attempt to write Evan's life story

Evan does merit a full length biography particularly if it draws on previously unpublished personal memories and letters. There is an exciting prospect of such a work to come based on a large collection of Evan's letters (as well as those written by his second wife, Olga) which are held in private hands. [27]

Nonetheless, this compilation also draws on many of Evan's letters in the Tredegar House Archives and elsewhere in the public domain. [28]

Evan Outed!

Several of the *Bright Young Things* were homosexual. Generally this way of life was not safe to be widely spoken about freely, as the law of the land at that time forbid its practises. The fear of exposure almost never dampened Evan's private life, it fuelled his carefree, flamboyant life style, and his wealth and position gave him a certain insulation inside the Establishment's closet.

Among the first to actually *out* Evan, and attribute the word "*homosexual*" to him was the prolific writer and biographer, H Montgomery Hyde, in 1970. [29] A Socialist's eye was also cast by Roy Jenkins, in 2004 when he added in a personal memoir about important Welsh families and their demise that "*the last of the [Morgan] line was a homosexual aesthete more at home in an Evelyn Waugh novel than a coal owners conference..*"[30]

Evan in Bali, Indonesia: *Tuan Raja*

"*....the last paradise on earth*"[31]

Evan's frivolous, precarious existence made a lasting impact in some unexpected portholes. According to the diaries of Donald Friend, the Australian artist who spent a long period of his life on the Island of Bali, Indonesia, Evan is recalled by those that knew him there in the 1930's as *Tuan Raja*, a curious phallic symbol of sorts who did "*awful things.... liberated by wealth and motivated, oddly enough by blasphemy...[careering] about in a sea of liquor – polluting sacred springs and desecrating temples.*" [32].

This picture of excess is corroborated by references to Evan's fondness for visiting Indonesia, Thailand and North Africa where he found obliging and liberated natives. [33]

Evan romped his way from the dreary coal stained Valleys of South Wales all the way up to the Royal Palaces of Europe. The Morgan family's money and status being derived from land, coalmines, the railways and the docks, and which maintained the ample Morgan seat at Tredegar House, near Newport, South Wales, as well as it's other lesser properties, including (the now ruined) Ruperra Castle,[34]

The Tredegar heir in waiting annoyed, shocked and alarmed many of his dour, conservative minded relatives, including his father, Courtenay Morgan, the 3rd Lord Tredegar, albeit the latter often displayed his own level of hypocrisy and double standards.

The wider clans were always anxious to protect the Morgan family name and legacy, as well as their own associations. Some thought Evan's larking about was amusing, others averted their eyes in horror. Evan wanted to be liked: his antics often came down to that short, simple premise.

The Scottish writer (Sir) Compton Mackenzie[35] records Evan as among those friends who died in 1949, saying poignantly:

"….Evan Tredegar died, and with all his absurdities I miss..[ed] him sadly…." [36]

VISCOUNT TREDEGAR

A MODERN DILETTANTE
Viscount Tredegar, who died at his home near Horsham yesterday at the age of 55, was a man of many parts to whom the word *dilettante* may appropriately be applied.

Obituaries refer to Evan as *"a dilettante"* [37] This is one of the euphemisms of the period for a homosexual man,[38] a situation that had to be painfully covered up, in Britain, before the law reform of the swinging sixties. [39]

Tributes to Evan Morgan catalogue his *"life of travel and adventure"* [40], and describe him as extravagant and wasteful and by every sinew, a fantasist and escapist. It is easy to see why from such alleged deeds (or misdeeds) as:

"… slumming [it] in Jerusalem, and being a fellow guest with [actor] Charlie Chaplin at a supper given by the notorious [silent movie star] Fatty Arbuckle[41]…he was once disguised as a Moor in Algiers, and

thrown bodily out of a mosque. He took part in a pilgrimage through the Holy Land, touching at Bethlehem, Nazareth, Galilee and Lebanon and made a walking tour across France... He ....rubbed shoulders with poets and painters, supped with [opera star] Caruso, foregathered with priests and actors, Sinn Feiners and rabbis. He cherished the memory of a breathless chase by a German Submarine when as a King's Messenger he was taking a passage in a French destroyer...... " [42]

How much sustainable truth and hard core exists at heart of these feats or their importance and value to anyone else but the storyteller (invariably, this being Evan himself) remains a grain of sand in a desert wasteland. Some tales are corroborated, whilst others are almost certainly myths.

Evan's Estate

The Morgan Family Seat of Tredegar House, Newport, South Wales

A few months after Evan's death, the press reported an estate of little real value, gobbled up by death duties and unpaid taxes by the estates, in default of non-payment of these duties by several of the past Lords Tredegar. In truth there was no option left to the surviving family, that being Evan's elderly uncle Frederic, who became the Fifth Lord Tredegar, [43] but to hand things on to his respective son, Evan's cousin, John Morgan, who from 1954-1962 became the last Baron, the Sixth Lord Tredegar. He left no male heir. [44]

There was prominent newspaper coverage of Evan's last estate. As in this example:

PEER LEAVES £2,500,000. Second Viscount Tredegar, of Tredegar Park, Newport, Mon, and Honeywood House, Oakwood Hill, Dorking, Surrey, poet, author, artist, a Papal chamberlain and oblate of Buckfast Abbey left unsettled estate valued at £199.136 gross (net value nil), and settled land at £2,357.083, making a total of £2,556,221 (details of estate duty not yet available). [45]

Evan's final financial affairs

Official files in National Archives, Kew,[46] relating to Evan's final financial affairs offer an intriguing muddle worth closer inspection.

In this glimpse of Evan, space only allows a brief mention of the vital part played by the lawyers acting on behalf of the Tredegar Settled Lands to answer the Inland Revenue's large claims. Whilst at the same time (and to much merit) securing, albeit in truth to save the Morgan family's face, the *full settlement* of accounts for local Newport, London and Surrey tradesmen. This included reaching a satisfactory compromise with Evan's key annuitants, including his ex-wife, Olga.[47] The proceeds from the death of Evan's mother Katharine a few months after her son (and with it the release to Evan's estate of the residue of her original marriage settlement) also brought some relief to reducing the sums owed to the tax authorities. The last Tredegar heir, John Morgan, was consoled with enough wealth remaining intact from legacies and heirlooms to enable him to live in comfort and exile in the tax haven of Monte Carlo.

Evan's Catholic conversion and death wish

In his mid-twenties Evan converted from the family's Anglican base to the Roman Catholic faith.

One obituary says Evan *"was converted [to Roman Catholic faith] by the Archbishop of Algiers, in the First World War. [48] There was no doubt however that the seeds were sown long before when he was at Oxford. He came under the influence of many leaders in art and literature, meeting Augustus John, the great artist, [Jacob] Epstein, the sculptor Mr Hilaire Belloc and Mr G K Chesterton [both poets and literary figures]. He was received into the Roman Catholic Church in*

1919 after being demobilised from the Army and was confirmed by Cardinal Amettee,[49] Lord Bishop of Paris. "[50]

Evan's last wish was to be buried at Buckfast Abbey, Devon, whose Benedictine monks he had befriended, and in his sad last weeks whilst dying, he had requested that regular Mass be held for the repose of his soul. [51]

With his usual bravado he'd promised the residue of the proceeds of his final estate to Buckfast Abbey on account of *"my sincere attachment to the Abbot and Monks serving God and Our Lady St Mary ".* [52] Sadly the reality was that this was an empty promise, for despite the headlines of millions of pounds of worth, the Tredegar coffers were empty and the family Estate (with the exception of heirlooms and legacies) was in a state of malignant insolvency.

Evan's Requiem Mass at Buckfast Abbey

Private Cemetery : Buckfast Abbey : Today

Evan's body travelled from his mother's home of Honeywood House, Dorking in Surrey the previous Sunday evening, in April 1949. With candles lighting up the Abbey's golden altar and golden candelabra above, the solemn Requiem Mass was conducted by the parish priest, the Rev Raphael Stones, OSB.[53] The monks of the Abbey choir led the singing unaccompanied by any music.

The top of the coffin was embossed with a full-length cross, and the inscription on the name plate was " *Evan Frederic Morgan, Viscount Tredegar . Born July 13 1893, died April 27, 1949. R.I.P.*"

To the chanting of the Abbey's monks, the brothers in surplices carried the processional cross and candle bearers followed them, as the coffin was borne on a wheeled bier to the small private cemetery in the Abbey grounds, where the internment took place.

Evan Morgan's modest Catholic funeral at Buckfast Abbey with a handful of mourners and its few floral tributes was followed by a number of Memorial Services in Newport, Monmouthshire, the site of the Viscount's home seat of Tredegar House, Tredegar Park and also at Farm Street, London.

Evan's Three Executors meet at Honeywood House, Dorking

The three mourners gathered together to pronounce judgement on the contents of the mysterious black boxes, left by Evan. Two of the men were related in blood : they were cousins, and, in turn, cousins of the recently departed, Evan Frederic Morgan, the last Viscount Tredegar. The third gatherer was a Solicitor and Trustee of the Tredegar Settled Lands[54]

Honeywood House, Dorking

In a scene resembling the meeting of the three witches at the commencement of the Scottish play by Shakespeare, the hurly burley had already been done. With the funeral rites over a serious task lay before the conspirators. What had Evan left behind in the mysterious boxes in his final last home at Honeywood House, Dorking?

His last will and testament was clear enough. It stipulated:

"To such of my friends Henry Maxwell (son of W B Maxwell) and Cyril Hartman B. Lit of University College Oxford as shall be living at my death and if more than one equally between them all my books concerning myself or written by myself at present in the sitting room at Honeywood House aforesaid and all documents of a personal nature whether comprising manuscripts in my own hand or typescript together with all my personal letters and papers contained in several tins and other boxes and without imposing any binding or legal obligation on them I express my desire that they will from the information to be obtained from such books papers and documents be able to write a biography of my life." [55]

At the time neither Henry Maxwell [56] nor Hartmann (Cyril Hughes Hartmann [57]) was aware of the burden Evan had placed on them. When approached on the subject of Evan's biography in the years that followed they could only answer that they were hardly aware of Evan's wishes, albeit they knew Evan wanted *someone* to write his life story and they were unaware of the aforementioned boxes and papers. The material had certainly *not* come into their hands.

Evan proves a burden on his Executors

The decision made by Evan's Executors, Charles Alexander Carnegie, 11th Earl of Southesk,[58] Raymond Alexander Carnegie[59] and Theodore Henry Edgcome Edwards to spurious efficiency, resulted in an act of censorship. This reflected the time and era of Britain in 1949. Since Evan was a homosexual and homosexuality was outlawed by the law of the land, these three wise men had no stomach for a scandal of *any* dimension, the contents of the box and any other records must be destroyed and Evan's scandalous past erased. It was how things were done. It was fulfilled as an act of terror, Evan's life over, he must be denied martyrdom and his secrets expunged. The good name of the family must be preserved.

One, probably at worst false, at best allegorical account says that across the length and breadth of the family's outposts an edict was heard to torch everything about and written by Evan Frederic Morgan. It was even said that the funeral pyres burned in some places for hours.

Although such a reference as the latter scene is almost certainly fictitious, it represents the fear that had passed through Evan's conservative minded, royally linked family.

So many false stories have been created about Evan Morgan simply to amuse, to dramatise his actions and deeds and excuse chaos in humour and allegory, in what amounts to a sometimes wicked, selfish and sordid existence, a life of extravagance and improvidence. What redeeming legacy there is of Evan is hard to declare. He was " *a(n) accomplished exponent and a patron of art and literature'*[60], a minor poet (with a few sparks of genius), an animal lover, a witty companion and storyteller especially in great gatherings of guests (of all shades and genders and proclivities, literary, occult and stately) invited by him to Tredegar House, South Wales in the 1930s and 1940s. Evan merits this sketch to at least connect and record the many faces of this unconventional *one-off* aristocratic figure.

Let's take a look at Evan's family roots.

II

Evan's Birth, Parents and Family Roots

Evan Frederic Morgan was born into nineteenth century aristocracy, balancing lengthy and notable Welsh and Scottish antecedents. He was heir to the Morgan/ Tredegar family honours. His birth on 13 July 1893 was at No 33, Cadogan Terrace, Chelsea, London. A smart address, comprising eight bedrooms, one bathroom and five reception rooms.

The child's father was of Welsh birth, Captain Courtenay Charles Evan Morgan (1867-1934) and Evan's mother Lady Katharine Agnes Blanche Carnegie (1867-1949) was Scottish. The couple had married in Scotland at Katharine's family home of Kinnaird Castle, near Brechin in 1890. Evan was their first child, followed by a daughter, Gwyneth Ericka Morgan, a sister to Evan, two years later in 1895, she died in mysterious circumstances in 1924, aged 29. Gwyneth is the subject of *A Beautiful Nuisance: The Life and Death of the Hon.*

Gwyneth Ericka Morgan by the same authors as this present compilation. [61]

Evan's father Courtenay was a soldier, and the son of Colonel Hon. Freddie Morgan, a Welsh landowner and Tory MP and his Scottish wife, Charlotte Williamson. [62] Katharine was the daughter of Sir James Carnegie, 9th Earl of Southesk and Lady Susan Murray of Kinnaird Castle in the Highlands of Scotland. [63]

The Morgan Family Crest

The new born child was the nephew of Colonel Freddie's brother, the unmarried Godfrey Charles Morgan, the second Lord Tredegar. In 1893, Godfrey was aged 64 described as *"still the sprightliest bachelor in Monmouthshire "*. The heir to the Barony of Tredegar was firstly Evan's grandfather Freddie, then Courtenay, and ultimately Evan who inherited the family titles from 1934.

The Morgan London Town House

The Morgans had a long standing town house in London at 39, Portman Square with a domestic entourage of butler, housekeeper and servants, some of whom travelled from the family's Welsh Estates of Ruperra Castle (the home of the heir to Tredegar) and the family's main seat of Tredegar House, near the town of Newport, close to the villages of Draethen and Rudry in a triangle between Caerphilly, Newport and Cardiff.

Several Morgan men were Members of Parliament representing almost without any gap in many centuries their Brecon and Monmouthshire land, coal, docks, and railway interests. The Morgans were once dubbed *The Kings of South Wales*. [64] Evan adored repeating that he was descended from the Welsh Princes.

Hunting and country pursuits

Evan's Welsh family were typical country squires. The Morgan men spent much of their time on these lands, comprising over 40,000 acres, playing a full part in the civic proceedings, industry and land use of the adjoining towns and villages. As sporting men, they enjoyed the full range of the country pursuits of the leisurely class, especially horse riding and fox and badger hunting.

One commentator records:
"Lord Tredegar, and his brother, Colonel the Hon. FC Morgan, are constantly to be seen in the saddle ...the Principality being their favourite battleground."

The *Monmouthshire Merlin* of 1883 described Freddie as *"A Knight of the Shire, a keen sportsman, and a spirited country gentleman"*. The same paper equally praised Godfrey's reputation for supporting charitable causes.

Philanthropy was one thing, business sense, quite another. One single stretch of railway on the Tredegar Estate, known as *The Golden Mile* earned the family a considerable income from their toll of one penny per ton of coal hauled. Most Morgan men were masculine and heroic. One of Evan's father's cousins described them as follows:

"In their history there was not one melancholy Celt amongst us, not one with that brooding mysticism, as in modern times we have been taught to believe was the inherent quality of Welshmen. They were strong men, fighting men, some thinking men, but all active workers who seemed to find a delight in living." [65]

Courtenay didn't fit this manly mould of Morgan men. He was molly cuddled by his mother, Charlotte Anne Williamson (who died in 1891). In part, this unyielding care was on account of Charlotte losing her first born son who lived only a few hours. [66]

Hon. Frederick Courtenay Morgan   *Godfrey Morgan, 2nd Lord Tredegar*

Besides a younger brother, Frederic (Freddie) Courtenay had two older sisters, Blanche and Violet.[67] But this excessive mother love weakened Courtenay's father's and uncle's aspirations of him being a gallant warrior, as they had been, having both fought in the bloody Crimean War. Courtenay was not a fighting man, he was not academically gifted either, the army was the family's choice, not his own. Courtenay was often sick with nerves. He enjoyed the sea (which his uncle Godfrey abhorred on account of his harsh experiences of seasickness on his way to the Crimean). Courtenay was bullied by his father and uncle, but he hid his feelings, under a state of seemingly natural morose and knuckled into the family pattern for hunting and shooting and breeding dogs for the sake of a quiet life.

Evan was in few ways like his father, he was more outwardly foppish and on top of all else he suffered more from a very weak chest, than from the nervous dispositions that troubled his parents. Both men were riddled with bad genes. But it was inherited genes that also gave Evan an appreciation of culture and he preferred art and music and poetry, a combination that reflected the deeper passions of his Carnegie maternal grandfather, James, 9th Earl of Southesk, who had enjoyed a life of adventure in the Canadian wilderness [68] and wrote poetry.

Evan's parents' loveless marriage was an arranged affair between the Morgan and Carnegie Estate brokers and it was a business deal from the start. Katharine hated Wales. The parties soon tired of each other, and although they remained married (on paper) for the rest of their lives, they were an odd coupling. In fact they were together off and on for the first two decades but Courtenay took mistresses or allowed himself to be burdened by his female relatives. These women made Katharine sick with wrath, and this led to her retreating, for comfort, to darkened rooms and solitude, a trait she continued throughout her life. [69] But for several years she was strong enough to dedicate herself to her own pleasures, travelling and being a patron of the arts and eventually moved during the First World War, to her own house near Dorking, Surrey of Honeywood House, which Evan shared with her in his later life and in the weeks before his death. Katharine later moved to London but she only survived her son by a matter of months. [70]

Evan's father, Courtenay Morgan become Lord Tredegar in 1913. The old London town house at 39 Portman Square was put on the market to raise funds for death duties. So a new London house was taken from 1914 onwards at 45, Grosvenor Square and Katharine and Evan lived there during part of the London season.

Evan's flights of fancy began early in his approach to life, he had to think and act for himself. There was no adequate or constant male

role model in his ordinary domestic life. The small, sick, spoilt, consumptive child saw little of his father Courtenay, except if he was on leave from the army[71] and on good enough terms with his estranged wife, the bipolar Katharine Carnegie[72] to have the children for a summer holiday or a Christmas treat. Evan was affected by his father and mother's tantrums. He enjoyed pampering from a labyrinth of servants, governesses and nursemaids. His frail sister Gwyneth was poor company as she often ill or withdrawn and ultimately was sent away to a boarding school.

The Morgan children had little love or parental attention shown them, however Katharine wrote and dedicated a children's story book *The Crimson Ducks* to her two offspring. Apart from the actual process of giving birth to them this was her only concrete display of any act of motherhood.

There was some attention paid to Evan and his sister during excursions to visit relatives including their paternal grandfather Freddie, a dominating Aunt Violet and several Morgan great aunts and cousins in Wales. They also holidayed with their maternal grandparents in the Highlands of Scotland. The Morgans and the Carnegies owned large country estates, with many hundreds of tenants.

Evan's Maternal Grandparents

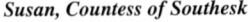

Susan, Countess of Southesk   *James Carnegie, 9th Earl of Southesk*

Evan was given a sense of all things bright and beautiful and of good worth in the classics of great literature and poetry by his mother's family, especially his maternal grandparents James Carnegie, 9th Earl of Southesk a scholar and published poet, and his dutiful, talented second wife, and Countess, Susan Murray, who grew up in Royal circles at Windsor, her mother was a Lady of the Bedchamber to Queen Victoria.

But the growing Evan rejected the life style of the country house brigade which his paternal uncle, Godfrey Morgan, Lord Tredegar, hero of the Crimean's Charge of the Light Brigade, best epitomised. Godfrey was a Master of Hounds, as was Evan's bossy parental aunt, Violet Mundy. The young Evan's attachment was of a genuine love for wild animals, and birds, and this was at odds with the family's participation in shooting and hunting of them in cruel sports, and with their leading profile amongst the local hunts folk. Landowners like the Morgans had no conscience at all over the killing of foxes and otters and birds and game. Evan abhorred the utter cruelty of such slaughter. He was known to sabotage gin traps and the like, that would maim and kill wandering animals. There was concern that Evan was just not cut out for ultimately becoming one day the Lord of the Manor.

Evan's father Courtenay had a troubled record of his own in complying with the strict obligations to the Morgan family. Courtenay was a shy, awkward figure. His father Freddie (the next brother to the bachelor Godfrey, Lord Tredegar and thus heir in waiting to the family titles) had been a veteran Member of Parliament (as many of the Morgan men) and this job was mapped out as being Courtenay's destiny too. He loathed being groomed for politics, showed little spark, but grudgingly conceded that his name go forward as the Conservative candidate for South Monmouthshire. But his heart was not in the task.

Courtenay was later swept away in politics by others around him. He displayed the same lack of rigour in his home life and role played his other duties including that of being a husband and father of two children. He was not cut out to try to win a seat in Parliament. He was humiliated in the general election of 1905 and the mantle of this was eventually passed on to a more charismatic cousin, Leolin Forestier-Walker, who did enter Parliament a few years later. [73] Courtenay had a lacklustre army career too, he preferred spending money on yachts and sailing, or generally travelling abroad, and playing golf [74] rather than meeting his family obligations.

A short burst of normality in the period to 1901-1905 witnessed the only measurable period when Courtenay and Katharine actually lived part of the time together under the same roof, at Ashford Court, Ludlow. But the record of the Butler's Book for the household maintained meticulously by the good and faithful servant (William Sayzeland [75]) shows constant attempts by Katharine to escape rather than spend any length of time in the matrimonial home. [76]

Welsh and Scottish family connections brought Evan (and Gwyneth) into contact with their cousins in Wales, England and Scotland.

Evan and Gwyneth had several older cousins on the Carnegie side, on account of their grandfather's two marriages. Katharine was a daughter from the second marriage. There were however a few cousins who became regular companions with the Morgan children on holidays and family gatherings.

Among Evan's closest male cousins on his father's side were the only sons of Blanche and Violet [77] but it was Raymond Rodakowski, a good looking, sporty, gung-ho type, on his mother's side whom Evan absolutely adored. Upon Rodakowski's death in 1916 (he was an officer in the Irish Guards[78]) Evan wrote a moving dedication entitled *Vale*. [79] Raymond's sister, Susan (known as Suki) was also a closely bonded, loving relative of both Evan and Gwyneth.[80]

III

Evan's Education and Coming of Age

Schooldays : Brighton

In 1902 the nine-year-old Hon. Evan Morgan was chosen as a train bearer to the Prince of Wales (later King George V) on the occasion of the Prince laying the foundation stone of the University College, Cardiff, South Wales.

Rich children of aristocratic families were usually sent away to boarding schools. In the choice of Courtenay's formal schooling – it was a harsh regime from the word go. He first attended at William Lee's School in Brighton. That school was famed for turning out scholarship winners and for breaking boys into the great English public schools. Courtenay later went to Eton.

In the choice of schooling for Evan, his health and being regularly abroad prevented him being enrolled for indeterminate terms at either a preparatory or public School.   He did attend a boarding school in Brighton where an incident is recorded of him being the subject of a attempted kidnap by two women, who intended to smuggle him to France – and seek ransom money for his safe return. The kidnap attempt was aborted by Katharine who found a letter from Evan referring to him being met by his "aunts" as being completely untrue – and the perpetrators of the crime were thus outdone. [81]

Evan then went on to Eton College. Here he was separated from his beloved sister- which was especially hard for Gwyneth – they had shared much together and were close at times. They only had each other for comfort, their parents were remote, and family life dysfunctional. As she was a girl – Gwyneth's schooling was far less important but she was educated at several good girls schools with other daughters of Society figures.

Evan at Eton College 1907-10

Photograph from Acroflita, Ltd.

ETON, THE MOST FAMOUS OF THE ANCIENT PUBLIC SCHOOLS OF ENGLAND

Evan Morgan's time at Eton College is sparsely recorded in the school's archives. He was not academically brilliant nor shone at sports or games. Evan appears buried beneath the Eton's files with a curious anonymity as "E.F.Morgan".

He was enrolled at Eton from the summer term of 1907 until the Lent leavings of 1910. He was in the house of an M.D.Hill. [82] His tutor was a Robert Booker. [83] Little else is clear about Evan's time at Eton

27

which was constantly interrupted by bouts of ill health. These resulted in his mother taking him abroad to seek much better climes in order to assist her son's erratic breathing. No photographs of Evan are held in the collections at Eton College . [84]

Evan's masters, Messrs Hill and Booker (who were both Oxford University men) may have had no more than a passing impact on the Tredegar heir. But perhaps Hill developed the lonely boy's interest in exotic birds and animals, which was later to form such a part of one of Evan's side shows at Tredegar Park. Here he had constructed an aviary and animal compound of out of the ordinary pets of kangaroos, including a boxing kangaroo named Somerset, four macaws, one of whom was named Peter and the most famous of all, Blue Boy (whom Evan taught to swear and appear unexpectedly out of the flies in his trousers) and a honey bear called Alice.

Perhaps the Eton schoolmasters generated a preference for Evan's eventual choice of study at Oxford University. Christ Church, Oxford. This college had seen other Morgan men amongst its number from previous generations. But like his great grandfather, Charles Morgan Robinson Morgan, the first Lord Tredegar, Evan left Oxford without taking a degree. The latter prompted one of Evan's University friends to comment years later *"I do not know what , if anything, Evan was supposed to be reading at Oxford. I never saw the slightest evidence of work in his rooms, and he did not take a degree. I don't suppose he ever had the slightest intention of doing so."*[85]

Evan the Painter and Exhibitor in the Paris Salon

The *Western Mail,* one of the local newspapers serving South Wales makes a few references to the young Evan. He attended his grandfather Freddie's funeral in 1909 and was reminded of the importance of his great uncle Godfrey's heavenly departure in 1913, as he was one of the chief mourners. He merits a description at the time of the latter.

"The young [Tredegar] heir Master Evan as he has been familiarly known is tall like his father (who stands over 6 ft). He and his mother Lady Katharine Morgan have wintered abroad as Master Evan's strength has not fully matured. The Young heir has developed considerable artistic ability...."

One of Evan's comforts whilst recuperating from bouts of chest and lung infections was art, he much enjoyed sketching and painting. In 1913 he achieved the accolade of having two of his paintings exhibited in the influential portal of the Paris Salon. His two pictures were *La Dame aux Camellias* and *Thamar*.[86]

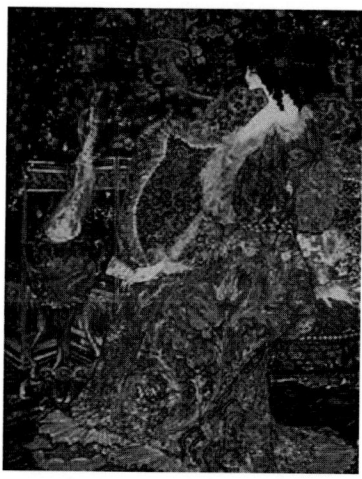

A painting by Evan Morgan (private collection)

Shadows Behind Evan's Coming Of Age in 1914

As the Tredegar heir, Evan was excited at the prospect of his coming of age.[87] He was due to spend his 21st birthday in London, amidst grand celebrations but this merriment was scuttled after a terrible boating tragedy on the Thames in early July, ending in the death of his 25-year- old baronet friend, Sir Denis Anson [88] after a silly prank went wrong. As a result, a sombre mood ripped through Evan's social crowd, dimming festivities and dampening party spirits. [89] On top of which was the ever growing prospect of a world war. Evan escaped to Nice for livelier fare, where he fell into the company of the Nina Hamnett, (later dubbed the Queen of Bohemia) who at the time was studying art in Paris. [90]

On 13 July 1914, Evan did celebrate his coming of age of 21 at Tredegar House, with generous tokens of esteem shown by his family and the Estate tenants. Next day he joined his father on board the steam yacht *Liberty* (which later in 1914 became a hospital ship[91]) to collect Prince Arthur of Connaught[92] at the port of Avonmouth on the Bristol Channel. They sailed the short distance to Newport where the Prince opened the new lock of the Alexandra Dock, followed by speeches at a very grand luncheon.[93]

Evan as a young man : aspiring poet and Tredegar heir

Evan's meetings with Royalty were to be a fairly regular occurrence, especially after his mother's (half) nephew Charles Carnegie (the heir to the Southesk Earldom) married Princess Maud Duff a granddaughter of King Edward VII. Prince Arthur of Connaught was already married to Maud's elder sister, Princess Alexandra. It was later said that Evan was a particular favourite of Queen Mary of Teck (wife of George V). When Evan holidayed to Scotland in 1931, he prized having a photograph taken with Queen Mary, he was always proud to show off to visitors *"his bedside table [was] littered with photographs of royalty in silver frames* [94]*."*

Evan and the Queen shared an incurable passion for collecting jade. [95] He also had an impressive Chinese collection of Ming porcelain. [96] It seems *"Evan was close friends with the Chinese Ambassador (and wife) and on more than one occasion threw a 'Chinese-style' party for them at [his London home at] 13 South Audley Street."* [97]

A witness to Evan's collecting habit in his early years at Oxford University records: *" One arrived in a typically Evanish apartment, overcrowded with objects d'art, mostly Chinese - he had a wonderful collection of early jade - ....they were his personal property, he said, unlike the heirlooms at Tredegar; they were part of him, and he proposed to live and die with them..."* [98]

Evan (back row, far right) with Queen Mary and Members of the Carnegie Family 1931

Whilst Evan was lying low, away from the gathering war storms in London, he had fulfilled his part in some Morgan obligations in Newport, but his father, Courtenay had no success in persuading Evan to move to his rightful abode in Wales. As heir to the Barony of Tredegar - by tradition - he should have been residing at Ruperra Castle. Despite changes to improve its facilities, Evan was content, whilst planning to be an undergraduate to live off and on at Oxford. The new town house in London at 45 Grosvenor Square served also for Gwyneth's demanding year ahead as a debutante. [99]

IV

Evan's Oxford Days

As war threatened every family and the fibre of the nation Evan went up to Christ Church Oxford in October 1914, where his tutor was John Murray. At Oxford Evan was one of the founders of the Oxford Celtic Society. He became that Society's vice-president.

Location of Evan's Rooms at Christ Church, Oxford,
Ground Floor of Canterbury

Evan - as Seen By Cyril Hughes Hartmann at Oxford

Cyril Hughes Hartmann (who was willed by Evan to write his biography from the contents of the mysterious black box left behind at Honeywood House) has preserved a marvellously affectionate portrait of Evan. It ranges from the time he first met him (at Oxford) and runs through the years until his death.[100] Hartmann was a boarder and friend at Charterhouse School with Evan's cousin, Raymond Rosakowski. They were all studying at Oxford together. In the 1920s Hartmann also became a very active correspondent with Evan's Aunt Nellie (his mother's sister) Lady Helena Carnegie.[101] We have Hartmann to thank in his Memoirs for the pleasure of seeing a more honest and sincere Evan, one who did not have to show-off the whole time and always take the lead. Hartmann recalls several placid and uneventful months they spent together in Spain (when he was doing some research work on Spanish sea power). Overriding all this was the bond of love they shared for Raymond Rodakowski.

From Hartmann's unique piece we find a description of Evan's rooms at Oxford:

" the walls were hung with a sort of mosaic of silks, velvets, brocades, and embroideries, mostly Persian, Russian, and Chinese, and this patchwork was overlaid with countless pictures, many of them original Beardsley drawings and Beardsley paintings by Evan himself [including one of his exhibition pieces in Paris] " La Dame aux Camellias". [102]

How Evan Saw Himself in Letters to Cyril Hughes Hartmann

Adding more weight to this genuinely warm friendship between Cyril and Evan are many letters in Evan's file at Tredegar House written by Evan to Cyril (whom he addressed on paper as *"Kyrile"* and usually started each letter with affectionate terms such as *"My Dear"* or *" Dearest".* These letters (presented to the House by Cyril's son, the late George Hughes Hartmann) give a most marvellous, intimate insight into Evan's life, fantasies and thinking between 1917 and 1925. [103] Here are to be found the great concern by Evan over his long labours as a poet. A desire to be recognised (in the face of bashings from the critics) and at least to ask that his friends show mercy in their reading of his poetic works. There are also Evan's deliberations about his succession of illnesses, [104] the glory of the short time he studied at Oxford, but more so of the joys of hanging around the rooms of fellow students. Evan is often overwhelming in his admissions of love for his friends (such as Cyril and others mentioned by name). Evan's foreign travels can be traced from this remarkable series of letters including some curiously erotic tales of close encounters with dancers, prostitutes (male and female) and all kinds of sexual conquests and fantasies. The narratives include lashings of Evan's time spent in North Africa (Algiers), in Spain (Madrid and Seville, including sometime there with Cyril and others) and in Lisbon Portugal, at the British Legation, where Evan's straight laced uncle Sir Lancelot Carnegie[105] was a diplomat and later British ambassador.

Evan's Mother Fixation

Katharine, Lady Tredegar

Evan composed flowery poetry about his adolescent passions and about his mother, whom he doted on (but would not admit). Despite this love he chose to mock and ridicule her with descriptions of her affinity with birds and even of the making of birds nests, big enough to sit in and roost. These references to Katharine are strewn across memoirs and diaries among Evan's circle. [106]

Those narratives that repeat Evan's original offensive and inaccurate references to Katharine avian habits should be treated with the contempt they deserve. [107]

Whilst at Oxford Evan enjoyed the sham of making jibes at his mother to make himself more interesting and attractive. Also to stand out amongst the more handsome, talented in an attempt to less conventional among his peer group. It helped Evan's popularity spouting what he thought were furiously funny fables about his dotty, eccentric Mama. [108]

Sadly Katharine (or Kassie as she was often addressed or sometimes Kats[109]) was a sick woman in part, on account of the trauma of her husband's serial adultery coupled with a complex mix of nervous diseases, some inherited, some thrust upon her from the pressures of a wretched married life.

Katharine was a lonely eccentric, shy, passive by nature, terrified of noise, (ultimately crippled by arthritis) who was uprooted from the place she loved the most, growing up in the Highlands of Scotland and plunged head-first into a miserable, loveless marriage to a dull, irritating man, who was obsessed only with himself and self pleasure. She never aspired to being the chatelaine of Tredegar House so this hardly helped Courtenay in his important role as Lord Tredegar, but she could not be blamed for being in this state or much less mocked. But these sneers by Evan of his mother found a following – and the repetition of Katharine's bird woman foibles are evident in references to her, particularly by people whom she never met. Some references go as far to say Katharine was as mad as a hatter. [110] There are however two very good, accurate and sensitive portraits of the real Katharine in *The Bright Twenties* by Cecil Roberts and *The Bonus of Laughter* by Alan Pryce Jones. [111] In addition Aldous Huxley and Frances Stevenson record in their diaries nothing less than praise, and admiration of how nice they found Katharine as a companion and hostess. In one letter Huxley describes her as "*a very delightful person*"[112] a sentiment repeated by Stevenson in saying Katharine was such *"a dear"*.[113]

Frances (who was David Lloyd George's private secretary and second wife) was a regular guest with Katharine (and Augustus John) at nights out in London at the opera, Katherine maintained a box at Covent Garden.

One of the Lady Tredegars is mentioned as being taken as a lover by the Welsh artist, Augustus John. [114] Although Lady Katharine was amused to support struggling artists and she was painted at least twice by John, and liked him, she is a surprising inclusion as one of the *"list of girls"*[115] conquered by John, in any case he found Katharine *"a trying subject"*[116]. The more likely of candidates for John's bed was Evan's first wife, Lois Sturt, who had an artists' studio in Chelsea, where John himself also sometime lived and worked. [117]

Evan is capable of spinning such an immoral tale about his mother. But when Evan was serious about telling lies and for making flattering remarks he pursued good looking young men and boys in order to play out his fantasies. He could also be spiteful and concurrently *"could be most charming and most bitchy."*[118]

Whilst attending Christ Church, Evan was often absent from his studies. Indeed he didn't aim to study at all. He had no intention of learning or aspiring to reading for a degree. Oxford was for socialising and fun and making conquests. Evan snared people and collected them much as he did his animal collection.

Young Evan

Evan was not quite the picture of Adonis as a youth. He was lanky, gaunt, underweight and chronically diseased from consumption. A painting of him by Ambrose McEvoy from the period reveals his frailty coupled with a miserable attempt at growing a moustache. [119]

The centre of Evan's grand social life, and a sheltered haven away from the great war raging in Europe was at Garsington Manor, [120] the large Oxfordshire home of the Morrells (Philip and Ottoline[121]) which attracted poets and artists galore.

The Bloomsbury' coterie headed here too but snubbed many of Garsington's foppish pansy wing, including Evan. Yet Virginia Woolfe (who later rejected publication by her Hogarth Press of Evan's 1921 novel *Trial by Ordeal*[122]) and Lytton Strachey each record fleeting references to Evan in their diaries. These portrayals are more negative than positive but seem well drawn.

Woolfe records somewhat cleverly*"Evan Morgan, a little red absurdity, with a beak of a nose, no chin, and a general likeness to a very callow but student Bantam cock, who has run to legs and neck."* [123]

Woolfe first met Evan at Garsington in 1917, when *"less talent and more pose"* was present in the 24 year-old Evan. [124]

Strachey (thirteen years older than Evan and (like Evan called an escapist) records in a letter his take on the "*immature*" [125] Evan aged 23.

" Then there was Evan – considerably different from my imaginations. I had envisioned a pale, slightly mysterious and small creature; and there appeared a tall bright-coloured youth with a paroqueet [sic] nose, and an assured manner, and the general appearance of a refined old woman of high birth." [126]

Evan liked any comment about himself! He portrayed the saint, the demon, the romantic figure and the bohemian alternately. [127] But in truth he was often just naughty and decadent in his taste for extremes and had a fascination for certain dark proclivities too. These included participation in secret societies and that extended to taking part in taboo rituals. His indulgences were dangerous, he lusted over younger members of his own sex with the gluttony of a satyr. He was often tactless and almost always insincere. He was in reality incapable of love. But Evan wanted to be liked and would attempt somersaults to win favour with the crowd across both sexes.

One friend highlights that *"there was nothing effeminate about him [Evan].. however much he may have liked good-looking young men..."* [128]

Among his contemporaries Evan had a saving feature, to guarantee him inclusion, he was very, very rich. He paid the bills and more, with £2000 a quarter being an average Evan outlay. [129] He could afford to offer to treat and create and fulfil his own and others people dreams and follies and he was often to be seen at *'The Randolph'*, the city's premier hotel in Oxford. Even after leaving Oxford University Evan was to be found there at weekends hosting fancy dress parties. [130]

Evan invited friends and strangers from near and far to these orgies. One unlikely friend was the actor-songwriter, Billy Milton [131]. Upon visiting Evan's suite at *The Randolph* with another friend in order to see Evan's costume, Milton recalls in his memoirs:

" Evan phoned to invite us both to his suite for a preview of the costume he intended to wear that night. It was late breakfast-time when I knocked at his door. On opening it, there was his Lordship standing before the window stark naked [132]*except for a tiny wasp of grey-oyster*

tulle covering his 'Brighton rock'… I presumed he was illustrating his family motto 'Ready to Serve'." [133]

Evan was predatory by nature with exhibitionist tendencies. He dressed up in the manner of the poet Percy B Shelley. One comment on seeing Evan was *" his beautifully cut and bejewelled cloths – an 18th century figure come to life again")*[134] . He also regularly donned the fancy dress costume of a female explorer named Rosita Forbes, who had been the first Western woman to conquer the deserts of Libya. [135] But there was a darker, more sinister side to Evan when he dressed up as a mystic figure called the *"Black Monk… a member of a secret occult circle with only 13 members."* [136] Evan did more than merely dabble in the occult, he read and studied about it fervently in the occult journals, and believed in its mysterious power and influence. [137]

Perhaps he did not *always* see it that way, and one commentator remarks that he ultimately became *"frightened of occult practices"*.[138] But early in his youth this dark interest snowballed into liaisons, in some cases lasting many years in black magic circles and an acquaintance with the Prince of Darkness on earth, the notorious Satanist and drug fiend Aleister Crowley. [139] Crowley's testimony suggests that Evan kept a well equipped magic room (usually written as Magick Room) at Tredegar House.[140] But its actual location is unknown. Evan's cousin, Alan Stewart, who lived in Tredegar House in the 1930s and 1940s, has *no* recollection of seeing the room in question.[141]

Cabaret
Theatre
Club

The Cave
of the
Golden
Calf

9, Heddon Street
Regent Street

In Evan's development years his interest in the supernatural was almost certainly a part of his boy worship of the composer Philip Hestletine, better known as Peter Warlock[142], who was a part of the occult's inner circle. Hestletine moved at close quarters with Evan during their overlapping years together at Eton College and Oxford. Together, they shared close confidantes in other young rising stars in poetry circles, including Tommy Earp and the sculptor, Jacob Epstein. [143]

Curious evidence exists of Evan (and his mother[144]) having an association with the *Cave of the Golden Calf* which was full of bohemians earning its description as *"the first English avant-garde night club and cabaret"*[145] before the Great War. It quickly became a centre for artists and poets living and passing through London.

Evan had a confident flair for being appealing, although was usually compulsive and flirty. In his day-to-day conduct working class targets such as clerks, valets, waiters, porters and sailors were vulnerable from an equal measure of verbal assaults and compliments.[146] Once Evan had taken a dislike to someone he was vile, but when he took a shine to a boy (and any companions of whatever class or gender) the hold had to be complete and total. He invited them in droves to clubs, parties and restaurants, and quickly forgot their names after they'd served a purpose, which might have only been to decorate a table at an event. Closer contact was kept clandestine as the actual acts intended and committed were against the law.

Evan surrounded himself with appealing bystanders. When he became Lord Tredegar the pool of grooms, wigged footmen and young valets swelled to include Evan's personal array of his favourite beauties. The servants who were a party to family secrets were often retained beyond their usefulness. [147]

On his father's death, one Tredegar retainer was the Steward, Mr North, who also acted as Evan's butler. Evan thought it would also be amusing to seek out for hire a Mr South, East and West![148]

Evan always had followers in tow and as many again side lined or spurned, as he moved on through the pack like a locust. He had few close or continuing relationships with any of these conquests. Men and boys and some women existed merely as an object or a conquest, they were used or conquered and then shown the exit but always with a sufficient reward given of money or jewellery or both.

V
Café Royal and Eiffel Tower Restaurant, London

Café Royal

When not prancing about Oxford, Evan was a member of a group of artists and literati who met and drank together in London's Café Royal [149]and later at a restaurant called *La Tour Eiffel,* The Eiffel Tower based at 1, Percy Street, off Tottenham Court Road. Other watering holes included the Fitzroy Tavern, in Bloomsbury [150] and the 17 Club, which was a creation of Leonard Woolf.[151]

Evan was not without enemies. He was more than once the victim of some determined pranksters. In 1914 rumours caused some newspapers to issue a statement saying that Evan intended to marry. It is however not impossible that Evan was the actual source of the story.

The Times published this notice *"We are requested to state that a report of the engagement of the Hon. Evan Morgan (not published in The Times) is without foundation."* [152]

Adrian Allinson's impressions of the Café Royal 1915-6

Despite the austere war time conditions prevailing the artist Adrian Allinson[153] captures in his painting of the restaurant from 1915-16 the restless spirit and free style of some of Evan's contemporaries of the Café Royal.   The figures in the picture line up as Dorelia and Augustus John[154], David Sampson, P G Konody, the art critic[155], Alan Odle (whom *The Times* [156] describes as " *a famous decadent*" [157]) Nancy Cunard[158], Horace de Vere Cole[159], Iris Tree[160] and finally Evan. Allinson appears in the picture too, along with a waiter named Mario in the background. [161]

Evan was more the odd man out, he was adopted into the group as he was rich and had been talked about as being flashy and liberal with his spending in Oxford. The majority of the coterie had joined forces whilst studying at the Slade Art College, in Chelsea. Evan was a soft touch and forked out money to ensure he was included. He worshipped them as idols, they possessed much greater talent. He copied their manners and the pastimes of several of the Café Royal regulars like the eccentric Odle (who modelled his life and appearance on another of Evan's heroes, Aubrey Beardsley) and like Evan was a consumptive and drank heavily. Evan adored Beardsley's drawings, his rooms at Oxford were covered in his works and illustrations.   Other members of the same Café Royal group of artists and writers included Jacob Epstein, Wyndham Lewis [162],

41

Robert Nichols, [163] Alvaro Guevara [164] and occasionally the strange figure of Ronald Firbank.[165]

Several members of the coterie were attracted to same-sex pair-offs. Some attracted attention from both sexes. There was a underlying melancholy (which was thought of as "fun" and " just sex") of partner swapping and orgies without the commitment of love or even a genuine relationship.

Nancy Cunard[166] was a sexual opportunist among the women. She was branded a rebel from the moment when, in 1914, she daringly lit a cigarette in the Café Royal. Respectable women did not then smoke in public. She referred to her own inner core at the Café Royal as "*a Corrupt Coterie*", and among these members were "*the poets and painters Osbert Sitwell, Evan Morgan, Iris Tree, Alvaro "Chile" Guevra, Robert Nichols and Augustus John.*" [167]

Nancy's crowd could see she was keen on Evan. The biographer of Alvaro Guevara (one of Nancy's silent admirers) " *had always been bewildered by her passion for that queer Evan Morgan, with whose eccentricities he [Alvaro] were only too familiar.*" [168]

The years spent at the Slade and at Oxford University, overlapped several members in the configuration of the group, the various factions grew to a strength of several dozen.[169] In addition to drinking, dining and dancing at the Café Royal, the group made its own mark on another restaurant, the avant-garde inspired café, Eiffel Tower, in London's Percy Street. This became very much their home turf and sanctuary.

One description of the latter establishment is typical "*the 'Eiffel Tower' was .. what the old Café Royal had been to the Nineties... a small room with perhaps seven tables...The Austrian (chef) Rudolf Stulik[170] who ran it had a large belly ike a football which went before him..*" [171] Stulik (like Rosa Lewis of the Cavendish Hotel, another favourite reserve of Evan) applied a Robin Hood attitude towards outstanding bills, which meant that those like Evan with excess money, were often quite willingly fleeced.

A watercolour painting survives by William Roberts of *The Vorticists*[172] of an assembly of people at the Eiffel Tower Restaurant in the spring of 1915 adding many more artists and poets as well as the others previously listed. [173]

Odder still characters, near museum pieces and camp followers from London's bohemian past occasionally visited (and were toasted) in the protected surrounds of The Eiffel Tower and Café Royal. *The Souls* [174] (who were so dreadfully depleted by the Great War) limped in and out regardless of death's cruel sting. Another odd ball among the veterans was Lord Alfred Douglas, (the lover and assassin of Oscar Wilde, whose sacred home had once been his own table at the Café Royal) and who several years later (in penury and near death) was generously helped by Evan and Evan's second wife, Olga. [175]

Evan and the Drug Culture

For decades an illicit drug culture involving the smoking of hashish and opium with the inhalation of smaller quantities of cocaine and heroin existed in London's West End, supplied by London's East End, from the Capital's docklands. The close London–Paris connections and overlapping circles – fostered by artists and the aristocracy - also led to drugs being imported into England. The "epidemic" really began during the Great War and the Café Royal crowd then had its share of high class drug users. There was street trading of drugs in the West End. In wider circles it became commonplace to take cocaine, nicknamed *"snow "* and *"H"* - heroin – as recreational drugs - and the use of these substances increased into the 1920s and beyond.

Evan admits to having taken cocaine but was not a serious user [176], although some of his social acquaintances, including Augustus John, Iris Tree, Jacob Epstein and Lady Diana Cooper[177] were habitually affected by drugs. [178] Evan's troubled sister Gwyneth, was plunged into the sordid world of drugs, through her association with Brilliant Billy Chang, who operated out of Limehouse from his own cover of a West End restaurant. [179]

.

Evan the budding Poet is published

Two of Evan's Books of Poetry – The Soldier Poet with his father

From 1915 until 1919 Evan contributed poetry to a magazine *The New Age*.[180]

On publication of Evan's first volume of verse, entitled *Fragments*, in 1916, he was thrilled at being described as *"a new soldier poet"*. [181] Evan was indeed a soldier, he joined the Welsh Guards in June 1915.[182] Whether he was received as a poet or not was more in the balance. Reviews of *Fragments* were mixed. He held on tightly to being dubbed *"from the same literary set as the late Rupert Brooke."* [183] Over the years that followed Evan published several other volumes of poetry. [184]

Evan was sought out by fellow writers for his patronage. One of Evan's friends, Wyndham Lewis wrote to his mother from an army camp at Horsham in August 1916 *"Evan Morgan was to visit Pound on Sunday last, and was expected to loosen his purse strings. But as I have not heard from Pound, I presume he has not done so…"* [185]

VI
Evan's Great War

Evan in Uniform

Evan was hardly cut out for *any* kind of military service in wartime. His friend Philip Hestletine reveals that Evan was on the point of a nervous breakdown only three months before joining the army. [186] In February, 1916 Evan suffered a *"severe attack of pleurisy…[in his] right lung…..[telling Cyril Hartmann it was] mentally speaking corridors of torture.. "* [187]

As a result Evan was put under the care of Dr Byres Moir, [188] a physician who offered homeopathic treatments, in his London consulting rooms.

Evan's army service was a sham since he was repeatedly unwell and did not start let alone finish any soldiers training. Mocking Evan's tall, thin, skeleton physique his Welsh friend, the painter Augustus John records facetiously after receiving the news of the warrior Evan:

"Evan Morgan has joined the Welsh Guards but 'his figure has to be altered slightly to meet the regulations, so he is now being stretched in various ways" [189].

Evan wrote to Cyril Hartmann (at Oxford) on 25 July 1916 from Lyme Regis *"I have just had a very severe operation for a bad abscess in the left ear and I am down here recovering : tis divine."* [190] Hartmann kept Evan busy by sending him some of his own short stories to critique. [191]

Evan was lying low for another reason. His 23rd birthday party on 13 July 1916 had got out of hand. Augustus John remarks that Evan's antics always reached extremes for a country at war, telling another friend:*"Evan Morgan gave a very stupid birthday party' yesterday! "*[192]

There are several updates about Evan's non-service in his army years amongst Augustus John's letters in the National Library of Wales. The great bearded Welsh painter was a guest at Evan's mother's home at Honeywood House. During the remainder of 1916 he was commissioned to paint Katharine and completed two portraits of her[193] and also Evan, and asked him to paint *" a head of him"*[194] at Honeywood. The other John references are dominated by revelations that Evan was at the seaside (Margate and Bournemouth are both mentioned) on sick leave from the army. War torn Europe had ended Evan's usual recuperation on the French and Italian Riviera. Later, whilst the War in Europe was still raging Evan managed to visit Algiers in North Africa, to rest whilst carrying out the duties of a King's Messenger (a sort of glorified courier carrying documents from Embassy to Embassy) at the same time. [195]

Evan briefly held an attachment in North Africa with the HQ staff of French General Robert Nivelle, whose war began well, but after being held responsible for massive army casualties was expelled to the desert, where he spent the rest of the war, ignored.[196]

Evan's father Courtenay Morgan

As the Great War took its dramatic toll on the aristocratic families of Britain, the losses were personally felt when Evan's own cousins fell in battle. Several did. [197] Courtenay felt only shame that Evan was not made of stronger stuff. Eventually Evan was found a new safe haven in which to languish in during the remainder of the war away, in Whitehall.

Evan In Whitehall

In the summer of 1917, Evan sustained an accident to the cartilage of his left knee. He hobbled about on two sticks to his office, a far cry from the rat infested trenches. He had a safe post secured for him at the start of the year in the Ministry of Labour, in London's Whitehall. Evan's boss, in the coalition government headed by David Lloyd George was John Hodge MP. [198] Evan worked (as an unpaid private secretary) to Hodge's parliamentary secretary, W (William) C Bridgeman (later Lord Bridgeman). Bridgeman did all the hard work which suited Hodge and Evan.

Evan's position in Whitehall proved to be of some good purpose. The writer/ poet Robert Graves (who had spent some holiday time with Evan cycling the highways and byways of the countryside around Oxford) wrote to him to ask for a word to be passed up the

46

establishment line about the plight of their fellow writer, Siegfried Sassoon, who was on the verge of crisis of conscience (which was excused as mental breakdown) about the morality of the War. Evan agreed to help his fellow poets. For once Evan was in the right place at the right time to secure this commendable footnote to his own history as well as the history of the War. [199]

Evan's time in Whitehall ended with the breakdown of his health in 1917-18, when he was exiled to North Africa. But his experience in the civil service resulted in 1919 in his selection for further duties, and thus relief from almost any kind of army service with his attachment to Sir George Riddell who headed the British Press Corps at the Paris Peace Talks at Versailles. [200] The Paris lights and nightclubs proved a pull for Evan, although he visited the cocktail receptions where one observer remarked he *"was as brilliantly amusing as ever."* [201] He also joined the tennis brigade around the politicians, in case of an offer of a further job in Whitehall might arise.

Despite an unremarkable war Evan was included in his old public school's *List of Etonians Who fought in the Great War.* [202]

Evan and W H Davies and at the Eisteddfod

Evan in the War Years

Evan's erstwhile Welsh links surfaced during the autumn of 1917. In February of that year he presented the bronze bust by (his chum) Jacob Epstein of the *"Super tramp"* poet W H Davies to Davies' own home town- also the Morgan seat- of Newport, South Wales. It can be seen in Newport Museum to this day. Then in September (with his health stable) he was at the year's *Eisteddfod* Evan received full bardic honours:

"September 6, 1917 - Birkenhead

The Gorsedd held its second session in the early hours of this morning. Several women and men were decorated with bardic honours, each candidate being led to the logan stone (Maen Llog) by two of the Welsh bards, by whom they were presented to the Archdruid. They included the Hon Evan Morgan, Lord Tredegar's poet son….."

Meanwhile Evan's time in the army and in government was only marked with more fall backs on his incurable genetic illnesses.

Evan and Frances Stevenson, private secretary to David Lloyd George

Frances Stevenson

Also whilst working in Whitehall (from 1917) Evan hatched a dastardly plan to personally appeal himself to Frances Stevenson, who at the time of Evan's encroachment was secretary to the Prime Minister, David Lloyd George.[203]

A series of letters and diary entries (held by the Parliamentary Archives) reveal the hounding and harassment committed by Evan, in order to put himself in a position where he would be somehow be offered a post in the Lloyd George's inner sanctum at No 10 Downing Street.

Evan remarks in one letter to Frances:

"I am so glad that you have decided to call me Evan" and adds factiously:

"It is so much shorter and all my friends fall into it almost at once; even strangers talk of me as Evan Morgan though they have never met me, at least so I am told; Mr Morgan doesn't exist."[204]

Evan demonstrated increasing familiarity with the Prime Minister in a reference to Lloyd George whilst still showing off the foppery of a modern day Sir Percy Blakeney:

"How is the great little man? Sometimes one's triumphs, as indeed his last speech was, are more wearing than one's defeats; Russia must be an infernal nuisance to him, coupled with the insidious wiles of the Vatican; and you once suggested that I with the mind of a clematis, decorative but quite useless should plunge my soul in the turgid vortex of Politics!"[205]

Eventually (although first flattered) Stevenson saw through Evan's plan and insincerity and branded him " *a hopeless liar...clever but thoroughly degenerate*".[206]

The grooming of Stevenson – designed to get closer to Lloyd George - even included an offer by Evan to Frances of marriage, which he leaked to his own followers as an affair of the heart. [207]

On 27 October 1917, Evan wrote to Frances Stevenson at 10 Downing Street in very personal terms, from the *Knowle Hotel,* Sidmouth, [208] saying he was *"resting and writing "*. He composed poetry specially for her delight – *"a few lines written just above the*

Hotel, on an exceedingly romantic hill crowned with a wood" [209] and generally kept up his stalking campaign.

"One day I want to come and work at No 10. I don't much care what at, but I feel your chief could make some sort of use of me."[210]

Of immense appeal to Evan in retreat at Sidmouth was that *The Knowle* had its own aviary. [211]

Also appealing no doubt, to Evan's sense for seeking thrills and stories to dine out on was that several wealthy residents at *The Knowle* had suffered jewel robberies However, Evan had truly come to *The Knowle* to seek a retreat. He wrote to Frances Stevenson :

"the air is a decided improvement on London and its draining atmosphere; here at least one can take in, instead of giving out all the time, and if only friends would stop bombarding me with a lot of unnecessary gossip and scandal life might be more or less peaceful..."
[212]

Invitations were launched by Evan for Frances to dine with him and join him at the opera in London. Evan's favourite place to show-off his prey was the Savoy Hotel, commenting in one letter to Frances, " *[the] Savoy Hotel is more amusing than the mausoleum Claridges, or the synagogue Ritz."* [213]

By January 1918 Evan had left his job in government. An announcement stated:-

" The Hon Evan Morgan who has been ordered abroad on sick leave, has arrived at Algiers" [214]

This was proceeded by a flurry of activity involving four telegrams from Evan to Frances Stevenson. Evan was now using Frances as a proverbial post-box:

These are intriguing notes. [215]

19 January 1918 FRANCE "ARRIVED FIRST STAGE AFTER GOOD JOURNEY JUST PROCEEDING PARIS = EVAN MORGAN"

20 January 1918 PARIS "ARRIVED 2nd STAGE PROCEEDING 3rd PROBABLES TOMORROW WITH LETTERS TO CONSUL FROM BRITISH EMBASSY = EVAN MORGAN "

24 January 1918 MARSEILLES "ARRIVED 3rd STAGE LEAVING FORD 4th STAGE PROBABLY FRIDAY. COULD YOU INFORM MY MOTHER ALL WELL = EVAN MORGAN"

27 January 1918 ALGIER "ARRIVED ALGIERS SAFE THIS MORNING COULD YOU LET MY HOME KNOW WRITING = EVAN MORGAN OASIS"

The Oasis was an hotel in Algiers. Evan's mission – secret or even vital to the war effort did not result in any great feat, beyond him carrying out some improvised duties relaying dispatches between countries. But Evan played the part as though he was Keen or Tree playing Hamlet. [216]

Another announcement followed to update Evan's military status.

"Evan Morgan is now on half pay list as a result of illness."[217]

Evan's friend Aldous Huxley reflected in a letter dated 18 April to Lewis Guilgud at Garsington:- *"Men of a certain age grow sad remembering'* and *"Utterly no news – a letter from Evan the other day describing the picturesque beauties of nature in Algeria."*[218]

Evan's beauties were almost certainly all young African men!

Evan was still pursuing Frances (and a job with Lloyd George) at the Paris Peace Conference, in 1919. He could not resist showing off, as demonstrated in this story recalled by Frances where Evan had pulled strings to get hard to get opera seats:

"….. the last time that I accepted an invitation from the future Lord Tredegar. He had found it difficult to secure good seats at the [Paris] Opera, and it did not take me long to realise, when we arrived there that LG (Lloyd George) was the person Evan was expected to escort, NOT ME! The red carpet was down, and important officials awaited the arrival of the distinguished foreign statesman, though being Frenchmen they made the best of the situation. But I was very angry. "
[219]

VII

Evan and Osmond Esmonde

Evan with an admirer

Evan was made aware in 1917-8 that Osmond Esmonde, [220] a fellow student at Oxford (three years his junior, pictured with Evan above) had confided in a third party that he had *"feelings"* for Evan. [221] A close friendship followed between them.

Evan and Ronald Firbank

Ronald Firbank

Later there was one figure who was for a time completely consumed by Evan, Ronald Firbank. Evan's affair with the oddball fantasy writer Firbank ended at a point of anger by Firbank over Evan's waspish behaviour in declining a book dedication. This resulted in all the books being withdrawn and pulped.

Ronald Firbank Author of The Flower Beneath the Foot

According to one of Firbank's biographers he " *frequented the Eiffel Tower, but irregularly.*" [222] The unique characteristic at the Eiffel Towe "*of six tables*" suited Firbank who was immensely shy and nervous. But another Firbank commentator declares that Evan was someone whom Ronald "*nursed intense longings.*" [223]

Evan was seven years younger than the openly camp'ish Firbank, who despite his tendency to sit alone in a corner, donned make up and put nail polish on his fingernails. Evan's account of their first meeting was of a "*tall Sherlock Holmes-like figure, the face characteristically half covered with the coat collar held up with the right hand and one long hand in an Aubrey Beardsley attitude pointing out towards infinity, [who] suddenly whispered in my ear 'Your name is Rameses'* [224]

Firbank thought Evan must "*therefore, be possessed of cosmic secrets.*" [225] He subsequently took Evan to see his supposed Egyptian likeness (a mummy in the British Museum), halting before a statue of Ramses II but "*a sarcophagus in which lay an age-emaciated shrilled discovery – a fanciful reproduction by the Ancient Egyptian rulers and the concept of reincarnation.* "[226]

Firbank was fascinated by Egyptian antiquities and its influence on his Roman Catholicism. He had visited Egypt to attempt to entangle the mystery of the Sphinx. Both Firbank and Morgan were also interested in the writings on magical rituals of Aleister Crowley.

Evan said he had enjoyed Firbank's companionship saying he was *"a unique character of cameo fantasy"*, [227] and looked on him *"as one might some rare bird to be cherished for its exquisite exotic qualities rather than as a human being.."*[228]

But the nearness of the relationship of choice acquaintance between them was of great concern to Evan's boorish Papa, Courtenay Morgan, Lord Tredegar.

In 1919 Firbank began work on a play called *The Princess Zoubaroff.* The following year the play was published by Grant Richards on 26 November 1920. A dedication to Evan (by Firbank) was removed at the last minute at Evan's insistence.

The dedication declared *"To the Hon. Evan Morgan in Souvenir Amicale of a 'Previous Incarnation'."* [229]

Firbank was furious, firing off comments that he had always thought Morgan *" a little fool"* [230]declaring in retrospect that it was *" a relief not to have a cad's name on the first page".*[231]

The Flower Beneath The Foot

In 1921 Firbank travelled through Italy and France and began work (to avenge Evan's actions) by writing *The Flower Beneath the Foot*, with Evan viciously portrayed in it as Hon. Eddy Monteith, son of Lord Intregar of Intreger Hall. Originally (in the early drafts of *Flower*) Eddy was called the *"Hon. Heaven Organ"*. The latter highly suggestive name was later removed as it was lewd (which Firbank didn't mind!) but was also deemed libellous (which Firbank's publisher did mind!)

Did Firbank ever have any genuine feelings for Evan or was it all a game, merely research for his book?

Gerald Berners, like Evan an eccentric British peer, writing about Firbank said:

"I don't think he wished for intimacy. I think he was terrified by the idea of being subjected to any kind of tie or obligation.."[232]

Evan also subscribed his name in 1922 to a bizarre presentation to Firbank. According to Ifan Kyrle Fletcher[233] :

"While he (Firbank) was in Rome during the winter of 1922 a few friends offered him proof of their affection and esteem. They procured a life size reproduction of that particular statue of Psyche which through an accident, has lost the crown of its head and has instead a marble plateau. On this convenient memorial plaque they inscribed their names – Gerald Tyrwhitt, Evan Morgan, Aldous Huxley and some others. With solemnity the statue was sent to Firbank at the Hotel Quirinale...." [234]

Firbank remains a genius of absurd fiction with characters as comically drawn as those of the immortals, Edward Lear or Joe Orton. Between Evan and Firbank there was more commonality in sexual deviance, gestures, style, and lusting after youths. Evan's friendship with Ronald Firbank was probably driven by Firbank's desire without it being carnal.

With Firbank, Evan found himself on the side of being stalked rather than stalker (as with Frances Stevenson).

There is no doubt about Firbank's talent to amuse and shock. He did this with the mastery of comic genius, in a series of books, all still in print, with images of blasphemy and sexual innuendo in excess, but which cannot fail to make us laugh out loud with their absurd truths. Firbank observed people with the precision of cat stalking a mouse. Evan had not one iota of the same talent. Evan's best wit lay with the quick retort and the occasional acid drop.

Firbank's motives at portraying Evan as Eddy in *"Flower"* are a lot more damning than Huxley's comic character creation, Ivor. But both these books are worth reading to make up your own mind. [235]

VIII

Evan's Attempt to renounce his birthright for The Catholic Church

THE HON. EVAN MORGAN.
Origin of the Monastery Rumour.
DETESTATION OF SOCIETY LIFE.

As with his *'affaire'* with Firbank, Evan was always in danger of imploding and taking with him the entire sum total of the Morgan family's reputation in one single action. His treatment of Frances Stevenson was reprehensible. The underlying liaison with Firbank also caused shock waves, especially as it was suggested that concurrently Evan was chasing a civil service post as a Private Secretary to a Cabinet Minister. [236]

Evan disgraced himself with friends, mocked his family, and irritated Society hosts and hostesses. This was unacceptable to his father and his ultra conservative Scottish and Royal cousins. Evan behaved like a fop, a dandy and was usually indulged by others because of his wealth. But those who were his so-called friends often scorned him. It put him out of the running certainly for all short lists in Whitehall or anything other than a casual post in the diplomatic service.

When the four years of war neared an end in June 1918, Evan was back in Wales. He was in the company of David Windsor, the Prince of Wales and others in a *Who's Who* of out of town Society folk. The Prince was in Wales to receive the freedom of Cardiff. However, it seems not even the court jester Evan could amuse or make him happy. Perhaps the Prince had been warned to give Evan as wide a berth as possible.[237]   Among David Windsor's later ladies in waiting was Hon. Lois Sturt, whom it was said found favour too with David's younger brother the dashing Prince George.[238]

People dismissed the more sordid sights in Evan's many chequered relationships, he was sheltered, as were others like him, by an Establishment cover-up or just turning the proverbial blind eye.

Aldous Huxley and his book which features
Ivor Lombard based on Evan

However, Katharine was leaned upon by her Royal relatives to act to contain her son's activities. She roped in Aldous Huxley to try to reign Evan in and give the heir apparent a sense of purpose. She told Huxley she was also prepared to fund a six month trip abroad, with Huxley acting as Evan's companion and minder.

 Huxley biographer reveals further insight:

"Lady Tredegar was worried about Evan's dissolute lifestyle and, thought, as Huxley put it 'that my respectable middle-aged temperament would act as a slight brake to Evan's whirligig habits.' . Lady Tredegar had reason to be concerned.." [239]

But the plan was dashed as the war was still raging and finally abandoned over the difficulties to obtain passports were marred with red tape.

Moving into the post-war freedom when travel restrictions were lifted it was only a year before Evan made the news headlines with gusto – when in 1920 the rumours started circulating (from USA, where Evan was on a long term holiday[240]) that he was to renounce his birthright and become a Catholic priest. His older second cousin, Charles (Chat) Williamson, also a homosexual had done precisely that some years before. [241] Ensuring he secured the maximum affect, the Tredegar heir refused to deny rumours and encouraged announcements he was to became a monk in the USA.

But he could not fool friends like Aldous Huxley, who knew him at close quarters.

Evan's Spin off on becoming a Monk

As with Frances Stevenson, Huxley was another victim of Evan's impish, although pre-meditated flatteries, but he eventually saw through Evan. Huxley was vulnerable to being picked up and spoilt but the two men were intellectually mismatched, with Huxley vastly superior. [242] He first met Evan at Garsington, where he had moved in with Ottoline Morrell [243] and her husband for the duration of the Great War. [244]

Initially Huxley rejoiced in his friendship with Evan.

"I have been having numbers of curious events with Evan – he is an adventurous person, a man of action, and he is very salutary in stirring up my contemplative lethargy – with the result we have the greatest fun"[245]

No one had taken much notice of Huxley before. He described Evan as *"my great new friend … the inimitable Evan Morgan"* ……. *his fabulous wealth is a wishing-cap that gives him whatever he wants…"* [246]

During Evan's attachment to Huxley, Evan's mother got involved in trying to see that Huxley took Evan under his wing. Katharine had whisked Huxley off to lunch at least once [247] to sing Evan's praises and persuade him to give Evan succour and protection from those in the coterie that were a bad influence. What Katharine didn't realise was that it was Evan who was often the worst behaved member of the group.

But it was clear to Huxley that this talk of renouncing 'everything' was Evan only attempting to disturb his family's peace and have his cake and eat it!

"Evan Morgan was talking of assuming holy orders, or a monastic life...the tale about Evan Morgan is, so far as I am aware, a cock and bull affair, I have never seen a man less monastic than he was when I saw him three or fours days ago".[248]

This doubt remained in later years when Huxley was asked about it:

"this was one of the occasions on which Morgan was talking of assuming holy orders or the monastic life. His Catholic spiritual advisers always managed to dissuade him.."[249]

Another observer remarked of Evan's conversion to the Catholic Faith :

"Evan Morgan s'est fait Catholique par volupti.."[250]

It was as if Evan had got the whole idea from a Ronald Firbank sub-plot. The most spoilt, extrovert, aristocrat in Britain renounces everything for a life of obedience and prayer and total sacrifice, dedicated to God and the poor of the world. The absurdity was plain to everyone, but Evan's father was naïve enough to be furious. Both his children had been a trouble to him.

It was left to Katharine to attempt to dispel the vapours over Evan's plan to *"renounce his title and relinquish his claim to his father's estate...in order to enter a Catholic monastery."*[251]

Katharine panicked, as well she might, even dismissing Evan becoming a Catholic. She was reported as saying:

"My son, who has lately returned from an extended visit to America, has spent the weekend with me. He has now gone to Oxford but I am fully acquainted with his plans and I hope you will contradict the story. So far from becoming a monk, he has not even joined the Catholic Church."[252]

In fact the truth behind Evan's deception and deviousness done largely to irk his father, (albeit Courtenay was away from the breaking news on a Mediterranean cruise) was that he had only secured himself a place in which to spend a quiet period recuperating from illness at the old Franciscan Catholic Mission of Santa Barbara in the USA "[253]

Nevertheless in the years that followed Evan did adhere himself in several ways to the centre of the Roman Catholic Church in Rome, including performing Papal service.

Evan and the Vatican

Evan in his Papal Knight costume

Evan was once entreated by the Pope to carry a Papal blessing to Lourdes. This required Evan to walk across France from Chambery to Lourdes, a journey which lasted fifty six days at twenty five kilometres a day. [254]

Evan also proudly carried up his duties at the Vatican as a Knight of the Order of Malta. This required him to participate in Papal rites and religious celebrations. [255] Evan's other titles (derived more from patronage than actual merit [256]) was as a Privy Chamberlain of the Cape and Sword (sometimes recorded as Sword and Cape) at the Papal Court to two Popes, Pope Benedict XV and Pope Pius XI. [257]

Evan's title was that of *"a lay appointment of Chamberlain to the Pope, a life position which entailed his attendance for duty at The*

Vatican once a year. This meant his absence from the county for three weeks or a month once a year." [258]

Vatican Secret Archives: Evan's application to be a Papal Chamberlain

The background to Evan's dalliances at the Vatican is revealed by original documents from the Vatican Secrets Archives.[259] One document actually shows that Evan was first nominated by the Archbishop of Cardiff. A letter recommending Evan to the post of Papal Chamberlain exists, signed by Pope Benedict XV. However *before* the necessary confirmation was given the Pope died. A later letter (written by Evan, in Italian) follows up the application before the new Pope, Pius XI. Thus Evan was only ever in reality a Chamberlain to Pius, and this was confirmed *after* he became Pope.

Naturally Evan adored his Papal costume. Commenting on the picture of Evan in his Papal outfit by Catherine Mann[260] The Vice Prefect of the Vatican Secrets Archives said: :

"the black/lace outfit is not that of a papal knight, but of a "cappa and spada" person." i.e. a chamberlain of honour, a secular, a layman, a post of honour involving no regular duties. " [261]

Evan's finest hour as a Papal Chamberlain

Without doubt Evan was present helping to fulfil a pivotal role when King George V and Queen Mary had an audience with Pope Pius XI, in Rome in 1923.

"Royal visit to the Pope. Reception at the Vatican. King George V and Queen Mary had an audience with Pope…….. " The members of the papal household, including the five English Private Chamberlains Viscount Campden, Mr O'Neill, Mr W Kerr, Count Curteis, Hon Evan Morgan and Mr Johnson were presented" [262]

A document in the Vatican Secrets Archives gives full details of this important Royal visit. [263]

Evan and the Cardinal

Cardinal Gasquet, [264] was one of the English Cardinals in the Vatican who befriended Evan. Shane Leslie [265] (a friend of Evan) has this brief extract in his biography of Gasquet [266] taken from the Cardinal's own diary :

"12 April Evan Morgan to tea." [this may be 1924 or 1925]

Leslie writes *"Evan Morgan ([later] Lord Tredegar had come into the Cardinal's perspective in 1924 and had afforded him much entertainment and some anxiety. A convert from High Society to the Church …. he had entered the Beda College (with his suite) to pursue his studies for the Papal Diplomacy…the Pope [Pius] himself took an interest in his case advising him to marry.."* [267]

Leslie refers to the latter in his memoirs *"I saw him [Evan] through a matrimonial essay which Pius XI unadvisedly bade him try when his heart was set on the priesthood. His quaint character made Roman excitement when he entered Beda College"* [268]

Evan as a student at Beda College, Rome

Evan later enrolled as a student at Beda College, Rome in 1924. [269] . This English – Catholic establishment was intended for older men, training for the priesthood. The building was situated in 67, Via San Niccolo da Tolentino near the Piazza Barberini.

A Catholic insider points out that a strict, almost certainly holy atmosphere pervaded at Beda in the 1920s. The regime was orthodox and fools and knaves were not tolerated. The Rector during Evan's short time there was Horace K Mann[270] who had the experience of being an uncompromising headmaster in a socially challenging part of Newcastle.

Evan's generous patronage of the Catholic Church protected him for a while, but it did not make him invisible. It was the same as when Evan was at Oxford University ten years before, he was not conscientious and had personally little desire or incentive to want to learn or study.

There are stories of Evan hurtling through Rome " *in his Rolls-Royce, kitted out with a drinks cabinet and a portable altar..*" [271]

A Catholic scholar who lives in Rome and who had friends from various social backgrounds who trained for the priesthood at Beda comments on this :

"The upper classes... have outstanding eccentrics - who, since they usually had more resources are more visible than the far more numerous of the middle classes. They also cultivate even more illusions. Fun bits about Rome, where in those days the Beda College was in Via San Nicola da Tolentino - which I know only too well. Doubt the bit about the altar in the car, not about the provision of drinks however...."[272]

There are narratives (albeit written long after Evan was dead) of Evan's frivolous attitude including sending his servant (probably a valet) to classes at Beda:

"Evan Morgan took liberties of a kind that raised doubts as to the worth of his vocation. He maintained a luxury suite at the Bernini Hotel not far from the seminary and there he entertained his friends in the style to which he was accustomed. He rarely attended the Gregorian University. Instead he would send one of his servants in his place, dressed in a cassock, to sit through lectures and take notes..."[273]

Curiously one memoir writer, a diplomat, attached to the British Legation at the Vatican claims he occupied the room at Beda College previously allocated to Evan:

"Beda College..I knew this well. I went to live there for several weeks until I could find a permanent home. I was assigned the room which had been occupied by the Hon. Evan Morgan...who in course of his varied and eccentric life had thought he would "try his vocation" to the priesthood. He had given up the attempt, but had left behind a collection of sumptuously bound religious and philosophical [works] ..."[274]

On a visit to the current premises of Beda College in 2009, a one page sheet, representing Evan's historical details kept there was provided. The inquiry into the whereabouts of any other material was snubbed albeit with some possible accuracy in the answers received that in the move of the premises files had been lost, and other old records destroyed in a fire and during the second world war. No search in the basement Archives could be easily undertaken on account of the health hazard from dust. [275]

A reference traced elsewhere resolved the likely reason why Evan left Beda under a cloud, in 1925, and explained the reason why the present Rector could not possibly take an interest in an inquiry about the Tredegar heir.

In 1925 " *The Rector of the Beda eventually instructed him [Evan] to leave when it was discovered that Morgan , the aspirant to a priestly life of celibacy, had imprudently fallen in love with an Italian youth.*" [276]

However there is a conflict of truth regarding the stories of just how fast and loose Evan was whilst he was supposed to be studying at Beda.

In a letter dated 10 April 1924 to Augustus John,[277] Evan expressed a wish that John would come to Rome asking him to paint the Madonna with the Infant Jesus, and offering John the sum of £500. The inference is that Evan intended to be away studying for seven years. He remarks that if the picture was completed within that timescale he could put it into the private chapel he hoped to have there.

Evan did not cut himself off from the rat-pack of Rome. He certainly participated in the Catholic and non-Catholic pleasures of the Eternal City, facilitated and importuned with his friends including the journalist, Cecil Roberts (who mentions some remarkable tales about Evan in a number of places in his very readable volumes of autobiography[278]) and the composer Lord (Gerald) Berners (a close friend of Firbank too) who had villas there. Several writers refer to Evan remaining a part of the visiting swarms of English and American writers, poets and travellers. Evan was also on good terms, socially with several countries diplomats and representatives serving in the Vatican, sometimes referred to as The Holy See. As a result he was introduced to many up and coming Catholic Papal personalities; and some stories attributed to these associations are blown up by soothsayers as containing wild elements of sexual impropriety and cloak and dagger. [279]

Evan in Dublin and Reveals the Secrets of the Vatican

THEATRE ROYAL LECTURE—A group of people who spoke at the Theatre Royal, Dublin, yesterday, in aid of the funds of the St. Vincent de Paul Society. Seated in front: The Rev. J. B. O'Connell, S.J.; the Hon. Evan Morgan and Mr. T. A. Finlay, K.C. At back: The Rev. Thomas Ryan, S.J.; Captain Ware and the Rev. M. Kirwan, S.J.

Evan In Dublin To Give a Lecture on the Vatican

From the late 1920s until the 1940s Evan gave a number of serious public lectures, reflecting his strongly felt passions and interests on art and including presentations on the poet John Donne at the Royal Society of Literature, in London. [280]

Evan also gave a lecture in Theatre Royal, Dublin on 23 November 1930 (under the auspices of the Society of St Vincent de Paul) on his *"Sojourn in the Vatican".*[281]

In his introduction The Rev J N O' Connell, CC said Evan had *"rendered such signal service to the [Catholic] Church that the Pope had conferred on him many honours".*[282]

Evan (to loud applause) *"outlined various ceremonies, scenes and episodes in the great Palace of the Vatican, of which he had been privileged to be a witness. He described the circumstances in which he became a convert to Roman Catholicism and of the urge that he felt to go to Rome to the source of that religion. He sketched his experiences and difficulties in gaining admission to the Vatican and to an audience with the Pope. Of the late Pope Benedict XV, Evan] said that, above all, he was a great diplomat, and, in his opinion, no other man could have dealt so magnificently with the troubles of that awful period of the Great War as His Holiness did. Having dealt in detail with the Palace in the Vatican and with St Peter's [Evan] went on to speak of the lure of Rome. It was, he said something beyond the five senses – something which touched the fourth estate of man. It was something terrific – he supposed it was the presence of the bodies of the Saints. [Evan] told of the holding of the Conclave of Cardinals to elect, under spiritual guidance, a new Pope, and caused amusement by describing how he persisted in gaining permission to be present at the final preparations for the Conclave.*[283] *Evan spoke of the flutter caused in the Vatican when, on being selected by the Conclave the new Pope received the announcement with the words "I will accept". "I am Pius, and I will give a blessing to the city and to the world." The statement [Evan continued] was made without a second's hesitation spoken under Divine inspiration he had in that he was to be the new Pope-King..*" [284]

Evan also told his audience that he had *"had the supreme privilege of taking Mr Bewley, the first Irish Free State Minister, to the Vatican..."*
[285]

Evan counted among his friends other Irishmen including the poet W B Yeats, who shared with Evan a great curiosity for the supernatural. On one occasion when they were both at Renvyle House as guests of Oliver St John Gogarty, an attempt by Evan to contact the other side and exorcise the Renvyle ghost resulted in a near death experience of fright as Evan collapsed in horror at the spirits he had invoked. [286]

Another acquaintance was the novelist L A G Strong,[287] who although English born, had a good Irish heritage from his mother and grandparents. He recalls Evan being a regular visitor to Dublin. He says Evan was

"the most astounding conversationalist I had heard"...[288]*... "his conversation was calculated – the word is exact – to startle the unsophisticated. Anecdote after anecdote of Paris and Marseilles would ripple from his lips, and one worthy young man after another would rise white-faced and leave the room. This was Evan's parlour game;*

like many devout Catholics, he allowed his fancy and his tongue great freedom.." [289]

IX
Evan Morgan 1920s

Evan adored the company of the highbrow heavyweight literary and artistic figures of the day. At Oxford, Hilaire Belloc advised him on Catholicism and religious conversion and G K Chesterton did the same. Evan celebrated the start of the year 1924 with a new book of poetry, AT DAWN: POEMS, PROFANE AND RELIGIOUS containing works addressed to Nancy Cunard, Alfred Noyes[290], Aldous Huxley and W B Yeats.....Noyes wrote a forward.

It was described as an *"eloquent volume"*.

The noted society photographer, Ceil Beaton described Evan in " *the discarded portraits* " of those he recalled from the 1920s and 1930s as *"very birdlike and spiky".* [291]

Throughout the 1920s Evan's health remained erratic with the need for regular periods in nursing homes.

In a letter to his old boss, William Bridgeman, (congratulating the latter on becoming Home Secretary in a new government under Bonar Law) he writes:

"I have been a good month in a nursing home with my usual chest trouble.." [292]

Evan refused to be beaten by the limitations of his badly crippled frame, and continued to aim to live life to the full. He had nurtured ambitions to work for Prime Minister, David Lloyd George, but this was ended by the Prime Minister's resignation.[293]

Evan spent time in Paris and Rome but was back in London in between.

Augustus John records:

"Paris is full of 'homo-sexualists of both kinds who dance together to the prurient strains of the saxophone". [294]

67

Evan in his heyday as one of the Bright Young People

Evan's Parties : London

Parties and cavortings of various shapes and forms gripped the *Bright Young Things*, untamed fancy dress events were replaced by a variety of outrageous themed events including pyjama parties, baby parties, bottle parties, costermonger romps, midnight night bathing and treasure hunts in cars (also known as 'chasing clues'). These were all judged on their wickedness and depth of depravity.

Brian Howard[295] a member of the *Bright Young's Things 'A' List* was shocked at the goings on at one party given by Evan:

"……. another night I went to the most horrible party given by Evan Morgan,, which began at the Eiffel Tower and ended at somebody's bedroom at Prince's Hotel in Jermyn Street. I rushed out, clutching my remaining bits of virtue – bundled them into a taxi, and trundled home. I've never seen anything so stupendously naughty, even in Oxford! Never again – as I value my reputation." [296]

Some more morally responsible comment below on Evan's parties, especially of his birthday bashes, balances Howard's horror, a man whose own extremes often topped Evan's behaviour, manner of dress and strange company .

This was how Cyril Hughes Hartmann recollected these parties:

"Evan was the most generous of hosts and fortunately possessed the means to gratify his taste for entertaining. The parties he gave on his birthday, July 13th, were fantastic. Nobody else in England would have, or could have, gathered together the people he asked to them – Royalty, Diplomacy, Literature, Art, Music, the Stage, Smart Society, Complete Nonentities. The parties at Claridge's in 1926, and at Boulestin's, in 1927, were especially memorable. At the latter the galaxy of Royalties was headed by the Princess Royal, Duchess of Fife. Chesterton and Belloc were also present. But there would be little purpose in reeling off a list of celebrities of 1927. The point is that this diversified array of rank, beauty, talent, and distinction in almost every field consisted of Evan's intimate friends and not of casual acquaintances. The seating arrangement at dinner, though apparently haphazard, had been planned by the host with great care and sometimes with a Puckish sense of humour." [297]

Boulestin's in Southampton Street, Covent Garden was one of the most select and expensive French restaurants in central London. Evan had a financial stake in the place with its proprietor Xavier Marcel Boulestin, a legendry figure in world cuisine. [298]

Evan was also active on the London Club circuit with memberships of six well-known gentleman's establishments including the Carlton, The Guards and The Fine Arts Club.

The Hoaxer and Evan's 34th Birthday in 1927

There was an attempt by a hoaxer to derail Evan's 1927 birthday party by issuing forged invitations. In the absence of a wife (albeit Evan was only a year away from marrying Hon. Lois Sturt) he asked his good friend Lady Juliet Duff [299] to act as hostess to the invited guests arriving at Boulestin's restaurant. Among Evan's Royal guests were the Princess Royal, Princess Maud (Evan's cousin by marriage) and Prince and Princess Arthur of Connaught, so there was some police security in place with such VIPs in attendance. Lady Juliet discovered that a hoaxer was at work, from telephone enquiries she received from guests who were not on her list though phoned ahead to check some details. There had been a mischief at work at another big Society event when Lord Kylsant's daughter's wedding was nearly wrecked by a practical joker. Lady Juliet immediately issued a second set of invitations with her own personal signatures on them. She also published a warning in the London newspapers, and thought she had put an end to the matter. But a score of angry and determined guests appeared (in good faith) at the restaurant, and crashed in. Only the presence of the squad of police prevented the undesirables from drawing up chairs and sitting down beside members of the Royal family. Evan for once was not amused.

Evan and Nancy Cunard

A book that reveals Nancy Cunard

Evan's episodes with women were as bizarre as his flirting with Ronald Firbank. The serious pursuit of him by Nancy Cunard (who would have given anything to be Mrs Evan Morgan (without any matrimonial obligations) is a good example of Evan completely out of his depth. Nancy like Ronald Firbank did everything to stalk and trap Evan into capitulation.

In 1916 Nancy married a muscular, cricket-mad Australian soldier, named Sidney Fairbairn[300] to gasps of horror from her parents and shell shock from the Coterie. She had strung out her ambitions upon Evan's title, and this drove him into a corner.

Evan was turned cold by these attentions. The attraction and attempted ensnaring by Nancy was more a game of hunting an untamed animal than anything about love.

Nancy Cunard

But Nancy wanted revenge as the woman Evan scorned. One biographer of Nancy sums this up neatly, with a reference to an astonishing display by her in public at her wedding to Sidney Fairbairn, when she was still harbouring a desire to have Evan :

"Evan Morgan had not reciprocated the attraction she felt for him……
[so] on catching sight of Evan …. at the reception, [Nancy] tore off her
bridal wreath and flung it on the ground."[301]

The marriage to Fairbairn, which ended after eighteen months was made ineffective by Sidney going to war, and Nancy's further romances[302] it finally finished in divorce. [303]

Evan and Politics : At Home and Abroad

In 1926 Evan left his flirtation with Roman Catholicism behind when he was adopted as prospective Conservative candidate for Limehouse in London's East End. The Morgans had long standing property and charitable interests thereabouts.[304]

Some said Evan lost his natural sparkle during this time. Evan's old friend Augustus John records:

"Had a talk with Evan Morgan. There seems to be a great deal wrong with him."[305]

VISCOUNT'S DAUGHTER STILL MISSING

The Hon. Gwyneth Morgan, daughter of Viscount Tredegar, who disappeared in dense fog on December 11 and is still missing. *The Daily Mirror* is informed that although her family do not suspect foul play their anxiety is great.

Evan's only sibling Gwyneth, whose body was found in the River Thames in 1925

These were the years following his sister Gwyneth's tragic death. This tragedy was followed by the sad death of another female cousin, Rose Hoare, in a car crash in 1927. [306] Evan only just dodged suffering a complete nervous breakdown.

Evan was still ably entertaining his large number of carnal targets and hangers-on:

1927 : " Evan Morgan comes with his usual big party to dinner. He pays for the meal and does all the talking. ..since becoming politician he seems to have lost the romantic and ascetic that he used to have." [307]

Evan was usually accompanied on his travels about the countryside by selection of birds, monkeys and rats.

1928: " A wet Sunday and with seating for 60 we lunched 103, plus eleven chauffeurs. Evan Morgan said he'd never seen so many people in so small a place. He didn't make it any better himself by bringing down his Australian crow which ran amok and pecked girls' ankles, having first laid an egg upstairs on his dressing table."[308]

A further (and original) prank was for Evan to produce four chinchilla rats and hand them round after dinner to be admired, after which the creatures were allowed to play hide and seek among the cushions of a big divan. [309]

In some social quarters Evan was never invited along. His hatred of the cruelty of blood sports meant he was excluded from invites by the owners of the great estates where shooting parties were the seasonal norm. Several other landowners and peers (and peeresses) snubbed Evan in favour of a rising range of younger new personalities with the seeds of these friendships formed in Paris and Monte Carlo, places which Evan enjoyed (he was sometimes to be found on the Continent and London [310]) in literary circles but he loved Rome and North Africa and the Dutch East Indies more.

In between all the frivolity, Evan attended receptions at 10 Downing Street, served on Hospital Committees in London's East End. He was also the President of The Royal Gwent Hospital, in Newport, South Wales and was instrumental in approaching the Queen to become first Royal Patron of the hospital. *"personally I will always remember with pleasure the part I was privileged to take on this memorable occasion"*. The hospital had received The Friars as a Convalescent Home for Women Patients, from Courtenay (it had long been the residence of Octavius Morgan).

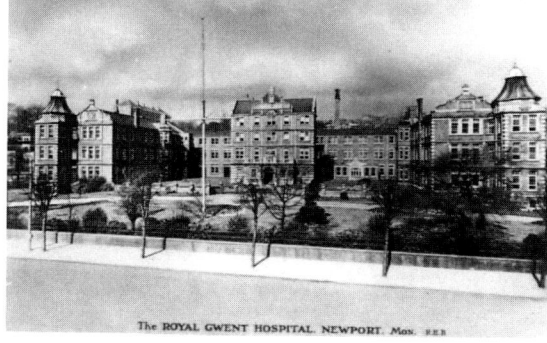

The ROYAL GWENT HOSPITAL. NEWPORT. Mon. 828

73

Evan fraternised with Royalty at horse racing meetings and concerts to raise money for hospital charities. [311] At several of these functions Evan was accompanied by the Hon. Lois Sturt, whom he married in 1928. [312]

X

Marriages and Mayhem

Evan marries Hon. Lois Sturt

Lois, Evan's first wife was the daughter of a peer, Lord Alington of Crichel, Dorset. She preferred much older men than Evan and had a long affair with Reggie Herbert, 15th Earl of Pembroke and Montgomery from 1920-5. A large number of Reggie's love letters to Lois survive. [313] The affair was ended by Lois' mother's appeal to Reggie, which paved the way for Lois to be resettled into an arranged marriage.

Hon Lois Sturt   Evan Morgan

Lois trained as a painter and had a studio in Chelsea. She later went on the stage and became a film actress. [314] The painter, Wyndham Lewis records that Lois was:

"the most beautiful of all the debutantes : that rarest of all things in England, a dark, plump beauty.." [315]

She was a key name in the *Bright Young Things* heyday, she *chased clues*[316] with her friends, the Royal Princes (sons of the King and Queen), was fined for speeding (meriting a mass of news headlines) she even killed a man with her motor car (which was less widely reported). [317]

One of Lois' contemporaries was the novelist Barbara Cartland. She recalls affectionately of Lois on film:

"Lois Sturt, Lady Alington's daughter, was the only one of my real close friends who was lucky enough to get into the movies. She had a part in The Glorious Adventure as Nell Gwynne. She couldn't have been better cast. She was real life pure 'Restoration'. She had dark flashing eyes, was impetuous, fearless and completely unpredictable. There was nothing she wouldn't do. She loved dressing up and was to be in all the pageants I produced. She always had rather unusual men in love with her and finally she married Viscount Tredegar, who was a character straight out of fiction." [318]

Lois and Evan at Tredegar House

Lois had absolutely no expectations of Evan as a man let alone as a husband. Their pairing was arranged to prevent scandals overwhelming both parties as a result of their affairs with men.

"Lois Sturt, Lord Alington's sister (and a jolly good sort), married the Hon Evan Morgan..." in **1928.** [319] So records the actress Ruby Miller[320] who enlarges the coverage about this in her memoires :

"Their wedding took place at Brompton Oratory, and Lois looked like a mediaeval picture, in her wedding gown of gold lame, with a golden veil and gold leaves, and a huge sheaf of crimson roses." [321]

The Golden Bride

In order to marry Evan, Lois went through the process of being received into the Roman Catholic Church. [322]

It was no ordinary marriage. Breaking with tradition the wedding reception was given the night *before* the nuptuals. Next day Evan was served, as only Evan could, by having *two* best men. [323] The ceremony was conducted by the Archbishop of Cardiff.

Rosa Lewis of the Cavendish

Rosa's Life Story

One of guests was Rosa Lewis - of Duchess of Jermyn Street fame - who ran the notorious Cavendish Hotel – a sanctuary for all the *Bright Young Things* – who were present as friends of the couple.

On seeing the Archbishop of Cardiff in his full scarlet robes – Rosa cried out in a loud voice:

" *Oh there's the Pope, at last I've seen the Pope*"

Several whispered, " *It's not the Pope.*"

Rosa would have none of it, insisting *"Of course it's the Pope, Evan would not be married by anyone but the Pope. "*[324]

Another narrative shows why Evan was easy to carcicature over his infatuation with being a Vatican emissary:

" *[Evan was] once represented running down Victoria Station in Papal uniform to the amazement of a trainload of cocottes and British holiday-makers to stop the Golden Arrow with the agonised cry : 'Secret papers for the Holy Father!' "*

Sir Francis Rose provides a believable anecdote of Evan landing from a ocean liner for a Eucharistic Congress wearing his Papal garb. The Press mistook him for the Papal Nuncio (Cardinal Mercier of Belguim), which Evan did not discourage or correct. This led to the whole of the reception Committee kneeling and kissing Evan's ring.....all with the constant fashing of the photographers.[325]

After the Wedding

After a six week honeymoon on the continent, the Morgans took up residence in a flat at 30, St James' Place, whilst a large house was built for them in South Street, Mayfair.

The role of Hon. Mrs Evan Morgan was to test Lois more than any part she'd played on stage or screen.

Yet despite a volatile pairing, the two parties actually liked each other, the fondness was genuine, at least in the early years. [326] Yet in the end Los stabbed deep with an attack on Evan, taking proceedings against him for divorce on the grounds of his homosexual activities.

Evan and Lois' London Home in South Street, Mayfair

The matrimonial home for the Morgans was eventually occupied at 40 South Street, Mayfair, after more than a year of rebuilding. One newspaper report, from 1929 expounds on the luxury inside:

"The house has been reconstructed on Italian lines and a most original cocktail hatch, is fitted on the ground, floor. This is hidden behind movable panels in the dining room wall, and when the panels are opened an electric sign flashes the words: 'The Road to Ruin.' The walls of Mrs. Morgan's bathroom are covered with an iridescent preparation which is a Dutch invention resembling the inside of an oyster shell-and is made in small squares, like mosaic work. The ceiling is of glow through in which sunlight lamps send showers of golden light...."[327]

Christabel Aberconway, Evan's Neighbour in South Street

The Morgan neighbours were equally as sensational, flamboyant and rich. At 38 South Street lived the industrialist Henry McLaren (from 1934 Lord Aberconway) and his eccentric, outspoken wife, Christabel.[328] Evan often sought refuge from Lois' wrath at No 38.
[329]

Evan Fund Raising in East End

The East End was utterly promiscuous and bi-sexual [330]

During the late 1920s and early 1930s Evan spent playing more sombre games with politics and good causes. Lois and her charismatic, bisexual brother Naps (Napier Sturt, Lord Alington[331]) were active at the same time in municipal elections in the East End of London. [332]

Lois' and Naps Election leaflet

Evan took on some challenging world issues, including the plight of Romans Catholics being suppressed in Mexico. [333] He is often cited as a fundraiser for various good causes. An example of this from 1929 sees him in the favourite guise of private chamberlain to Pope Pius XI, raising funds at a private dinner

"for the purpose of aiding the Talmud Torahs, Hebrew religious school, of Whitechapel, London's East End." [334] At this event held at Evan's home he declared in explanation of his interest in the Talmud Torahs

"that he felt that modern times require the unswerving guidance of morality and ethics" [335] *adding that he foresaw " an early fight between the religious and the anti-religionist"* [336] *and " that the forces of law prevail against pernicious Bolshevism"* to create *" A bulwark against these forces"* [337].

Spurred by boxing enthusiast Antony Knebworth[338], the handsome fellow Tory candidate for Shoreditch, Evan also took a shine to supporting the East's End's manly activity of boxing and introduced several of his Royal friends to a recreational and financial involvement in the sport. [339] There were always parties afterwards, fuelled by drink, drugs and sex. Newcomers were broken in quickly. Francis Rose recalls a night (with Evan, Prince George, later Duke of Kent and Naps Alington [340]), *"I left at dawn, slept all day, and then woke to my first hangover".* [341]

Evan also bravely[342] contested the 1929 General Election standing at Stepney, Limehouse against Labour's future Prime Minister, Clement Attlee[343] but in 1931 he stood down as Conservative candidate in Cardiff to make way for a candidate representing the cause of the "National" government. [344]

Evan the bird tamer bitten by a wolf and goes to Canada

Evan loved animals. He had a unique ability with all forms of wildlife - but particularly birds. One friend remarked :

"There was something extremely bird-like about the way he held his head, and would cock it to one side when listening to one or when about to ask a question. His eyelids were hooded, and he gave me, indeed, very much the impression of some wild bird of prey, caged perhaps

certainly never tamed, his way with birds was fantastic. I have seen him, against all advice...go into the cage of a Siberian owl of almost chilling ferocity, which could have clawed his eyes out....[and the bird] settled peacefully and happily upon his shoulder." [345]

Evan was only occasionally outwitted by an animal. But he was bitten on the finger by a wolf at a reception, which was held at London Zoo, on the eve of leaving Britain on a two month Empire Tour (with other Parliamentarians) of Canada.[346] He recovered quickly when, hypodermics super-charged with antiseptic were plunged into his skin, and opium administered. [347]

Evan caused widespread controversy in Canada with unfortunate comments about the backward nature of some of the places the group visited. There were howls of hostility about particular comments that :

" on a trip through the Peace River Country in northern Alberta .. he could not see much hope for the area..with so great a lack of comforts, no interest in the humanities and a marked absence of medical and surgical aid "

Evan learned that he had a lack of judgement in understanding the rough and tumble of politics and diplomacy. It was left to other colleagues to explain that Evan was still recovering from a wound sustained from a wolf. There were those who many had wanted Evan thrown to wolves by his comments about Canada. He was not invited there again.

Evan and Lois Co-exist together then Split

Into the 1930s, the Morgans co-existed in their home at South Street Mayfair. Their rows were notorious. Henry Maxwell recalls:

"[Lois] was a boisterous, life-loving, large-hearted person, who tended to do everything to excess. The marriage with E was stormy from the first, and Lois was wildly unfaithful to him, and each was always coming home and finding the other in bed with someone else....." [348]

But despite the domestic chaos Evan and Lois enjoyed trips away together to the West Indies, Italy and Egypt. [349]

Later the two led virtually separated lives. Lois became well known on the horse racing circuit as an owner. Evan rose in support of the memory of dear friend Peter Warlock (who died in 1930) at a memorial concert the following year. [350] He also travelled extensively abroad, with trips to Nazi Germany. Some unexplained elements of that period may be laid to rest by a book due to be published in 2013. [351]

Lois racing colours

In 1932 Lois accompanied her father-in-law, Lord Tredegar on a cruise to Ceylon. [352] By early 1933 Lois had moved to her rented country house of Mumpumps in Surrey. It had its own swimming pool, here she was living a separate life away from Evan, breeding dogs - great danes - and hosting bathing parties, [353] with carefully selected guests, as well as holidaying abroad with male and female friends. She travelled frequently up and down to London with two male companions a zoologist, E G Boulenger [354] and *her lover, a hideous bald headed man*" [355] named Captain Alex (Tim)Freeman, an army officer, ten years older than Lois, who died in a nursing home in 1939.[356]

The Night William Butler Yeats was ejected by Lois

William Butler Yeats

Back in their 'only just married' days Alan Pryce-Jones observed that when Evan had had too many brandies he was given to harsh comments about Lois's friends and lovers. The zoologist Boulenger was already by then Lois's constant companion.

One evening is recalled when Pryce-Jones, the Irish poet William Butler Yeats and others were together for an evening of poetry and talk. However Evan and Lois had just had a huge row. She had chosen the same occasion to invite some of her racing friends round together with zoologist, Boulenger.

The two totally different groups sat down in the dining room, and it seems Yeats, who was accustomed to deference, was not best pleased.

When the men from his party were alone, Evan rose to make a speech. It was a long drunken ramble, the target being Mr Boulanger

"I think that we must congratulate Mr Boulanger. Thanks to his friendship with my wife, he can live in my houses as much as he likes, he can eat excellent food at my table, he can use my cars and my chauffeur. But I have to draw the line when he gives my wife the drugs prescribed for his fish."[357]

On hearing Evan's voice in rage, Lois had crept downstairs and was behind the door, listening. At these words, she flung the doors open – she had her tigerish side – and pointed dramatically round the room crying out:

"Leave the house!! All of you!! Now!!"[358]

Yeats was led away in bewilderment. He was taken out into the safety of the open air by one of the other guests, an up-and coming gossipy journalist named Godfrey Winn. Godfrey Winn was a regular feature of Evan's later parties at Tredegar House, reports of which appeared in the *Daily Mirror* during 1936-7.[359]

Godfrey Winn

83

Winn records the following:

" Tredegar Park, outside Newport where the parties were so large that there was a special plan for you to study, when you came downstairs for dinner, as to where you were sitting, my car always seemed to be the smallest in the drive.."[360]

Evan and the Catholic Poetry Society

The Catholic Poetry Society.

The Catholic Poetry Society in London has been fortunate in securing many distinguished literary people to assist in its aims. and, under the presidency of the Hon. Evan Morgan, the eldest son of Viscount Tredegar, the Society has achieved considerable success.

The first reading of the winter session was held yesterday at Mr. Morgan's London house, when Mr. Alfred Noyes, who has an international reputation, gave a reading.

THE HON. E. MORGAN.

Later in the session there will be readings by Mr. Shane Leslie, Mr. G. K. Chesterton, Mr. Compton Mackenzie, and the President of the Society. The Secretary of the Society is Mr. Maurice Leahy, of Leigh-on-Sea. Mr. E. V. Knox, the well-known *Punch* writer, is also a supporter of the Society.

The Hon. Evan Morgan, who is the author of several books, was received into the Roman Catholic Church in 1919.

Evan combined his literary interests with his Catholicism by helping to found the Catholic Poetry Society. Maurice Leahy[361] was secretary and co-founder in 1927. The Catholic Poetry Society lasted till 1935. Hon. Vice- Presidents and Associates were Alfred Noyes, and Shane Leslie.

Evan also composed the hymn *"Christ the King"* to be sung at the opening of new Liverpool Catholic Cathedral by Cardinal Bourne[362] in 1933.

Lois Angered and Hits Back

Lois could lose her temper with Evan about anything, but they always fell back into the quaint terms of their domestic arrangement.

Then mysteriously in 1933 Lois petitioned Evan for a divorce on the grounds that he had committed sodomy with two men. Neither of Evan's paramours was named but the events themselves were said to have taken place in England and Germany. This was the action of a vindictive woman set out to avenge, albeit the petition was subsequently refused and the proceedings were left to wither on the vine. [363] But the lurid accusations are listed in surviving papers in the National Archives, Kew. [364]

In 1934 Lois became Viscountess Tredegar, but she was rarely at Evan's side or got involved in any of the affairs of the Morgan Estate.

XI

Evan Becomes Viscount Tredegar

Evan's father, Courtenay frequently stayed at the Ritz Hotel in London. He openly lived there with one of his mistresses (to Katharine's anger [365]) , and died there in 1934.

Evan's father Courtenay died *"a blind old man"* [366] beaten by failing health at sixty-seven. His finest hour was commanding his yacht Liberty when he converted it to a hospital ship for use in the Great War.

Evan was abroad, on board the yacht of a millionaire friend when he heard the news about his father's death. At last Evan could take the family home Tredegar House into orbit.

"after the death of his father [Evan Morgan led] a life that approximates more to a poem than to reality." [367]

Evan however had one surprise in store for his critics. There was a real issue on the landed estates involving cruelty to animals that he felt strongly enough about to take action in the House of Lords, despite the Morgan men and their 'hunting and shooting' traditions.

Evan first sat in the House of Lords on 11th July 1934. In Parliament, on 5th December 1934, he introduced a Bill to prohibit the use of steel traps and moved at second reading his "Gin Traps (Prohibition) Bill " in the House of Lords in May 1935.   A gin trap was defined as " *one that catches mammals or birds alive by gripping a limb by means of jaws, teeth, or clamps in such a manner as to cause pain"*.

In Parliament Evan proclaimed that if they supported the Bill *"that they should give the world an example in kindness to animals."*

PROHIBITION OF GIN TRAPS

BILL SAID TO BE TOO DRASTIC

Despite an impressive, detailed speech by Evan[368] on the second reading of the Bill on 28 May 1935 the motion was rejected, but the reform was only kicked out by four votes, remarkable when one considers that the aristocracy enjoyed their sport. [369]

Evan's Shame Over Ruperra Castle's tenants

Ruperra Castle in Ruins

Animal lover Evan showed less humanity to his tenants on the Ruperra Castle Estate, he disconnected their water supply. [370]

This action followed Evan's decision to dismiss staff and put the Castle up for sale, with a view to paying off some of his father's death duties. [371]   Evan also turned against tenants on the fringes of the Estate by withdrawing their water source.

Mary Thomas lived at *Cwm Leyshon* cottage in Rudry from the 1920s onwards. It was an estate cottage with the *Retreat* next to it.   Mary's personal testimony survives, thanks to interviews conducted by local historian, Pat Jones-Jenkins (formerly Pat Moseley).[372]

"We had water in the garden until Evan stopped the water on us in the garden of the Retreat (one of a pair of cottages with Cwm Leyshon) when Grandfather and our uncle lived there and when[Lord] Tredegar sold under those conditions. Then when it was sold to Haskins and then to (?Evans)our rights were stopped . We had to go as far as Maenllwyd to get drinking water until the Council put a tap inside the gate. It was a hard way of living." [373]

Mary worked in the *Bothy* at Ruperra Castle cooking and cleaning for the gardener's boys in the left hand building of the block. The Head Gardener and his wife, the McKinnons lived on the right side.

"Evan wasn't very nice" [374] added Mary in comparing him with his father, Courtenay. Mary gives the following as an example of Evan's lack of courtesy to one of the oldest and loyalist of his estate workers:

"Angus McKinnon, the Head Gardener at Ruperra was awfully upset that Evan Morgan never said he was sorry when Mrs McKinnon died. With Evan's father it would have been different. He would go in and have a cup of tea with them at the Bothy. And he'd walk around the gardens with Mr McKinnon and both of them would sit on the front steps to talk. " [375]

Pat Jones-Jenkins (formerly Pat Moseley) and Chris Jones-Jenkins reflect on the change of style between Evan and his father:

"When Evan succeeded Courtenay as Lord Tredegar in 1934, Morgan Family visits to Ruperra became less frequent. To the long serving workers still in charge, it must have seemed strange after the activity of previous years. Possibly, in their old age, the slowing pace of things didn't bother them too much, but they must have been aware that it was the end of an era." [376]

A similar judgement is made of the decline of standards during Evan's years as the custodian of the Tredegar Estates by the late Roger Philips, who wrote a comprehensive history in 1990. [377]

Evan failed to sell Ruperra Castle, although its contents were sold off. Courteney Morgan *"spent a great deal of money on Ruperra.....where he wished Evan to live during his lifetime. But Evan refused to live there.*[378]

The army took over the Castle in the Second World War but a fire in 1941 severely destroyed its rooms and roof, leaving a ruin (and it is even more dilapidated today). Paradoxically, a friend whom Evan showed round Ruperra before the war, says he " *seemed proud of it...*" [379] The same man was with him " *during the war when he received news of it being burned out...[says] Evan was greatly distressed*" [380] by its destruction.

Lois and Evan in USA

In late December 1935 Lois went to America (perhaps with a view of kick starting her film career) and the following year she spent time in Jamaica with an American female friend. Evan also went to New York in February 1936, [381] but the Tredegars tragically did not see each other alive again, save for a passing glance at a reception in London in the summer of 1937 . [382] Evan also travelled for to benefit his health during in this period to hotter climes including the Canaries and the West Indies. On board the *SS Alondra* he encountered some Irish soldiers , who were part of the Irish Brigade, fighting in Spain. Evan was moved to melancholy, a rather more serious mood than this usual flirting with soldiers or sailors in his company. [383]

Death of Lois in Budapest

Lord Tredegar Flies to Budapest

VISCOUNTESS'S DEATH CAUSED BY HEART FAILURE

LADY TREDEGAR DIES AT 37

On 18 September 1937 Lois died from a heart attack[384]- whilst on holiday with Mme Louis Cartier, Countess Almasy in Budapest, Hungary. Lois' brother Naps (Lord) Alington rushed to the scene, hotly followed by Evan. Lois's death was at first a mystery and the body was placed in police charge. Naps Alington later issued a statement to the Press :

" ….There is no question of an inquest on Lady Tredegar. She had a heart attack ..at the home of her host, M Cartier and his wife, when she was preparing to go out to dinner. She died shortly afterwards".

Crichel House, Dorset

Lois was cremated in Vienna, Austria. Evan brought Lois' ashes back to England (her remains were carried onto the plane as hand luggage although Evan later told stories of the urn having it's own fare paid seat on the plane [385]). Naps met Evan at Croydon Airport and the ashes were *"conveyed to Crichel"* (the Alington home in Dorset) in a casket which was placed by Naps in the rose garden there. [386] A Requiem Mass for Lois was held at the same time.[387]

Tredegar House Estate

Tredegar Estates Offices, Newport

Whilst Evan gave the cold-shoulder to his Ruperra tenants, the main Tredegar Estate, with its Estate Office in the town of Newport continued to flourish until the early years of the Second World War.

Alan Carnegie Stewart applied for a job there in 1938. As Evan's half-cousin he was leapfrogged into being an articled pupil, without payment of any fee. However, Alan remembers that in order to be taken on he and his father were summoned by Evan to lunch:

"My father and I were invited to lunch, and when we arrived at Tredegar Park by taxi from Newport Station there was a footman to open the car door. Another footman to take our coats and a third footman to announce our arrival! When we sat down for lunch a footman stood behind each chair.

In those days there were 26 indoor servants and 25 gardeners in addition to the vast staff on the Estate…. The Estate Office itself had a staff of over 20, including an architect, draughtsmen, accountant and rent collectors, secretaries and typists.

The Estate had its own woodland staff, estate yard with all tradesmen, home farm and gamekeepers…" [388]

Alan worked in the Estate Office until he went to war. He recalls Princess Olga coming to live at Tredegar House, and she and Evan gave him and his wife Margaret, a cocktail shaker as a wedding present.

Alan retuned to the same job at the Estate Office after the war, (1947-8) by which time much of Tredegar House was virtually closed down, with white dust sheets covering the furniture and pictures. Evan was only very occasionally in residence. Arranged by Captain Ware, Alan and his wife, Margaret lived at Tredegar House, with their own bedroom and they used the Brown Room as their own sitting room. Alan finally left the Estate the year before Evan's death.[389]

One regret that Alan recounted was that in all the years he worked at the Estate Office, Evan never once visited the men and women working there. [390]

Other memoirs refer to Evan's short temper with staff, he delighted in a public dressing down, bordering on humiliation of footmen and lowly maids when something went wrong in the domestic arrangements of the house. Evan's guests thought it was all a part of the entertainment. Evan was a lover (as was his mother) of leaving windows open and letting cold air run through the rooms. Evan lashed out at those who closed the windows. An instance of Evan's forked tongue is remembered by Henry Maxwell:

"I recall one dinner, on a Sunday evening, when, most unusually, the food was not up to the normal standard. Evan was, it must be admitted, terribly quick-tempered, demanded to know, in pretty fierce language, what the hell was going on? Mr North, [the House Steward/ Butler] with great dignity, replied, "The dinner has had to be cooked by the kitchen maid, My Lord; Cook is not feeling herself." Evan hissed back at him "Oh, and who is she feeling then?" [391]

Tredegar House Parties and Guests

Evan and Friend

After succeeding to the Viscountcy, Evan's parties at Tredegar House were always sizable events. Many descriptions survive of these parties, and the colourful array of guests. These gatherings were glittering affairs, the mix of guests was often out of the ordinary.

Alan Pryce-Jones lists *"a Berlin hustler"*[392] amongst Evan's typical list of house guests at one or other of these *"vast and chaotic house parties"*[393] .

A distinguished diarist records one of the unnamed guests as being *"that international monument of depravity, X"* [394]

The long description of the mystery woman that follows suggests that this is most likely to be the Marchesa Luisa Casati. [395]

Marchesa Luisa Casati [396]

Exiled in London, with colossal debts, Evan and other admirers, (including Naps Alington [397]) had befriended Luisa, an eccentric Italian much painted and sculptured, who wore the most exotic costumes, once " *parading with a pair of leashed cheetahs and wearing live snakes as jewellery.*" [398] On one occasion for playfulness, Evan provoked a clash of personalities and egos when he invited the Marchesa and Aleister Crowley to his London home on the same evening. "*….the two collided and an argument ensued….*" [399] exactly as Evan planned.

Cecil Roberts

Cecil Roberts offers a description of Tredegar House as being

" crammed with pictures, tapestries, statues, silver and most valuable of all servants. [and his room was] beautiful. Reached by the fine Grinling Gibbons staircase." [400]

Cyril Hartmann adds his memory of Evan's house parties:

"With great reluctance I attended one or two of Evan's enormous and always heterogeneous house parties, when thirty or more people would sit down to every meal. It was not so bad during the day when one could choose one's own company and do whatever one liked, but after dinner there were always appallingly embarrassing parlour–games of the charade variety, to which Evan was particularly addicted. I always did my best to avoid taking part in these, but I could not always make my escape in time, and it was the one thing which Evan was completely merciless, even with old and other privileged friends..." [401]

And Evan More.....[402]

DISTINGUISHED GUESTS OF LORD TREDEGAR

Here are happy, smiling guests of Viscount Tredegar at Tredegar House. Left to right: Major B. Corbet, Mr. Mackenson, Mrs. Carnegie, the Countess of Carlisle, the Marchesa Godio-de-Godieo, Mr. H. G. Wells (novelist), Viscountess Massereene and Ferrard, Mrs. Richard Guinness, Mr. Derek Jackson (the Oxford don gentleman-rider, who rode his own horse, Princess Mir, in the Grand National), Mrs. Alan Pryce-Jones (a daughter of the First Lord of the Admiralty), Viscount Tredegar, Mr. Alan Pryce-Jones, Lord Faringdon, Captain H. Ware and Colonel Mason.

There is reference to the very long list of guests by many other writers who composed commentaries on Evan's parties with details of their own experiences as guests.

The hospitality was total and consuming. The pats of butter bore the Tredegar coronet. Evan the perfect host, was assisted by an excellent secretary-hostess Emily Sutherland. Alongside Sutherland was Evan's loyal estate manager, Captain Harry Ware who organised Evan's affairs behind and in front of stage. [403] A recent memoir by an American hones in affectionately on Sutherland and Ware's role in always carefully watching over any vulnerable young guests. [404]

Evan's godson Desmond Leslie[405] also refers to sitting the *"children's table"* (when aged 14) and later the more adult antics, the compulsory playing of a drawing rooms games, with Evan's favourite being *In the Manner of the Word,* [406] which he invented (with H G Wells and Mgr Ronnie Knox SJ [407]).

Another regular guest adds *"Evan was a great mimic. He was extraordinarily witty and entertaining, observant of people's foibles to a deadly degree and sparing them nothing! His strictures and observations were accompanied by a significant and resounding sniff! When he sniffed like that, one always knew that something pretty devastating was on its way."* [408]

On leaving Tredegar House after a weekend of fun bouquets of flowers always adorned guest's cars. ...this haven was a modern day *Shangri-La.*

One damper on all this gross and vulgar use of the Morgan money came from the diarist, Chips Channon .. in the 1930s : " *4 July, Tredegar; glorious house, but the feel and even smell of decay, of aristocracy in extremis, the sinister and the trivial, crucifixes and crocodiles..*"[409]

Honeywood House – Parties

Evan entertains his Carnegie Cousins at Honeywood House

Evan also invited numerous combinations of people to his mother's home in Surrey, Honeywood House.

Rafaelle, Duchess of Leinster[410] (pictured left)was among the more observant, and more cynical of Evan's guests there. She noted that Evan drank a whole bottle of brandy at night and did not turn a hair. She also comments that *"about the place was a weary housekeeper who had obviously been there a very long time."* [411] After being given drinks, Evan's special guests were shown up to his private chapel (on the first floor) and taken to see his valuable collection of rare ivory figures. Rafaelle's company comprised five young men (of various nationalities and ages) who, like her arrived at the local railway station and were ferried to the house.

The Duchess got more than she bargained for *"It was evident that the young men were not as used to brandy as my host. Hysteria was in the room...I couldn't bear another minute of it ..I went in search of someone to see if I could get a train [out]. No trains until the* morning."[412] Next day Rafaelle didn't wait around for breakfast. *"I got a taxi, and to my amazement, I found another guest also at the station. He looked completely used up, and whipped out a big white pill saying : 'If I don't take this I will die.'"* [413]

Katharine, Lady Tredegar was not much seen by Evan's friends visiting Honeywood. She is described as being *"..an invalid, leading an almost cloistered life. She appeared at mealtimes at Honeywood, but otherwise one saw very little of her. In London Evan never entertained his guests at his mother's house, but would invariably take them out to a restaurant, or rather, a series of restaurants or clubs, for Evan always made a night of it".*[414]

Evan's Menagerie

Evan's zoo included a boxing kangaroo

A weekend was never complete at Tredegar House without a visit by the guests to Evan's private zoo, in the grounds, which was maintained by a zookeeper, Mr Pitt.

As with the house parties, a number of records can be gleaned to learn more about Evan's prized menagerie.

"the feudal park was of wild beasts and tropical birds, for Evan was more successful in running a menagerie than a menage. .."

Evan had had part of the stables converted to contain the caged collection. One friend of Evan's parents recalls that there was *"a dog faced baboon called Bimbo....but one day Bimbo rang amok and was later sent to London Zoo...".* [415]

Another observer writes *"there was an aviary of rare birds, ibis, cranes, storks, toucans, parrots, pelicans and vultures. In the enclosure by the lake there was a boxing kangaroo. Evan invited us to take it on, but no one ventured, rumour saying that a former guest had been carried out on a stretcher! "* [416]

Another episode to cause great consternation was when a venomous widow spider escaped from its glass cage inside the house in the Gilt Room. A white faced footman eventually confided to Evan *" M'Lord.. the Widow's out....".*

The spider was eventually found climbing up the curtains! [417]

Several memoir writers refer to Evan, simply for amusement, letting his animals loose in the house, to the shrieks and horrors of guests and staff.

The cost of feeding Evan's collection of animals and birds ran into thousands of pounds a year.

Evan with Blue Boy

The science fiction writer, H G Wells, once dubbed 'the English Jules Verne' was a constant house guest. He was pecked by Blue Boy, Evan's notoriously bad mouthed parrot, and claimed he could never *"gratify that damn bird"*. [418] Evan's regular party piece was to have Blue Boy behave badly. In private, another trick was for the bird to bestow hammer blows from its head at great speed between Evan's toes, whilst he was standing naked in the bathroom.

A Honey Bear like Alice

Alice, a honey bear was another of Evan's animal treasures. She took a shine to one guests, the journalist, Godfrey Winn who is recorded as saying *" Yes, Alice was a blundering bundle of*

99

glamour. She even followed me about when I went there to stay. And when I showed signs of apprehension because Alice nibbled my trouser leg, Evan explained "Oh, that's only Alice's way of showing affection." [419]

Evan extraordinary power over birds is revealed in this story. When he called out " *Rosa!! Rosa!!* " across the lake at Tredegar, Rosa a duck, (probably called after Rosa Lewis of the Cavendish Hotel fame) came skimming out of the reeds. [420]

Evan's cousin Alan Stewart remembers Evan's concern for a pregnant kangaroo.

"Evan tried to resolve the mystery of whether a new born baby kangaroo finds its way to its mother pouch of its own accord or whether the mother kangaroo puts the baby in her pouch."

Alan explained that Evan sat up several nights in a row to watch this particular baby kangaroo being born to see what happened. [421]

There remains some doubt to the outcome of whether Evan solved the mystery or not!!

Evan always wanted to shock and amuse. Another relative provides this anecdote of Evan at his very best.

" I asked my father about Evan Morgan who he met as a young boy. He had various curious stories about him. Apparently he had my grandparents met at the station by an elephant when they went to stay with him and he had monkeys on the dining room table. Also he surrounded himself with powdered footmen for whom the job specification seemed to require a belief in homosexuality and communism. This apparently strained relations with my grandparents but he recalls him as being very entertaining. "[422]

Journalist Cecil Roberts, a life long friend of Evan (after saving his life one night in London after the Great War[423]) relates a story of Evan travelling abroad with some of his pets. Roberts was on a lecture tour of the USA in the 1930s and booking into a hotel in Kansas City when the desk clerk remarked:

"Hey we had another Britisher here a few days ago. A strange guy. He was travelling with a priest, a red haired youth, a baby panther, two snakes, a mongoose and a couple of bird cages"

Immediately Roberts asked: *"Was his name Tredegar?"* **The clerk replied:**

"Sure, that's it, Tredegar. We objected to his animals but he said they all slept with him."[424]

Stepping Out With Evan

A Close Up of the Peer Who is Everything

There are priceless anecdotes of Evan's assaults on some notable figures of his time. Money speaks, wealth could buy anything and anyone.

Charles Austin Sherman III vividly describes in his memoirs[425] how Evan in a *"coup"* [426] acquired the services of two of Frances's greatest entertainers for an evening at the famous Maxim's restaurant, Paris. The two stars were Maurice Chevalier and Edith Piaf.

Evan gate crashed his friend's parties too. He would take a group of his house guests to St Donat's Castle, in the Vale of Glamorgan, when that old citadel was the home of the American newspaper magnet William Randolph Hearst. The party motored down as a convoy from Tredegar House to find lashings of hospitality on offer from

Hearst *"in green knickers surrounded by a spill of stars from Hollywood..."* Numerous guests were later observed floating in the swimming pool which had once been the castle's old jousting ground.. Among Hearst regular invitees were the likes of Charlie Chaplin and Douglas Fairbanks Jnr and regular visitors were British film stars and politicians, with David Lloyd George being almost part of the furniture after he ceased to be Prime Minister.

Things didn't always go to plan. A story of Evan running into the painter Pablo Picasso is an example. Evan was in a restaurant (with one of his young men on display) when he spotted the great painter sitting alone on a terrace. Evan summoned the wine waiter to take a drink over to the legend with his compliments. Picasso eventually approached Evan, picking up *en route* to his table, a vase of flowers and as he moved in, proceeded to pour the vase and contents over Evan's head. [427]

Whether or not Evan came a cropper, these tales were repeated with relish at Evan's instigation.

XII

Evan's Last decade
Evan and Olga[428]

Lord Tredegar and Princess Olga Wed

VISCOUNT TREDEGAR TO MARRY HERE
"Day On Which Both Our Birthdays Fall"
HONEYMOON WITH RUSSIAN PRINCESS IN HIS BALI HOME

SINGAPORE REGISTER OFFICE CEREMONY

Evan knew his second wife Olga (a Russian Princess, and divorcee[429]) some time before he proposed marriage to her. She visited as a guest at Tredegar House in December 1937, with her dogs. [430] Evan was also on good terms with Olga's brother Count Voronzow Dasckow and later supported the latter's admission for residence in the USA. [431]

In November 1938, Evan announced at a dance in Newport (attended by Olga) that he was to marry the Princess. [432]

Olga and Evan

The real plans began in the Spring of 1939 with an announcement that they would marry in Rome and then honeymoon in Java, to be followed by time in *"the East Indes island of Bali where Lord Tredegar has a native style home…"* [433]

In the end the marriage took place on 13 March 1939 in Singapore, with a flurry of excitement among the Colonial authorities over Olga's nationality, but which was resolved without incident. [434] Sir Shenton Thomas, the Governor of the Straits Settlement was one of the guests at the wedding reception. Olga *"wore a white silk costume with hat and shoes to match. Baskets of orchids filled the room where the marriage ceremony was held…[Evan's] private secretary Capt. H Ware, and Mrs Sutherland, who accompanied Lord Tredegar's party to the East, were the witnesses. A special licence costing £8 was secured."* [435]

Evan's 2ⁿᵈ wife Princess Olga

Olga envisaged she would be more than just a show wife and might even be the mother to their children. Sadly she was to be at best disappointed, at worst fooled. Evan required his wives to be more like his mother. Added to this it was evident that his adoration of his faithful secretary Emily Sutherland, whom in fact he called Mother Sutherland or *Mother S* for short, it was a complex relationship!

Olga had sophisticated tastes in fashion and interior design, she transformed her living spaces of *The Red Room and Pink Room* into a glorious display of her style. An observer remarked that " *Princess Olga painted her fingernails with miniature scenes instead of nail varnish..*" [436]

She had appeared in the front cover of the fashionable *Tatler* magazine and was marked out as an iconic image of her time. Olga was a popular figure in Newport and she performed her public duties as Evan's wife earnestly and enthusiastically. She was much liked as Viscountess Tredegar. But in the end the marriage crumbled with the parties barely able to communicate with each other except through intermediaries.

In Olga's reminiscences, a wonderful story emerged about the bed she had

"When I married Lord Tredegar, my bedroom was the Pink bedroom, a bathroom was in the next door room and Lord Tredegar moved from the King's bedroom to the Passing Room. Shortly after the war started and due to staff and heating problems he moved back to the King's bedroom, and I moved to the Red Room and made the Blue Room into my sitting room. .. the bedrooms had four poster beds...the bed in the Pink Room was 9 ft square...this large bed ending its days in the dining room....

I visited Tredegar (House) in the 1960s with an old friend Mrs Noel Stevens. We had only meant to walk in the grounds, but the young Mother Superior asked us to come into the house and took us first of all into the dining room which the nuns has transformed into their Chapel. She took me up to the altar rail and asked me if I recognised the rails and altar, I was somewhat non-plussed and she gaily announced that it was my bed! " [437]

Evan and Crowley exposed

1943 was Evan's own *annus horribilis*. Two family deaths in January did not bode well. [438] In April, he suffered the indignity of the Court Martial. In July Olga divorced him, citing his *'incapacity'* [439] as the reason for the annulment. A note in the Tredegar House files is uncompromising

"Evan was sterile"[440]

Whilst the tribulations and the verdict of Evan's breaches of The Official Secrets Acts were withheld from the public, the press trumpeted the humiliating truth of Evan's failed marriage.

Friends were thin on the ground in these lonely months. It was in the summer of 1943, a few days before Evan reached his 50th birthday that his old charmer Aleister Crowley stayed for a few days as guest of honour at Tredegar House. [441]

Evan's compatriot, Augustus John spared no punches in a early letter to Evan (after John had completed several sketches of *The Great Beast* - as Crowley was known [442]) :

"Aleister Crowley is in no way admirable; I even doubt his carnal prowess. The face I have drawn is that of a vulgar charlatan - a coarse bad mystagogue." [443]

Another commentator remarked of Crowley (in 1927)

"I've bought AC's memoirs which are disappointing. For all his reputation he reads like a living example of Oscar's man who "wakes up every morning with bad resolutions and always breaks them." [444]

There is still further doubt expressed by one insider from the occult who points out from the testimony of another occultist present at the same visit to Evan's home *" that .. Crowley was by this time .. calmed down a lot.."*[445] . Moreover, *" Crowley* [who had] *once described Evan as the Adept of Adepts " may just have been trying to butter* [Evan] *up at the time..*[as he was].. *...desperately short of money."* [446]

There is no question that at the gathering there comprised plenty of reading from the occult scriptures and Crowley was impressed by seeing Evan's well equipped Magick Room. The assertion made that Evan enticed Crowley at this visit to induce some kind of horrific illness to descend upon his former commanding officer in the army, over Evan's Court Martial is not proven. It is however apparent from Crowley's published diaries, that Evan saw the *Great Beast* over some parts of 1943-4 .They regularly dined and wrote *"chits"* to each other. Emily Sutherland also showed an interest in the relationship. [447]

Evan In London in the Blitz

During the Blitz and whilst serving in the army at Wing House, Piccadilly, Evan could also be seen taking tea in the Palm Court of the Ritz Hotel or entertaining in the *"downstairs bar as it was underground...*[with the likes of] *Harold Nicolson, MP* [and] *if the air raid siren had gone.. the King and Queen of Albania used to appear and sit in a back room."* [448] Evan was equally at home in the Hotel Ritz in Paris, he had a compulsion for picking up men at the Lido and then wining and dining them. [449]

Dicky Buckle

Evan's London house at 13 South Audley Street had two direct bomb hits in May 1941, He then moved to Albany, Piccadilly, which also had a direct hit.

Some young men in their mid 20s, like Richard (Dicky) Buckle (later a distinguished ballet critic[450]) arrived during the period and stayed temporarily, *en route* to join their regiment to serve in the war. Buckle also visited Evan at Honeywood House after the War. [451]

13 South Audley Street became a nest for Evan to entertain his kindred spirits. This fact is recalled by Evan's great friend Conte Anthony (Tony) Mattei, [452] who served in war torn Italy with Dicky Buckle and who were comrades and later close friends. During and after the war, Evan hosted parties with Mattei. From the 1920s onwards, Evan's earlier London homes were a hub for a cluster of new and rising stars in the art world to meet, including portrait painters, sculptors [453] and their models. [454]

Another youth snatched by the tailcoat by Evan and given special treatment, including treats in London's finest dining establishments was Robert Harbinson[455], an Irishman from Belfast. He first fell under Evan's spell when, as a teenager he was attending a Church seminary near Cardiff that had links with Evan's Stewart relations. Years later Harbinson, who became an accomplished travel writer but social misfit (who broke several stories of sex-based conspiracies in high places [456]) included his seemingly innocent flirtations with Evan in his memoirs. [457]

Evan and Lord Alfred Douglas

A series of letters in the British Library provides insight into Evan's well meant campaign with the unlikely fellow patron, the birth and contraceptive goddess, Marie Stopes (who had a house near Dorking [458]) to provide support, and recognition to the aging Bosie (Lord Alfred) Douglas. Alfred was in a state of destitution. Representations to two Prime Ministers, Neville Chamberlain and Winston Churchill to get him a Civil List Pension failed miserably[459] as did a concurrent attempt to persuade any notable figures *"to join a committee to proclaim Douglas the greatest sonneteer since Shakespeare"* and so enable the Civil List application. Evan was mortified that Evelyn Waugh and Harold Nicolson would not help. Notwithstanding any thought of Douglas they reminded the conspirators of the works of Milton and Wordsworth . [460] Evan (and Olga) visited Douglas during his final years and tried to make him comfortable and provided basic items and treats.

Evan's Last Years : After the War

Evan and his Bronze Head and the Sculptor, Prince Bira of Siam

With his health unstable and fortunes declining Evan spent the winter of 1946 in his beloved Jamaica. Here he was lionised as *"a lineal descendant of Morgan the Pirate- sometime Island governor."* Evan had spent happy times here between the wars, sometimes with Lois in pursuit, to find herself the same hot spots. Evan was usually in the company of one his closest male companions of the previous decade (either at home in Wales or London or abroad) Prince Paul of Greece. As playboys Evan and the Prince were regular visitors to Jamaica from 1934 at least until Paul married in 1938. [461]

There are several lively texts that suggest Evan and Prince Paul not only shared a good friendship travelling and sailing but they passed around each other (and with a few notable dignitaries besides) the spoils and entanglements of their involvement with several male gigolos. [462]

Evan and Prince Paul of Greece

Evan's Last Male Conquests

Denham "Denny" Fouts

Two books published in the 1990s[463] repeat the same assertion that late in his life Evan took a shine to a gigolo named Denham "Denny" Fouts, who was of American descent. Denham had romped his way through America and Europe, in affairs with many notable figures but died a hopeless opium addict. [464]

When the pressure to commit himself emotionally to anyone (or anything) Evan had little staying power. He was never capable of meeting someone on equal terms. His relationships with the likes of Aldous Huxley, Frances Stevenson and Ronald Firbank all withered to nought quickly when Evan's victims discovered his selfishness, his warped nature, his congenital lies, perverted nature and thoughtless disloyalty. These and other friends soon avoided him like the plague. As we have noted the worst exhibition of Evan's bad behaviour involved a tussle with the fantasy novelist, Ronald Firbank over a well meant book dedication.

Evan's lusting for young men especially it seems those that were already marked out as being queer in the aftermath of other failed relationships or a reputation for being an easy prey. In this context was Evan's apparent fling with Alistair Graham[465], a figure often cited as being in part Waugh's inspiration for Sebastian Flyte in *Brideshead Revisited*. Resembling a scene with Oscar Wilde and Bosie being ejected from what they thought was a safe house for conducting their affair, Evan and Graham were prevented from continuing their sexual liaisons at the Cavendish Hotel, where Evan kept a suite of rooms (so had a pass key to the establishment). He was held in much regard by its colourful proprietor, Rosa Lewis,[466] primarily because he always paid his bills and indeed those of others too. Rosa always defended Evan against his critics as in the following exchange between her and another Cavendish dweller, a monocled guards officer:

"Upon my soul Rosa, why do you bother with pansies like that?

"Pansies!" retorted Rosa. "Who the hell do you think you are? I saw you leaching after that Lady Chatterley, like a tomcat on hot bricks. And when it comes to calling young Evan names I'd just like to ask where I'd be if it wasn't for pansies like him who pay the bills for scrimshanking buggers like you." [467]

Rosa Lewis was also especially fond of Graham, *"one of the moneyless young men who drinks were charged to older and richer customers"* [468] who served as a diplomat abroad. **Graham left Britain for foreign exile and many years later returned to the UK – to Wales where he lived out his days as a recluse.** [469]

Tredegar House files touch briefly on other lovers of Evan. [470] **One remarkable bed companion of Evan's (related by Henry Maxwell) was the 1920s, silent movie star Rudolf Valentino :**

Evan *"rather liked shocking people...and he was the reverse of secretive about any lurid episode in his past. He told more than once that he had had an affair with Rudolf Valentino.... And how Valentino's women fans would have lynched*
Him had they known." [471]

Surprisingly, even as Evan moved towards his last years he was contemplating marriage again. [472] **This was more of a cunning financial plan to save the Tredegar Estate from going under besides which Evan dreaded his inheritance being passed down to his cousin John, whom he hated.** [473]

What Evan Did In The Second World War

Evan in World War Two

111

The full story of what Evan did in the second World War is revealed in the transcript of the Court Martial. Evan (who loved birds more than he loved people) was the link between pigeon breeders in Britain and the military units and the Intelligence services using pigeons as a part of the war effort. It was covert work governed by the Official Secrets Act. Evan revealed information to several individuals who were not entitled to know anything about this work.

Address to the House of Lords, by the King

King George VI (whom Evan had greeted on horseback when the King and Queen visited Newport and Cardiff in 1937) informed the House of Peers that one of their number had been arrested.

The Lords acknowledged the King's message:

DIE MARTIS 13 APRILIS, 1943

Ordered, by the Lords Spiritual and Temporal of the United Kingdom of Great Britain and Northern Ireland in Parliament assembled, That an humble Address be presented to His Majesty to return the thanks of the House to His Majesty for His most gracious message which He has been pleased to make to this House of the reason for putting Major the Lord Tredegar under arrest.

(Signed) Henry J F Badeley
Cler: Parliamentor [474]

Evan in Army Uniform

The Court Martial of Evan Morgan

Monckton

When facing near certain imprisonment in 1943, after breaching the Official Secrets Act, Evan's champion, the great advocate of the Abdication crisis, Sir Walter Monckton[475] said his client was more at home in a Doge's Palace of 15th Century Venice than of modern times.[476] This perceptive remark, with other mitigating factors thrown in, not least about his upbringing and dysfunctional family, saved Evan's skin. The details about this Court Martial were not widely disclosed. When Evan died his army record was summed up in obituaries by stating *"He resigned his commission with the honorary rank of Captain in 1943 on account of* ill-health." [477] although this is supplemented by reference to him acting as *"Military County Social Welfare Officer for Monmouthshire and commanded the 3rd Monmouthshire Battalion of the Home Guard."*[478]

Nigel West's Book on MI5

Other references, fabled, flawed and fashioned, unless demonstrated otherwise by convincing new evidence persist elsewhere uncorrected, about Evan's war years. One instance of this was in a book by Nigel West[479] who is usually well informed, but was duped this time. He stated that Evan was *let off* prosecution by Court Martial for revealing military secrets in 1943 as a result of intervention to save him by MI5. [480] This clumsy blunder has been mentioned in other contexts and has propounded West's gaffe into other books[481] and across the Internet planting a wholly inaccurate and misleading account of what actually happened. As this book shows Evan did *not* get off the humiliating spectacle of a Court Martial for offences including that of silly, careless talk. He underwent a trial and a verdict was duly reached by the Army judges appointed to hear the allegations made against him.

National Archives File WO 71/1078

The transcript of the Court Martial in this book is uplifted from the Judicial Proceedings namely the official War Office file held by National Archives, Kew, WO 71/1078. This is reproduced in full and shows one of the less amusing faces of Evan Morgan. This work has been undertaken to set the record straight, and the coverage of the book is extended into tackling some of Evan's other many faces. But the latter is only Evan at a backward glance. There is plenty of room left for others to praise and bury Evan.

Evan and the Nazis

With many myths and legends flying around about Evan, it is especially important to clarify and correct the historical record, so far as is possible. An example is Evan's wartime service in the Second World War. This has been subject of quaint speculation with some extraordinary suggestions made. Unsubstantiated claims have been winkled out of gossip and unimportant coincidences by Evan fanciers, of him being a spy, an influential friend of several high ranking Nazis in Hitler's Germany, including Rudolph Hess, whom it is inferred (and is a most unlikely claim) that Evan saw Hess after his capture in Britain in 1941. Hess was held at Maindiff Court Military Hospital and POW Reception Centre outside Abergavenny. [482]

A few years ago the compilers of this book took part in a BBC Radio Wales programme *"A Meeting in Munich"* [483] which drew on hugely speculative revelations about Evan based on a curious document, a seating plan for a table at a restaurant and on no more than that. It is a fact that Evan once dined with some notable Nazis (and their sympathisers) at Bad Wiesse, near Munich, in 1932. And the odd-ball attendees included Rudolph Hess, Ernst Rohm and Edmund Heines. [484] Rohm and Heines (both gay) were executed on Hitler's orders in 1934. Among the British diners at that Munich restaurant table were other gay friends and acquaintances of the artist Sir Francis Rose[485] (who was one of Ernst Rohm's lovers[486]) including Evan and James Lonsdale-Bryans.[487] If they were planning anything, an orgy or re-enactment of some occult ceremony seems a more likely inference, than spying or plotting. It would be eight years later when war was eventually declared, if the story behind this was true would be a wonderful example of forward thinking. This was a Germany where homosexuality was rife, with clubs and *" diplomatic cocktail parties and orgies ..organised by highly-paid pimps.."* [488]

Evan's big night out with the Nazis is hardly convincing evidence of the Tredegar heir being anything other than a follower of fashion. The key player in making it all happen, for Evan to meet some prominent Nazis was Francis Rose. He was a close friend of Evan and one of only seven people who sent wreaths to Evan's funeral at Buckfast Abbey in 1949. [489] In his colourful, highly readable Memoirs (with many references to Evan's flamboyant side) Rose cautions about Evan's excesses:

"Evan Tredegar perhaps went too far in his fantasies when his passion for fancy dress led him to wear clerical dress at a party given by the disgraced and exiled Infante of Spain, Don Luis, Prince of Orleans where cocaine was served on silver salvers carried by Negro boys and powdered footmen." [490]

But for all his *"making mock"*[491] Rose later saw a fundamental change in Evan into a more restrained *"quiet, kind, religious man with deep faith who died ..in great peace with his religion."* [492] Evidence exists of a different kind, since a document seen in the Tredegar House records starkly that *" Evan died a religious maniac.."* [493] whilst another repeats a calmer pronouncement that Evan *" was consoled and sustained by his religion."*[494] Another note in the Tredegar House files indicates that Evan also took stock of his fading life by consulting a palmist.

"Evan Morgan used to attend a palmist called Madame Brena Rhodes of Newport where he would frequently burst out crying."[495]

Several of Evan's friends were based in Germany in the 1930s,[496] many young queer men flocked there, for hefty servings of *'divine decadence'* as is so wonderfully described by Christopher Isherwood in his famous Berlin stories.

Did Evan's parrot bite Hermann Goering?

It is also a complete myth about a further link cited by the war-mongers who see Evan as some kind of James Bond figure fraternising with Nazis, when Hermann Goering paid a trip to the Isle of Capri, Italy to see Mussolini. Moreover it is fiction to say that Evan's parrot bit Goering as is claimed in this declaration.

"One morning, Evan's parrot found its way into Goering's bedroom and, in the ensuing fracas to remove it, attached itself to the Reichsmarschall's face by biting firmly onto his nose. [497]

This fanciful epistle on another that first gained momentum in an article in *Encounter* magazine, in 1974.[498]

"In the 1930s, the Nazi period, Goering had paid a visit to Mussolini and had expressed a wish to see Capri. (It was not a success.) Lord Tredegar had the next suite at the Hotel Quisisana, and Tredegar's monkey bit the Field Marshal's nose."

It's the monkey now! It all sounds like one of Evan's vastly embellished tales.

It was the monkey, and indeed it was this particular creature who was guilty of a misdemeanour in a hotel in Capri. But the animal's target was not Goering, but a female guest. The whole fascinating story is told over three pages in *The Story of Axel Munthe*, published in 1953. [499] The monkey, named Patti, [500] was a gift to Evan from the King of Siam. [501] It was due to join the other Morgan exotic pets at his private zoo in the grounds of Tredegar House. The monkey lost heart before ever reaching Wales. At Capri Evan sought help from Axel Munthe, [502] known as a *"celebrated animal lover"* [503] who (although retired) had a home on the island.

Patti was duly fostered and nursed back to health again. Evan was encouraged by the reports to return to Capri to take Patti back to Wales. Whilst staying at an hotel Evan was warned to keep Patti on a long lead, but he rejected this as he thought it likely to irritate the beast. The monkey soon became unmanageable and the hotel politely requested that Evan remove the animal.

One escapade that had concerned the hotel was when " *Patti...had climbed out of the window in the night, crossed the open verandah, got into another room, settled himself on the chest of a woman suffering from heart trouble, who was in bed asleep, and begun tousling her hair with his long, thin fingers. The woman woke up, saw the gruesome creature reflected in the moonlight and let out an unearthly shriek."* [504] It took many weeks for the guest to recover from her ordeal. Evan was forced to remove Patti to the sanctuary of South Wales.

But what of Hermann Goering on Capri ? It was in fact Axel Munthe (and certainly not Evan) who met Goering there in January 1937. The event is recorded with photographs in the American Library of Congress. [505] Munthe (who opposed the Nazis) resisted an approach by Goering to buy the villa of San Michele, Munthe's precious home on the island. [506]

Evan's last time in Ireland and on Capri

At the end of his life Evan's religion (which he toyed with at times and even mocked) was a special comfort to the dying man. He made several visits to Ireland, [507] and was contemplating Irish citizenship. [508]

Yet there are still stories of Evan continuing to live life on all cylinders. He returned to Capri during this time, in the very last year of his life, only " *to be arrested for committing a public nuisance and sacrilege! [He was]....progressing quietly towards a beach to swim, harming nobody, clad simply in a sort of codpiece and collar of pearls from which hung his large jewelled crucifix, [when he] was seized and cast in a cell...".* [509] *It would seem that Evan was reported by some islanders who fell into the category of gracious living"* [510] possibly Miss Gracie Fields " *that vaudeville monster ...who [owned] half of Capri . [and saw Evan whilst].squinting through binoculars from the garden of her villa ..."* [511].

Poor Evan, to suffer such a dismal fate when he was so terribly ill, and although he was soon released from jail, his end was very near.

Evan took very seriously ill in Rome, but succeeded in returning to Britain where he was immediately admitted to the Middlesex Hospital. He was discharged but later died at his mother's Surrey home of Honeywood House. He was fifty-five years old.

Evan, towards the end of his life

Evan Mourned and Mourns

Cynthia Jebb[512] records in her diary for 19 May 1949:

"Tomorrow I go to Evan Tredegar's memorial service at the [Brompton] Oratory. He was a very old beau of mine. Mad, hectic, a curious mixture of being highly religious and not a little vicious; yet he was a good friend always, amusing, a generous host, and above all, he had beaucomp de race.,,,"

For the two years following Evan's death a single *In Memoriam* appeared in *The Times*

"Tredegar: Viscount Evan April 27th 1949. In loving memory of dear EVAN, so sadly missed. B.M."

B.M. was Baron George Marochetti (grandson of the famous sculptor of that surname) who died in 1952, aged 58. He was a journalist, diplomat and shipping and wine agent. His loss of Evan was clearly very personally felt. [513] This echoes Evan's own intimations that he placed in *The Times*, in memory of Raymond Rodakowski and the poem he wrote in love of Raymond.

Raymond Rodakowski
Vale

To R .R.

And so, you too, my last and oldest friend,
Have sped to regions that we cannot see;
Who in the battle's forefront found your end
And faced it with a soldier's chivalry.
And so to you too have fled and passed away,
Yet we shall meet again some happier day.

And you have paid the heaviest price of all,
An you have given more than many gave,
This life alone did your young senses call
Who nothing sought when you had found the grave:
On life you said there was, one life alone;
And that you gave, scare counting it your own.

You told me often there could be no God,
No life eternal, nought beyond the shroud,
And no uprising from the burial sod,
No Paradise behind the fleeting cloud:
Now have you solved that mystery and know
Whence we have come and wither we must go.

Last Words

Evan's Grave in the Private Cemetery at Buckfast Abbey
2nd Stone from the Left

Of Your Charity Pray for the Soul
Of Evan Frederic Morgan Viscount Tredegar of Tredegar Park
Newport, Monmouthshire

Like his hero, the poet John Donne, Evan believed in three separate lives *"of the body, of the intelligence, and of the soul".* [514]

His favourite lines from Donne are a fitting epitaph:

I am two fooles, I know
For loving and for saying so
In whining Poetry...

Evan wrote the following in Jamaica:

A Sonnet By Evan Morgan

Remember me sometimes, when the Sun is warm
Upon the blossoms dancing on the tree
Remember me! And if your heart must scorn
My weaknesses...let these trifles be
As fallen petals shaken to the ground
Soon to be scorched to ochre; let your heart
Be ever finding never what was found.
Something profound which only Souls impart
One to another in the breath of Spring
A glancing profile in mirroring water shines
Ever before me, that was never found
But was bequeathed; only a heart divines
Such loveliness when heart to heart is bound
Breathe not my name in anger nor in scorn
For both of us will yet again be born.

Despite his many foibles there will *never* be another Evan Morgan!

Aspects of Evan
The Last
Viscount Tredegar

The transcript of Evan's Court Martial for offences against the Official Secrets Acts

From National Archives, Kew File reference

WO 71/1078.

Part of the map referred to in the proceedings

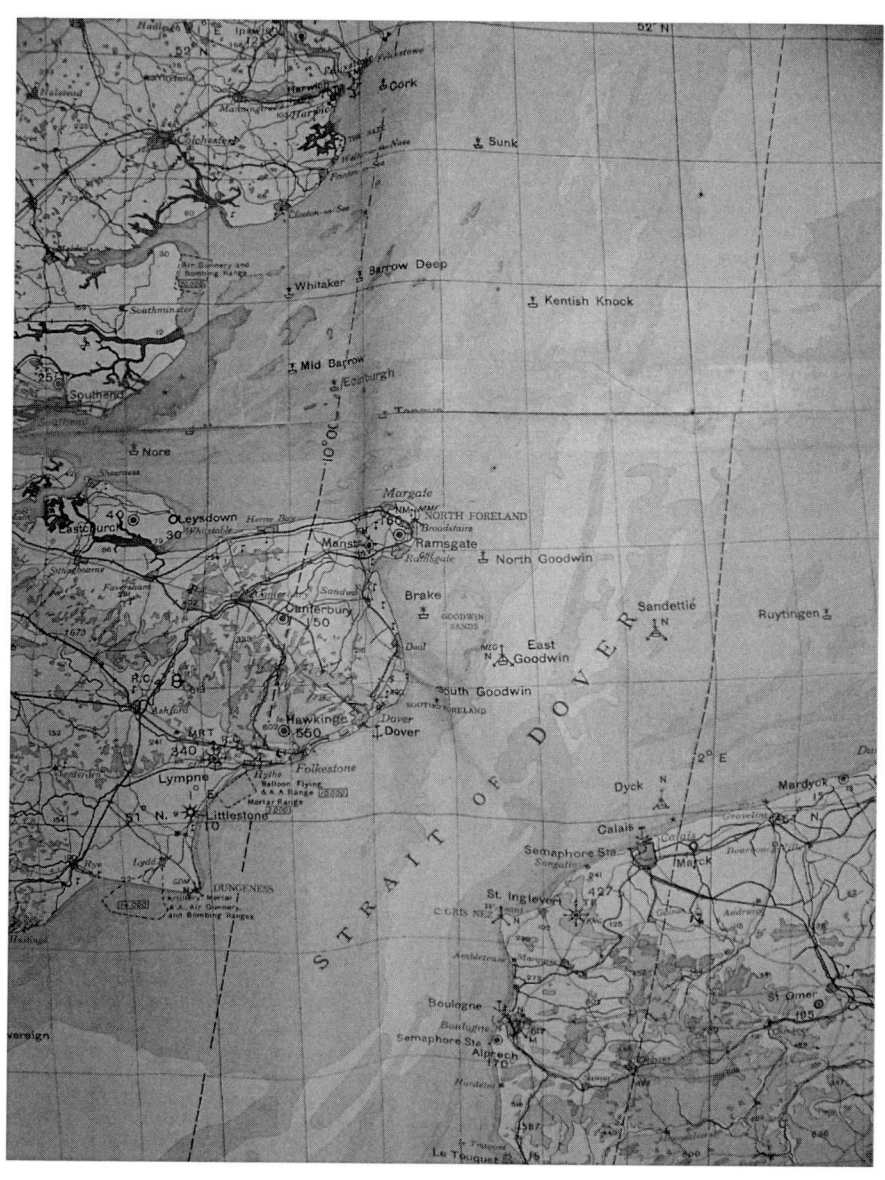

Part of the Map referred to in the transcript

SECRET

Trial by General Court Martial

TEMPORARY MAJOR (WAR SUBSTANTIVE CAPTAIN) THE
VISCOUNT TREDEGAR, Royal Corps of Signals, attached Holding
Battalion, Scots Guards

on

Monday, 19th April, 1943

PROCEDINGS

of a

GENERAL COURT MARTIAL

on

MONDAY, 19th APRIL 1943

upon the trial of

Temporary Major (War Substantive Captain) THE VISCOUNT
TREDEGAR, Royal Corps of Signals, attached Holding Battalion,
Scots Guards

London District Orders by   Lt. General Sir Arthur F Smith
KBE, CB, DSO, MC
Commanding the London
District
Dated at Leconfield House, W1
15th April 1943

PRESIDENT

Colonel J. K. PRESCOTT, Commanding Grenadier Guards

MEMBERS

Lt.-Col. F. JONES, Commanding No. 1 H.Q. Signals

Lt.-Col. A.B. PARKES. OBE, T. D. Commanding 30th Battalion, The Middlesex Regiment.

Major C.J. VERNON CENTWORTH, Grenadier Guards.

Major F. L. BLACKSTONE, 1st Battalion, The Leicestershire Regiment.

WAITING MEMBERS

Lt.-Colonel C.N. CORNISH, CBE, MC. Commanding Training Battalion, Grenadier Guards

Captain P. W. N. Lawrence, Training Battalion, Coldstream Guards.

JUDGE ADVOCATE

The order convening the court, the charge sheet and the summary of evidence are laid before the court.

The court satisfy themselves as provided by Rules of Procedure 22 and 23.

The accused is brought before the court.

The prosecutor is Lieutenant-Colonel NORMAN PARKES, [515] Military Department, Office of the Judge Advocate General.

Defending counsel are SIR WALTER MONCKTON, K.C.[516], and MR G.R.F. MORRIS.

At 1030 hours the trial commences.

The JUDGE ADVOCATE: The court have thought it right in this case to sit in camera and have made directions under sections 6(1)(a) & (b) of the Emergency Powers (Defence) Act, 1939.

The president is going to ask everybody in court to say nothing about anything they may have heard in connection with this case when they leave the court. I may say that these directions are made under a statute which provides severe penalties for any breach of its provisions.

This court, being satisfied that it is expedient in the interests of the defence of Realm so to do, directs:

> (a) that throughout the proceeding all persons except those directly concerned in the actual conduct of the trial shall be excluded; and
>
> (b) that no person shall disclose, save in the course of duty and subject to any directions of the Secretary of State for War, any information whatever with respect to the General Court-Martial for the trial of Temporary Major (War Substantive Captain) The Viscount Tredegar Royal Corps of Signals, attached Holding Battalion, Scots Guards".

> That order is duly signed by the president, the members and the judge advocate at London on the 19th April, 1943.

> The order convening the court is read, and is marked "G", signed by the president and attached to the proceedings.

> The names of the president and members of the court are read over in the hearing of the accused and they severally answer to their names.

The PRESIDENT: Do you object to be tried by me as a president, or by any of the officers whose names you have read over?

The ACCUSED: No.

> The president, members and judge advocate are duly sworn.

The JUDGE ADVOCATE: Do you object to Staff Sergeant-major R.A. Paynter, R.A.S.C, acting as shorthand writer?

The ACCUSED: No.
The shorthand writer is duly sworn.

The charge sheet is marked "B.2", signed by the president and attached to the proceedings.

THE JUDGE ADVOCATE: "The Accused, Temporary Major (War Substantive Captain) The Viscount Tredegar, Royal Corps of Signals, attached Holding Battalion, Scots Guards, an officer of the Regular Forces". Is that your correct name, rank, and description?

The ACCUSED: Yes. I am not actually of the Regular Forces.

Lt. Col PARKES: This officer's 199A shows him to have been appointed to an Emergency Commission. I think I am right in saying that that is the correct description of an officer holding a commission of that kind.

The JUDGE ADVOATE: Do you hold an Emergency Commission?

The ACCUSED: Yes

The JUDGE ADVOCATE: I think you are – at any rate technically – correctly described as an officer of the Regular Forces. It will not make any difference; it is only to show that you are subject to Military Law.

THE ACCUSED: Very well.

THE JUDGE ADVOCATE: The first charge is laid under section 41 of the Army Act. When on active service committing a civil offence, that is to say unlawful communication of information contrary to section 2 of the Official Secrets Act 1911, in that you, at Ipswich on or about 4th February 1943, having in your possession information as to carrier pigeon operations in enemy occupied territory which you had obtained owing to your position as a person holding office under His Majesty unlawfully communicated the same to Herbert Edward Keys and divers other civilians then present who were not persons to whom you were authorised to communicate it nor persons to whom it was in the interests of the State your duty to communicate it. How say you, do you plead guilty or not guilty to the first charge?

The ACCUSED: Not guilty.

THE JUDGE ADVOCATE: The second charge is laid under section 40 of the Army Act. When on active service conduct to the prejudice of good order and military discipline, in that you, at London on or about 3rd February 1943, when Officer Commanding Special Section, Carrier Pigeon Service, improperly informed Major C. Cassidy, M.C., Royal Army Medical Corps, who was then visiting your office that certain pins then affixed to a map of part of north-west Europe on the wall of the said office indicated localities connected with operations involving the dropping of carrier pigeons by parachute in enemy occupied territory. Do you plead guilty or not guilty to the second charge?

The ACCUSED: Not guilty.

The JUDGE ADVOCATE: The third charge is laid under section 41 of the Army Act. When on active service committing a civil offence, that is to say unlawful communication of information contrary to section 2 of the Official Secrets Act 1911 as amended by the Official Secrets Act 1920, in that you, at London on 15 March 1943, having in your possession information as to carrier pigeon operations in enemy occupied territory to which you had access owing your position as a person holding office under His Majesty unlawfully communicated the same to Nora McIntyre and Helen Margaret Isherwood, who were not persons to whom you were authorised to communicate it nor persons to whom it was in the interests of the State your duty to communicate it. Do you plead guilty or not guilty to the third charge?

The ACCUSED: Not guilty.

The JUDGE ADVOCATE: The charges are signed by Lt.-Col. Bland at Chelsea on the 13th April 1943. He commands the Holding Battalion of the Scots Guards.

The charge sheet is endorsed "To be tried by General-Court Martial" and is signed by Col. G. M. Cox, A.A.G., for the Lieutenant-General Commanding London District at London on the 15th April 1943.

Will you now listen to this question, which is perhaps more properly answered by your counsel? Do you wish to apply for an adjournment on the ground that any of the rules relating to procedure before trial have not been complied with and that you have been prejudiced thereby or on the ground that you have not had sufficient opportunity for preparing your defence?

THE ACCUSED: No

(The court and judge advocate decide that as there is a shorthand writer employed it is unnecessary to comply with the provisions of Rule of Procedure 83(B)).

Lt. Col PARKES: May it please the court. In this case you will hear evidence as to certain secret operations which are being carried on, and which have been for some time before carried on, by our Intelligence Service, involving the dropping in various parts of occupied Europe of carrier pigeons by means of parachute. You will hear that those operations are designed for two purposes. Sometimes such pigeons are dropped at particular localities where one of our agents on the continent is known to be so as to provide him with a means of communication with this country. In other cases pigeons are dropped in that way, not for any identified agent but in the hope that persons friendly to the Allied cause will get hold of the pigeon and send back messages which may be of value to us.

Those operations are directed by a department of Military Intelligence at the War Office known as MI 14. The pigeons are bred by civilian breeders all over the country who are organised in groups. These breeders are under the general direction of a military unit known as the Special Section, Carrier Pigeon, of the Royal Corps of Signals. The accused officer at the time you will be concerned with today was the commanding officer of that unit. His responsibility was to ensure that pigeons were bred and available for use by MI 14 for those operations abroad, the actual direction of the operations being the responsibility not of the accused officer but of MI 14.

The second officer had his headquarters at Wing House in Piccadilly, where he had an office. He had with him at that office a Capt. Kleyn, who will give evidence in this case. Capt. Kleyn is an officer of the Intelligence Service and he was attached to the accused so that he (Capt. Kleyn) would be able to convey to the aerodrome or aerodromes concerned from which the pigeons were to go such pigeons as might be required by the Intelligence Service.

As you will have gathered from hearing the charges read, they relate to three cases of alleged disclosure by the accused officer of information in regard to these operations. The operations carried out by MI 14 were recorded by Capt. Kleyn in an operational log book, wherein he showed the pigeons that went out day by day, their destinations, the places from which they returned and the nature of the messages that were brought back.

It appears that at the end of last year the accused officer acquired possession of these log books. I do not for one moment suggest that he obtained those log books for any improper purpose. Having them in his possession, he caused a summary to be made of certain of the portions. On the 4th January of this year he went to Ipswich where he met a group of civilian pigeon breeders. He met them in an hotel at that town – I gather for the purpose of encouraging those breeders to greater efforts in their work. He took with him a Sgt. Sutton and he took a summary of the operations of the pigeons provided by that group of breeders for the proceeding two years. The summary (which will be placed before you) recorded the numbers of pigeons that had been dropped by parachute in various parts of the continent – identifying the parts sometimes by country and sometimes more precisely by locality – and the numbers that returned.

You will hear from the lips of Sgt. Sutton that the accused officer read out that summary to those civilian breeders. You will hear evidence from a representative of MI 14, the officer responsible for these operations, that that information was secret and might be of use to the enemy. Indeed, one hardly requires evidence to show that information showing the localities in which pigeons have been dropped might be of use to the enemy, and still more when the locality is coupled with information showing the proportions of pigeons which return from that particular locality. That disclosure is the subject of the first charge.

I want to make it crystal clear that the prosecution in this case make no suggestion that the accused by any other motive than a desire to do his duty. I anticipate it will be quite clear when you have heard the evidence that the accused was anxious to encourage these civilians in their work. What is said by the prosecution is that he made an error of judgment – it may be when you have heard the evidence you will think a serious error of judgment – in disclosing information of that kind to a number of civilians. It is quite clear that they did not require that information for their work of pigeon breeding. That was on the 4th January.

On the 3rd February a Major Cassidy of the Royal Army Medical Corps employed at the War Office.

The JUDGE ADVOCATE: Are these firm dates? They are "on or about" in the charges.

Lt. Col. PARKES: The 4th January is a firm date. I think the witnesses will not be too clear about the 3rd February. The date of the last charge, however, is a precise one. I do not anticipate there will any dispute as to the dates.

SIR WALTER MONCKTON: There will be no dispute as to dates.

Lt. Col. PARKES: Major Cassidy was taken by a Major Carruthers (also employed at the War Office, under the Adjutant-General) to visit the accused officer in his office at Wing House. It was, I think, in the nature of a social visit. At any rate, it had nothing, you will hear, to do officially with the operational use of pigeons. Indeed, neither of these officers, Major Cassidy and Major Carruthers, was in any way concerned with work of that kind.

You will hear that in the course of conversation the accused indicated to Major Cassidy that these pigeons were used for operations in the occupied territories and that he showed him a live pigeon, a parachute and a container – a specimen of the kind used in these operations. Then he indicated on a large map (which will be placed before you) which was on the wall of his office a number of pins in the occupied territories of Europe. There will be some difference of recollection between the two witnesses, Major Cassidy and Major Carruthers, as to what the accused said, but it is suggested that the effect of what the accused said as to those pins was that they were connected with localities connected with these carrier pigeon operations.

It hardly requires evidence to show that the accused ought not to have disclosed the existence of information of that kind upon the wall of his office. At its lowest, the prosecution suggest that it was a bad example for the accused officer, holding the position that he did, to make that information known to an officer quite unconnected with this work. That is the subject of the second charge. It is suggested for your consideration that the accused's conduct on that occasion amounted to conduct to the prejudice of good order and military discipline.

Turning to the subject matter of the third charge, on the 15th March there were present at Wing House two Girl Guide Leaders. They were there, I think, for some publicity purpose. Some photographs had been taken on the roof of Wing House and after this had been done the accused officer invited these two visitors - their names are Miss Isherwood and Miss McIntyre – into his office. Accompanying them were a Subaltern Harvey of the A.T.S., who was attached officially to his section, and a Subaltern Mackenzie, who was a staff officer in the Pigeon Service.

One does not doubt that the accused's object, and only object, was to entertain these two young women who had visited his office for a purpose which was an official one in that it was connected with official publicity. Evidence will be given, however, that the accused drew the attention to a spot north-west of the Zuyder Zee, that he told them that there had been an enemy concentration and radio location station there, that a message had been brought back by pigeon from there and that within a very short time our planes had bombed the place.

Evidence will be given in fact in June of 1942 and again in November of 1942 messages had been received by pigeon as to those matters in that locality, and indeed those messages, or the effect of them, were recorded in the operational log books to which the accused had had access earlier in the year. It is suggested for your consideration that of necessity operational information of that kind must be highly secret and that the disclosure was improper in that if any hint reached the enemy of those facts the Gestapo would not lose a moment of time in combing the locality in question for persons who had sent any such message.

The accused then went on to have a live pigeon, a container and a parachute brought in by a sergeant and he demonstrated the use of them to these two Girl Guide Leaders. Evidence will be given that, as one might infer, the enemy probably had got specimens of these parachutes already, because they have been dropped in fairly large quantities on the continent. One cannot hope that some of them have not got into enemy hands. At the same time evidence from those who deal with these matters will be given that we have no evidence to show that they knew the precise way in which these are used.

The accused then went on to explain to these Girl Guide Leaders that different coloured containers for messages were used. Those are the little containers which are fastened to the pigeon's legs. He told them that the green ones were for real secret messages. Evidence will be given that that is a secret matter, and indeed one can appreciate that if it were universally known that these green containers contain secret information there might well be many inquisitive persons who happen to pick them up or get them who might be tempted to look at them and thereby delay their arrival at their proper destination, or indeed maliciously minded persons might know what containers ought to be stopped altogether from reaching their destination if possible.

The JUDGE ADVOCATE: I do not quite follow this part of the case. Is it secret information coming from the other side to us, or are you suggesting it is something we put in them going out?

Lt-Col. PARKES: Coming back here.

The JUDGE ADVOCATE: Is not it all secret?

Lt-Col. PARKES: I am sorry I did not make it clear. You will appreciate that the Pigeon Service is a much larger organisation than the Special Section. The Special Section is concerned with pigeons which are dropped in occupied territory. The Army, of course, has for many years made use of pigeons for ordinary military operations, and the ordinary military messages which might be used by the ordinary Army unit are in different coloured containers. It is the green ones which are used for this special work in occupied territory.

The JUDGE ADVOCATE: This particular organisation would be using green ones?

Lt-Col. PARKES: Yes. I think in fact they used one other colour as well. The evidence is that the accused told these young women that it was the green one that contained the secret information.

Sir WALTER MONCKTON: Are the green ones confined to this special work?

Lt-Col. PARKES: Yes, I think they are, though I should like to make sure it's clear that I do not anticipate the evidence will show that the accused told the girls that that was so. The evidence will show that the said: "These are the secret messages". That is the subject of the third charge, that is to say, the disclosures of those matters on that day to those young women.

The JUDGE ADVOCATE: Will you just make it quite clear – perhaps the court do not appreciate it – that the first and the third charges are in form different from the second charge, in that they are much more serious.

Lt-Col. PARKES: I propose in a moment to read the relevant portions of the Official Secrets Act.

I anticipate that you would like to know at once what the accused has said in regard to at any rate one of the matters with which you are concerned today. On the 6th April he was interviewed by the Deputy Director of Signals, who was his military superior, and he was informed of the allegations the subject of the third charge. I want to make it quite clear that at that time he was not told, and therefore had no opportunity of dealing with, any of the matters complained of in the first and second charges. He thereupon: made a statement which I anticipate you would like me to read to you now. Some of it deals with matters which are not relevant to this inquiry and unless my learned friend wishes me to do so I will not read those irrelevant portions.

SIR WALTER MONCKTON: I agree.

Lt.-Col. PARKES; The accused officer said: "I wish to make the following voluntary statement. I have been warned that anything I may say may be used in evidence. I am O.C. Special Section (Carrier Pigeon) Service and I work at Wing House, Piccadilly, W1. I assumed these duties during the first week in November 1942. I wish to apologise to the Director of Signals for what appears to be a grave breach of trust. With regard to the demonstration of the use of the container and parachute I did not consider this to be a secret as it has received wide publicity in the press. Lt.-Col. Cullinan" – that is the officer who was in charge of the Pigeon Service as a whole – "has frequently brought army officers into my room and ordered me to carry out this demonstration in their presence. I told the Girl Guide Leaders on 15th March 1943 that the green message containers were used in connection with pigeons bringing back information from occupied territory. I had no reason to think this information was secret. I have in my office a map showing England and part of the continent. This map has a number of coloured pins affixed to it. Those in England indicate the pigeon lofts in this country and those on the continent were affixed by a Dutchman, a Mr. Ray, who had recently escaped from Holland. He placed the pins at places in Holland where he knew there were Allied sympathisers who would be prepared to revolt against the enemy in the event of an Allied landing.

I did not point out to the Girl Guide Leaders a point N. W. of the Zuyder Zee. I remember telling them that at that point which I indicated on the map there had been an important enemy radio location station, information as to which had been brought back by a pigeon and that as a result within a very short time the RAF. laid it flat. This information was given to me by Col. Cullinan, who also told me that he had been congratulated by Guide Leaders. I further told them that pigeons were being dropped by parachute in Holland."

I now go to the top of the next page. "I did tell the Girl Guide Leaders on the 15th March 1943, that it was possible to drop pigeons at a specified place where the Intelligence Service knew that there was a person who would send back a message.

On Sunday, 21st March, Col. Cullinan told me that I had been reported by Subalterns Harvey and Mackenzie in respect of the incidents of 15th March. He suggested that I should have an operation which I had been contemplating for some time and that I should resign my appointment as O. C. Special Section, and that after the operation I should make a full apology to the Director of Signals for my indiscretion. Col. Cullinan told me not to report the matter to higher authority and that he did not intend to do so himself. The matter has remained in that state up to the present time".

That is the explanation that the accused has given in regard to the third charge. Before calling the evidence before you I think it would be of assistance if I invited your attention to the relevant portions of section of the Official Secrets Act under which the first and third charges are laid. Section 2 of the Act of 1911, which has been amended by Act of 1920, reads as follows, leaving out the words that do not apply to these charges: "If any persons having in his possession information which he has obtained or to which he has had access owing to his position as a person who holds or has held office under His Majesty communicates the information to any person other than a person to whom he is authorised to communicate it or a person to whom it is in the interest of the State his duty to communicate it, that person shall be guilty of a misdemeanour".

May I summarise the position? The first and third charges allege that civil offence which is created by that Statute for all persons serving the Crown. The second charge complains merely of the alleged military impropriety of the accused in the example that he set to another officer who happened to be in his room. It is alleged as a bad example as to security matters given by the accused in connection with this.

I will now call the witnesses before you.

No.P.4129534 L/Sjt. F.T. SUTTON is called in and having been duly sworn is examined by Lt.-Col. PARKES as follows:-

Q   No F.4129534 L/Sjt. F.T. Sutton, Royal Corps of Signals, are you an Area Serjeant at Special Section (Carrier Pigeon) R.C.S. at Wing House? A. Yes

Q   I want you to look at two operational log books. (Handed). Did you see those early in January of this year: A. Yes.

Q   In what circumstances? What happened? A. In Lord Tredegar's office, when I collected them to compile a summary.

Q   Who gave them to you? A. They were on the corner of the table and Lord Tredegar informed me that those were the books that he wanted to work upon.

Q   What did he want you to do? A. Compile a list of all the performances and returns compared with the losses of each individual loft.

Q   Did you do that? A. Yes.

Q   Did you give a copy of the summary that you prepared to Lord Tredegar? A. Yes

Q   What did he do with it; do you know? A. I do not know what further he did with it at the time.

Q   On the 4th January did you go down with him in Ipswich? A. Yes

Q   Was there a meeting there at which a number of pigeon breeders were present? A. Yes

Q   All the breeders of one group; is that right? A. Yes.

Q   Was Mr. Keys there himself? A. Yes.

Q   How many others were there? A. It would be 25 besides Mr. Keys.

Q   Were they all civilians? A. Yes.

Q   Where did the meeting take place? A. At the White Hart or White Horse Hotel.

Q   Were you present throughout? A. Yes.

Q   Did Lord Tredegar speak to them? A. Yes

Q   Will you quite shortly tell the court what sort of things Lord Tredegar said to them? A. Mainly he appealed for their co-operation to continue their services under him as they had done under the previous C.O.

Q   Have you seen the document before? (Handed). A. Yes.

Q   What is that? A. It is the list of Mr. Key's group which was compiled by me.

Q   You have told us you made a number of summaries, one for each of the groups.

The JUDGE ADVOCATE: He used a different name; he said "each loft". A.   Each loft and group.

139

Q   You never used the word "group"; you said "loft" and the prosecutor said "Group". I do not know what is the difference. It may be the same.

Lt. Col. PARKES: What is the difference?

A. There is no difference really, not so far as we are concerned operationally. We all term the groups actually as lofts because in a group there is a number of civilians employed. It concerns just one main loft,belonging to civilians in most cases.

SIR WALTER MONCKTON: Does that mean the whole group uses one loft? A. No. They are all formed under one P.S.O.

Lt. Col. PARKES: That is a Pigeon Supply Officer, is it? A. Yes

Q   Mr Keys was the Pigeon Supply Officer of that group? A. Yes

Q   Was there more than one loft in the group? A. There would be 26.

Q   Nevertheless you speak of it as one loft? A. Yes, from an operational point of view.

Q   What about that document I handed to you? A. That is the copy that was compiled for Mr. Key's group.

Q   What happened to that that day – anything? A. That day?

Q   Yes. A. The next time I saw it was when Lord Tredegar opened his file and read it out to the members at the meeting.

Q   He read that out, did he? A. Yes

Q   The whole of it? A. Yes.

Q   This is the actual document he read from, is it? A. That is correct. There was only that one made.

Lt. Col. PARKES: I think I shall have to read this.

IPSWICH	MR KEYS	SECRET
35 sent	11 returned	Ghent –Dunkirk
32 sent	9 returned	Belgium
23 sent	0 returned	Belgium-Holland
10 sent	0 returned	Rotterdam
3 sent	2 returned	Cherbourg
14 sent	1 returned	K. France-Lille-Arms-Bordeaux-Holland (x)
11 sent	0 returned	Denmark
6 sent	1 returned	Belgium
8 sent	1 returned	Belgium
3 sent	0 returned	France
8 sent	2 returned	Holland
12 sent	3 returned	Amsterdam
3 sent	0 returned	Belgium
12	3 returned	Belgium
16 sent	8 returned	Belgium
12 sent	3 returned	French Court
3 sent	0 returned	Holland
13 sent	1 returned	Belgium
10 sent	2 returned	Belgium
12 sent	2 returned	Holland
9 sent	2 returned	Holland
13 sent	3 returned	France
2 sent	1 returned	Belgium
11 sent	3 returned	Belgium
9 sent	6 returned	Belgium
2sent	o returned	Amiens
5 sent	4 returned	Amiens
2 sent	0 returned	N. Belgium
2 sent	0 returned	Holland
1 sent	0 returned	Belgium
3 sent	0 returned	Belgium
2 sent	0 returned	Belgium
12 sent	1 returned	Holland
6 sent	0 returned	France
5 sent	0 returned	Holland
2 sent	1 returned	Belgium
5 sent	1 returned	Belgium

Q   What period is covered by that? A. From April 1941 up to
     November 1942.

(List marked "R", signed by the president and attached to the proceedings).

Q   When he had read that out did any of the members of the group say anything?   A. Mr. Keys got up and said "The number is wrong", or words to that effect, "You have left out two".

THE JUDGE ADVOCATE: Left out two what?   A. He sent two returns. Lord Tredegar said "Oh, yes, Denmark, Copenhagen".

Lt. – Col. PARKES: Did he say "Copenhagen". A. Yes.

Q   Did he look at anything before he gave that answer? A. No, I do not think so.

Q   Or was he speaking from memory; don't you remember? A. No, I cannot remember.

<u>Cross-examined by Sir Walter Monckton</u>

Q   Is this the original or a copy? A. It is the original.

Q   That is the one that you actually yourself prepared? A. Yes.

Q   Did you type it yourself? A. Yes

Q   It did not get on to a file? A. No. It was only kept in Lord Tredegar's own personal file.

Q   It looks extremely clean for something that has been used was there not perhaps another copy? A. No. There was never another copy made out; I only made the one.

Lt.-Col PARKES: I think I ought to help you here, Sir Walter. I think that is not the actual copy. I myself removed the original from the file and it was pinned or fastened in. I suggested that a copy ought to be made and I think Capt. Kleyn has provided us with a typed copy. We should get the original.

SIR WALTER MONCKTON: I am much obliged for that. It did not look to me like one that had been used at a meeting. I ought to say that the accused told me he was sure the original had been filed, but this has not. While the original is being sent for, Sgt. Sutton, perhaps I may ask you some questions. The log books which were kept and from which you compiled this summary had a great deal more information than is on the summary: A. Oh, yes.

Q   The summary does not record dates? A. No.

Q   Nor does it record, as the log book would record, the name of the pilot who dropped the bird? A. No.

Q   That is in the log book? A. Yes

Q   You know the log books? A. Yes, I have seen them.

Q   And other particulars; for instance, the number of birds to identify it? A. No; none of that was put in the summary.

Q   It is in the log book but not in the summary? A. That is right.

Q   And what happens about the message? A. Nothing at all about that was put in the summary.

Q   It is all in the log book but not in the summary? A. Yes

Q   I have no doubt that you compiled the summary in accordance with instructions you got from Lord Tredegar? A. That is correct.

Q   All that you were putting in there was the number that went out, the number that got back and the places from which they came back? A. That is correct.

Q   Anything which would give further information, the nature of the message, the condition in which the bird came back or who dropped it, you were not to put in? A. Yes.

Q   Have you been for some time in this particular branch of the service? A. I joined them in July 1942.

Q   That was before Lord Tredegar became in charge of it? A. That is correct.

Q   Major Pearson was in charge of it then? A. Yes.

Q   In November of 1942 Major Tredegar took over? A. That is correct.

Q   He had been away, had not he, from May until November on sick leave? A. I never saw him until he came to take over command again, not from the time I came to the service.

Q   You did not see him till he came to command; that would be towards the end of 1942? A. That would be correct.

Q   A month or so before the occasion you are speaking of? A. Yes.

Q   You knew Mr. Keys and his group of – what do you call them, fanciers or breeders? A. That is correct.

Q   Did you know there was some anxiety as to whether Mr. Keys and his group were   going on? A. Yes, there was that anxiety.

Q   Did you know that Lord Tredegar had been sent by his C.O. to try and persuade him and his group to continue? A. Yes

Q   That was the whole object of the journey? A. That was the object of the journey.

Q   Did you know – do not tell us if you did not – that the C.S.O. under whom Lord Tredegar was serving knew that he was getting this summary prepared? A. Only from the fact that Lord Tredegar had informed us that it was on the C S O's instructions.

Q   He informed you that it was on the C.S.O's instructions that that this summary was being prepared? A. Yes.

Q   From the use which he made of it and from what he told you, you knew that he was using the limited information which you had put, under his instructions, into this summary in order to encourage the breeders and fanciers in that group to continue and not to give up? A. Do you mind saying that again?

Q   You knew the object of his journey was to persuade these people to go on? A. That is right.

Q   You knew that this summary was being prepared under the C.S.O's orders? A. That is correct.

Q   You heard him use the summary at the meeting? A. Yes.

Q   You heard him making use of it? A. Yes.

Q   Was not he using the information there to persuade these people to go on? A. I should imagine that was his idea.

Q   Giving them a bit of information to show that what they were doing was worthwhile? A. That could have been his idea.

Q   Do not let me suggest to you that this scheme was not a great success, but an awful lot of birds do not seem to come back. It sounded like somebody reading the results   of   football matches – 11-0; 10-1; 8-1, -- that sort of thing. A great many do not come back? A. Yes.

Q   These birds go through many hazards? A. Yes.

Q   They may be shot down over there or over here? A. We understand from the operational point of view what may happen to them.

Q   There are many hazards. I put it that way. A. Yes.

Q   There are live wires and all sorts of things? A. Yes.

Q   They are not all well-disposed at the other end where they are dropped; we know that, do not we? A. Yes, we know that.

Q   This had been going on for a long time, I suppose? We are in camera here and I shall be stopped if I ask you something I ought not to ask you. You knew that these birds had been going since April 1941? A. I was not aware of that, not until I arrived in July.

145

Q   Did Mr. Keys appear to you to know a good deal about it? A. Nothing more than his own operations side, the number of returns his group actually had.

Q   He knew all about that? A. Yes, he would, naturally.

Q   He seems to have known that two of them had been left out of the count which was given by the accused? A. I cannot say how he came by that figure at all.

Q   Of course, these groups and lofts have pigeons which, wherever they are dropped are going to come back to the home loft? A. That is the general rule.

Q   If all goes well? A. That is right.

Q   If the hazards are overcome. Of course they knew when success attends their efforts and pigeons do come in that they have come from some distance? A. Yes.

Q   Tell me about the message which they bring. They have messages in containers? A. That is right.

Q   There is no seal on the container, is there? A. No, there is no seal at all.

Q   Anybody who picked up the bird would be able to undo the container and take out the message? A. Yes, he could.

Q   I suppose from time to time people in this country do pick up the birds – for instance, if they are exhausted and come down – and undo the container? A. We only find that on very rare occasions.

Q   Such occasions have come to your knowledge? A. Only, as far as I know, on one occasion.

Q   There was one, was there not, in November of last year? A. It never came to my knowledge.

Q   You did not hear of a maid picking one up at one of these places – it happened to a German maid. You never heard anything of that? A. No.

Q   She said she picked up a message, which she read. You do not recollect that? A. No.

Q   Had this group of Mr. Keys' been going on for some time? A. I believe it had.

Q   In the course of this meeting, when Lord Tredegar was making his speech did he succeed in persuading them to continue? A. Yes, they continued their supply.

Q   Mr. Keys and his group would obviously know how many birds they had supplied? A. Yes.

Q   They would know how many came back? That is correct.

Q   As you say, they would a general idea of what they had been doing?

A.   That is right.

Q   The only thing they were getting from this summary was – to the extent to which it   appears in the summary – the actual spots from which the birds had returned? A. The actual places were mentioned on the sheet; that is right.

Re-examined by Lt.- Col. Parkes.

Q   Is that the original document that you prepared? A. Yes, that is right. I see a thing here.

THE JUDGE ADVOCATE: Are you satisfied with that now, Sir Walter?

SIR WALTER MONCKTON: Yes. I was not making any attack on him, but one always wants to get those things clear.

(Original list is substituted, marked "H", signed by the president and attached to the proceedings).

THE JUDGE ADVOCATE: Are you calling Mr. Keys:

Lt.-Col. PARKES: I do not propose to unless Sir Walter would like to cross examine him.

SIR WALTER MONCKTON: I do not want him.

The JUDGE ADVOCATE: This is a question I have been wanting to put to somebody, so if you can answer it will you help me? When the pigeon is dropped from the aircraft can it get out by itself? A. No.

Q   It is in a container, is it? A. Yes.

Q   If it is not released, does it die? A. It would do eventually, if it was left unnoticed for   any length of time.

Q   In addition to all the normal hazards, the bird has to be let out by somebody when it is dropped? A. Yes.

Q   Failing it being let free in a certain time, of course it must die? A. Yes.

Q   Every bird that comes back has been released from a container? A. Yes.

Q   Therefore it is rather interesting to know how many birds come back from any particular area, is not it? A. It would be interesting, I expect, to the people actually concerned?

Q   Because every one of those birds has been released by somebody? A. That is right.

Q   I suppose they do come back without messages sometimes? A. On some   occasions.

Q   Sometimes they have messages? A. Yes.

Q   This document was prepared, I gather, for the occasion of this particular meeting at Ipswich? A. No, I do not think so. No, it was not.

Q   How long before this meeting was it prepared? A. It was only prepared on the Saturday previous to the meeting. That would be the 2nd January. I had received instructions about it three weeks or more before that.

Q   From the accused? A. Yes.

Q   Three weeks before the meeting – is that what you say? -- you were instructed to make this out?

Q   You are right in saying it only related to this particular group, are you? A. No every loft and group was compiled on the summary – every loft and group we had. It was not that one summary; there were numbers made out.

Q   This particular one? A. That particular sheet, yes.

Q   Were you making out more than one summary? A. Yes, a summary of each loft   and group.

Q   You are only dealing with this particular one at Ipswich? A. Yes, at present.

Q   When was this one made out, the Ipswich one? A. That would be completed on the Saturday and the Sunday previous to the meeting.

Q   And the meeting was on what day? A. On the Monday.

Q   It was prepared on the Saturday or Sunday before the Monday? A. That is right.

The PRESIDENT: There is one thing I am not quite clear about. The defending counsel asked you just now; did the C.S.O. order this summary to be made and you said "Yes". Who did you mean by the "C.S.O."? A. I do not think I said "yes". I said according to information passed by my O.C. – he gave us the instructions on the instructions of the Chief Signals Officer.

A MEMBER OF THE COURT: You gathered that from the accused: that the Signals Officer had given those instructions? It was your impression from what the accused told you? A. That is correct.

The JUDGE ADVOCATE: Sir Walter, when the court or I put any questions it is a matter of course for counsel, if they wish to put any further questions, to ask the court at any time.

SIR WALTER MONCKTON: Perhaps I may ask one question on those questions. You got that impression long before these charges, the impression that he was giving you orders in accordance with instructions he had got from the C.S.O.? A. Yes.

Q   You got that before the meeting? A. Yes.

(The witness withdraws).

Lt-Col. PARKES: I do not propose to call Mr. Keys unless the defence wish to cross-examine.

SIR WALTER MONCKTON: I do not want him.

Major C. CASSIDY is called and having been duly sworn is examined by Lt.-Col PARKES as follows:-

Q   You are Major C. Cassidy? A. Yes.

Q   What appointment do you hold? I am D.A.D.C. A.N.D.2. (Statistics) at the War Office.

Q   Does your work bring you in touch with carrier pigeons in any way?

A.   No.

Q   The statistics are not pigeon statistics? A. No.

Q   In the early part of February of this year did you go to see the accused officer at Wing House? A. I did.

Q   Do you remember the date? A. I think it was the 3rd February.

Q   Was it in the afternoon? A. Yes, late afternoon.

Q   Did you go with anybody else? A. Major Carruthers.

Q   Did you know Lord Tredegar before then? A. No.

Q   What was the purpose of your visit? A. Major Carruthers took me up to introduce me to Lord Tredegar with a view to seeing his book of birds.

Q   You met Lord Tredegar in the room, did you? A. Yes.

Q   Were you, Lord Tredegar and Major Carruthers there together? A. Yes.

Q   Will you tell the court what happened? A. I was introduced to Lord Tredegar. Then somebody – I am not certain who – said "Let's show him the secret stuff".

Q   Was there anybody else besides Lord Tredegar, Major Carruthers and yourself there? A. Not at that time.

Q   It was one of those two? A. Yes.

Q   What was the "secret stuff"? A. Lord Tredegar sent for an H.C.O., who brought in a   pigeon, a container for a pigeon, a parachute, a bag of rations for the pigeon and a little folder with some instructions.

Q   Very shortly, what happened then? A. I was shown how the container worked, how how the pigeon was put into the container and how the parachute worked. I also gave a casual glance at the instructions.

Q   Was there a map on the wall? A. There was.

Q   Was it a map like that one? (Map produced). A. Yes.

THE JUDGE ADVOCATE: Is that supposed to be the same one? What is the scale of it?

Lt.-Col. PARKES: There will be evidence that that is the one which was on the wall. The scale is 1/500,000. (To the witness). Were there any pins in the map? A. There were.

Q   What sort of pins; do you remember? A. I cannot exactly remember what sort of pins they were rather distinctive pins. I thought they were glass headed but I understand they were not.

Q Was anything said about those pins? A. I was told that they marked points where pigeons were pin-pointed.

Q Was that the actual expression? A. That was the actual expression.

Q Was it explained at all? A. No.

Q Were these pins showing where pigeons were pin-pointed on the European portion or the English portion? A. There are pins on both portions, but the ones where pigeons were pin-pointed were on the European portion.

Q Can you remember what part of Europe? A. France, Belgium, and I think Holland.

Q Who said that about the pin-pointing? A. I think Lord Tredegar.

Q Was anything else said about the pins or the work of pigeons on that occasion? A: I do not think so.

Cross-examined by Sir Walter Monckton.

Q May I assume there were a number of pins on the map? A. Yes.

Q Pretty thickly studded? A. Yes.

Q Do you happen to work in Wing House yourself? A. I do.

Q Do you work in an office below that in which Lord Tredegar worked? A. Yes.

Q I do not know if you did, but you probably knew when you went there what Lord Tredegar's job was? A. I did.

Q That he was in charge of the special section dealing with carrier pigeons? A. Yes.

Q Do you happen to know the office where his C.S.O. is, Col. Cullinan?

A.   No.

Q   This office in which Major Tredegar was   is one in which people went from time to time, to your knowledge – you have been in the building? A. I could not say who went into his office. That afternoon other people came into the office when this demonstration had finished.

Q   Coming and going? A. Col. Cullinan went into the office afterwards and a civilian came into the office after that, but I could not say who went into his office.

Q   Was the map over his desk? A. Yes, on the wall behind his desk.

Q   So that anyone who came into the room would see a large map with a lot of pins on it? A. Yes.

Q   They might or might not notice whether the pins were glass headed or not? A. Yes.

Q   You thought at one time that they were, but now you appreciate that they were not? A. Yes. I gave them a casual glance.

Q   There was no secret about what his appointment was, was there? You knew   perfectly well what he was? A. It is in the War Office Directory.

Q   That makes it less secret perhaps. Somebody coming into the room of a man holding that appointment and seeing a large scale map, observing pins in England and in the Low Countries and France, would not want a great deal of ingenuity, would he, to jump to the conclusion that that was a place where pigeons were going to be used – each of those points? A. No I think it was the obvious thing.

Q   It is not a strain on the intelligence is it? A. No.

Q   You yourself are interested in birds, are you not – pigeons? A. Yes.

Q   Being interested in ornithology you knew that Major Tredegar was well qualified on that subject? A. I did.

Q   It was Major Curruthers who was a friend of his and yours was it?

A.   Yes.

Q   He was the person, not Lord Tredegar, who invited you to go in on this occasion? A. Yes.

Q   Knowing of your interest in birds? A. Yes.

Q   You yourself are also concerned, are you not, with the taking of micrograms, small photographs and things of that sort? A. No, I am actually concerned with that.

Q   Are you interested in that? A. I Photostat documents.

Q   Has it been suggested to you at any time the use of micrograms or Photostats of documents might be useful in connection with carrier pigeons as they are small to carry? A. That did arise.

Q   Was it discussed with Lord Tredegar at any time? A. It was not really discussed with him. I was asked if I could bring up a microgram slide.

Q   Whether you would bring one up to show him? A. No whether I could have a microgram slide enlarged.

Q   That was in the course of casual conversation with Lord Tredegar, was it? A. Yes.

Q   You are not going to pledge your recollection, are you that Lord Tredegar, said on that occasion that he would show you where the pigeons were pin-pointed? A. No I will not.

Q   I think when you are asked before you said you thought it was he but it could have been Major Carruthers? A. It might have been, yes. I would not be quite certain.

Q At any rate, whoever it was who said it was saying nothing which you could not have observed for yourself? **A.** That is quite true.

Q As to the display of the pigeon, the container and all that, it was the only occasion you had been there? **A.** That is the only occasion

Q So you did not know whether that had been shown to other people or on whose instructions, or anything of the kind? **A.** No, I had no idea whether it had been shown before.

Q It was just a box, a pigeon and a parachute, I take it? **A.** Yes, a container a parachute and a pigeon. Somebody said "Let's show him the secret stuff", you say? **A.** Yes.

Q You are not saying that that was Lord Tredegar? **A.** I am not certain who.

Q You do not know enough to know whether that is an expression which Lord Tredegar would use or whether he would say "Let's show him the act". You have never heard that said? **A.** I do not think so.

Q Can you be sure that was not what was said on this occasion, "Let's show him the act"? **A.** I do not think it was.

Q You are not going to pledge your recollection to use of the expression "secret stuff"? **A.** It was said.

Q By somebody. By whom you cannot say? **A.** No.

Re-examined by Ltl-Col. Parkes.

Q Whoever said it, at any rate the stuff was produced? **A.** Yes.

Q You say that before you went to that office you knew that Lord Tredegar commanded the special section of the Carrier Pigeon Service? **A.** Yes.

Q Did you know what the special section did? **A.** No

Q Did you have any idea before you went to this office? **A.** No.

155

Q   Did you know whether they were concerned with the occupied territories at all before you went there? A. No, I had no idea. I did not know where they came from

The JUDGE ADVOCATE: You say there were pins on the European side?

A.   Yes.

Q   And on the other side? A. Yes.

Q   Were they the same sort of pins; did you notice? A. I think so.

Q   You got the impression that they were the same sort of pins, wherever they were in the map? A. I think so. I gave it a very casual glance.

Q   The other person who was with you, Major Carruthers; did you know what he did? A. How do you mean?

Q   Do you know what his job is in the army? A. He is a D.A.A.G. in the A.G. Statistics.

Q   Do you know of your own knowledge whether he had got anything to do with pigeons? A. I do not know.

Q   Whoever was doing the talking, other than what you yourself said, it was either the accused or Major Carruthers; is that it? A.   The sergeant actually demonstrated the pigeon, the parachute and the container.

Q   Did the sergeant say anything which you attributed to – A. No.

Q   We can leave him out of it, can we? A. Yes.

Q   About "secret stuff" or the other bit about the pin-pointing? A.   Yes.

A MEMBER OF THE COURT: When you were shown this map with the pins you thought they were the same kind of pins on the European and the British side? A. I think so.

Q   Was it clearly explained to you what the pins represented? A. No.

Q   When they said that pigeons were pin-pointed, you had no idea what that meant? A. No. I surmised. I had no idea what it meant.

Q   What did you think it meant? A. I thought it meant it was places where the pigeons were meant to be dropped.

Q   Not necessarily places from which pigeons were to be released to be sent back to this country? A. That is what I meant when I said "dropped". I mean that they were released by parachute.

ANOTHER MEMBER: Before you went to that office had you ever heard of pigeons in containers being dropped over enemy territory? A. No.

THE JUDGE ADVOCATE: When you came out you had learned quite a lot, had not you, which you did not know before about pigeon dropping – after the demonstration, I mean? A. Yes. I had learned that pigeons were dropped by parachute, which I did not know before.

(The witness withdraws).

Major R. H. CARRUTHERS is called in and having been duly sworn is examined by Lt-Col. Parkes as follows:

Q   Major R. H. Carruthers, General List; is that your right description?

A.   Yes.

Q   Are you the D.A.A. C. in A.G. Statistics at the War Office? A. Yes.

Q   Does your work bring you into contact at all with carrier pigeons?

A.   No.

Q   On the afternoon of a day which we believe to be the 3rd February did you go with Major Cassidy to see Lord Tredegar in his office at Wing House? A. I did

Q   Did you know Lord Tredegar before? A. Very well.

Q   Will you tell the court what happened while you were in there with Major Cassidy and Lord Tredegar? A. Yes. I had occasion to visit Major Cassidy at Wing House that afternoon and in the course of conversation with Major Cassidy I asked him if he had met Lord Tredegar.

Q   I want you really to describe what happened when you were in the room with Lord Tredegar. A. I was responsible for taking Major Cassidy down to Lord Tredegar's room. When we arrived there we were both shown by Lord Tredegar an atlas which he had in which Major Cassidy was particularly interested. It was an atlas showing the different parts of the world where different animals came from.

Q   Was anything said about pigeons? A. Something was said about pigeons. Major Cassidy looked at a skeleton of a pigeon which was standing on top of a bookcase in the room and the conversation turned to pigeons.

Q   What was said about pigeons? A. I do not actually remember how it opened. I imagine that possibly what really happened was that Major Cassidy said he had seen plenty of pigeons round Wing House. I think he said at times he had found it difficult to get into the lift for these pigeons.

Q   Was a pigeon produced while you were there? A. Yes.

Q   How came that to be produced? A. Lord Tredegar sent for a sergeant who brought a pigeon into the room.

Q   Did he say anything, either just before or when he sent for the pigeon, about what he was going to send for? A. I do not recollect what words he actually used before he sent for the pigeon. I think he must have said: "I will show you one of my pigeons". At any rate, he sent for the sergeant, who brought a pigeon in.

Q   Did you make any suggestion yourself of any kind in regard to seeing a pigeon? A. No.

Q   You are sure? A. Yes.

Q   So a pigeon, a container and a parachute were brought in; is that right? A. A container and a parachute were brought in.

Q   Then there was some demonstration by the sergeant, was there? A. That is so.

Q   We have heard that a map like this was on the wall. (Map produced). Do you remember seeing a map like that there? A. That certainly seems very similar to a map I did see on the wall.

Q   Were there any pins affixed to it? A. Yes; the, map was covered in pins.

Q   Did England have any pins in it? A. Yes, there were a lot of pins.

Q   What about the continent? A. There were a lot of pins on the continent.

Q   Was anything said by anybody about the pins? A. I think there was a scale on the map, an adjustable scale, which I think I looked at and moved to some place on the coast to read off the distance. I do not remember anything being actually said about the pins. I had seen that map before myself. I had been in that room before and I had seen the map on a previous occasion.

Cross-examined by Sir Walter Monckton.

Q   Anyone who came into the room would see the map, because it was always there? A. It was always there when I was there.

Q   It always had the pins on it when you saw it? A. Yes.

Q   Had you seen a demonstration of the container and the bird before?

A.   No.

Q   The sergeant was sent for, was he? A. Yes.

Q   And he brought the bird and the container? A. Yes.

Q   That was all the new material you got on that occasion? A. Yes.

Lt.-Col. PARKES: No re-examination.

The JUDGE ADVOCATE: Was this the accused's own room, a room he had to himself? A. It was his own room.

Q   How many times had you been in there before? A. I should think quite half a dozen

Q   The stranger in the room on that occasion was Major Cassidy? A. That is so.

Q   You have given us all the recollection you can about the conversation? A. Yes. I had a very detached interest in this conversation. I had been in this room before. I was sick at the time. The next morning, I actually went off to Millbank and was given sick leave. I was just recuperating from 'flu. I had introduced Major Cassidy to Lord Tredegar, and as I say, my interest was to some extent detached.

The PRESIDENT: Although you had not seen the demonstration before you did not take any interest in it? A. I took some interest in the demonstration, yes.

(The witness withdraws).

SUBALTERN J. C. HARVEY is called in and having been duly sworn is examined by Lt.-Col. PARKES as follows:

Q   You are Subaltern J. C. Harvey? A. T. S? A. Yes

Q   Are you an officer of No. 1 (London District) Group, A. T. S.?
A. Yes.

Q   On the 15th March of this year were you attached for duty to the Special Section (Carrier Pigeon) Royal Corps of Signals?
A. Yes.

Q   Had you been there for a week or so before that day? A. Yes.

Q   On the afternoon of the 15th March were some photographs taken on the roof of   Wing House? A. Yes.

Q   Were they in connection with a Girl Guide publicity scheme?
A. They were.

Q   It was a matter that Lord Tredegar by his duty was concerned with, was it? A. I think so.

Q   After these photographs had been taken did you go down with Lord Tredegar to his office? A. Yes. I do not think I actually went down with him.

Q   Who went down with? A. A Subaltern Mackenzie and I went down.

Q   To Lord Tredegar's office? A. Yes, with Miss Isherwood and Miss McIntryre.

Q   Were they Girl Guide officials who had been present on the roof for the purpose of the photograph? A. Yes.

Q   So there were the four of you and Lord Tredegar in his office together; is that right? A. Yes.

Q   Was your attention attracted by anything to anything that happened while you were there in his office? A. Yes.

Q   Just tell the court what it was that you noticed. A. Subaltern Mackenzie and I were talking. The first thing that attracted my attention was hearing something to the effect   that
Lord Tredegar was saying enemy radio location and concentrations – or something to that effect.

Q   Was he doing anything then? A. Yes, he pointed to a place on the map which was on the wall.

Q   Look at this map. (Map produced). Is this the map which was on the wall and to which he pointed? A. It is.

Q   I want you to show the court where he pointed. A. I cannot tell you the exact place but somewhere here (indicating).

The JUDGE ADVOCATE: Where is it on the map?

Lt- Col. PARKES: Is it the portion of land which is north-west of the Zuyder Zee. How did he point; with what? A. With his finger.

Q   Will you show the court, if you can remember, how close to the map his finger went as he pointed? A. I should think about like that (illustrating). I do not know; it was   definitely very near the map.

Q   What did he say after that? A. News of which had been brought over to this by pigeon.

Q   And then? A. That a very short time afterwards – I think he said four and a half hours, but I am not absolutely certain. I cannot tell you exactly the time he said; I think he said four and a half hours, but anyhow a short time afterwards we had bombed that point or attacked that point. These are not his exact words.

Q   You heard him say that and point to the map? A. Yes.

Q   To whom was he saying it? A. To the two Girl Guide Leaders that were present in the room. They were beside him, by the map.

Q   They were where? A. They were beside the map where he was, the other side of the desk.

Q   What happened after that? Did you see a live pigeon that day? A. Oh, yes. I was trying to think of the sequence.

Q Have we got the sequence right now? A. Yes. A sergeant demonstrated how the pigeon was dropped by aeroplane and how the parachute worked.

Q Was there a real pigeon to demonstrate with? A. Yes. The sergeant put the pigeon into a container, a cardboard container, closed it, and then demonstrated to us, as far as he could without opening the parachute, how it worked.

Q How came the sergeant to do that; whose suggestion was that? A. Major Tredegar asked him to show his act, I think he called it.

Q Was anything else said? A. I think it was during that time that Major Tredegar took an envelope out of a cupboard.

Q I do not want to worry about that. Anything else? A. A Major came into the room, Major Cassidy, bringing photographic enlargements.

Q That does not matter. Did anything else happen? (After a pause). Just think of the events of that afternoon.

The JUDGE ADVOCATE: There must be a limit to the time of the lady thinking. *(sic)*

Lt.-Col. PARKES: If there is nothing else that you remember I will not trouble you any further.

Cross-examined by Sir Walter Monckton

Q Am I right in thinking that during the week you were on this duty, just before this occasion, you were sharing a table with Major Tredegar, working on his table in the room? A. Yes.

Q I went to get first of all the circumstances of the Girl Guide visit. We have heard   and no doubt you know – that there were a great many pigeons about from time to time at Wing House? A. Yes.

Q Is this what happened about Girl Guides. Was there, on the instructions of the C.S.O. assistance given to the publicity in relation to Wings for Victory efforts by Girl Guides? A. I assume that was so. I was not on that side.

Q   Would Subaltern Mackenzie be able to say about that? A. Yes.

Q   You were on the roof, were you? A. Yes.

Q   There were some pigeons due to come in. I gather some came and some did not; is that right? A. That is correct.

Q   There were cinematograph machines and the Press? A. Yes.

Q   And photographs? A. Yes.

Q   Did a great number of pigeons fail to turn up? A. I do not know.

Q   Was Subaltern Mackenzie the publicity officer? A. Yes, she dealt with all that.

Q   At any rate, did you know, sharing his room, that Major Tredegar had been detailed by the C.S.O. to do what he could to entertain on that occasion those who were there? A. I do not think the C.O. was present. Major Tredegar was second in command. I presume he would normally do it.

Q   Whether or not he had specific instructions? A. Yes.

Q   Lady Baden-Powell was there on the roof? A. Yes.

Q   She went away afterwards? A. Yes.

Q   And these two Girl Guide Leaders were invited into the office by Major Tredegar? A. Yes.

Q   Did you hear a conversation they had with him about pigeons in general? A. No, I do not remember it because I was not paying much attention at the beginning at all.

Q   Does this help you? Do you remember their talking about whether pigeons were particularly brave birds? A. No.

Q   Do you remember him saying they would fly through anything, gas, shrapnel, shells, bombs, anything? Do you remember them asking him whether there had been any outstanding feats by pigeons in this war, A. No. I did state all I remembered here.

Q   Sometimes, you know, when you are reminded it comes back to our mind. A. Yes.

Q   It does not on this occasion? A. No, it does not.

Q   There is no doubt that you remember him mentioning a radio location station? A. Yes, and enemy concentrations.

Q   I am challenging that the radio location station was mentioned. Are you satisfied that the words "enemy concentration" were used? A. I said "radio location and enemy concentration".

Q   You are quite sure of that? A. Yes.

Q   All the time you were there this map was over his desk? A. Behind his desk.

Q   And rather above it, so that he could look at it beginning waist high?

A.   Yes.

Q   He was pointing to a place somewhere by the Hook of Holland? A. Yes, north-west of the Zuyder Zee.

Q   You showed us what he did. He did in fact point, did not he, with this instrument? A. No. As far as I remember he pointed with his finger.

Q   Did he not turn round and point like this with this thing? A. No, I do not think so.

Q   Are you sure one way or the other? A. I think it was his finger.

(Map marked "I", signed by the president and attached to the proceedings).

(The witness withdraws).

Miss NORA McINTYRE is called in and having been duly sworn is examined by Lt.-Col PARKES as follows:-

Q   Is your name Nora McIntyre? A. Yes.

Q   Are you an Assistant Secretary at Girl Guide Headquarters? A. I am.

Q   On the 15th March were you at Wing House, Piccadilly, in the afternoon? A. I was.

Q   After being on the roof did you go down to Lord Tredegar's office?

A.   Yes.

Q   Did you notice a map on the wall? A. Yes.

Q   A large map of north-west Europe? A. Yes.

Q   Did Lord Tredegar do or say anything in regard to that map that you can recall?   A. He pointed to a certain area on the map.

Q   What area was it, do you know? A. I am not quite sure of it. It was up in the right hand corner. That is all I can remember.

Q   Did he say anything about it? A. He told us that a pigeon had been dropped there and owing to that action had been taken which resulted in many – I think it was either lives or tons of shipping being saved. I cannot be certain which it was.

Q   Is there anything else that you can remember that he said about that matter? A. I cannot recall anything further.

Q   Before you went that afternoon did you know that pigeons were ever dropped on the continent? A. I cannot say I knew for certain but I knew they were dropped by parachute. It would be for this purpose of dropping them on the continent that they would use that.

166

Q   Did you see a pigeon that afternoon? A. Yes.

Q   What happened in regard to that? A. Lord Tredegar asked a sergeant to come down in order that we might see a pigeon container with a parachute. The sergeant brought down the container with the parachute on top and the pigeon was inside the container. They told us something of how the parachute worked and gave certain interesting information about it.

Q   Can you remember what the interesting information was at all? A. Just sort of showing the container and the parachute on top and that it was dropped from an aeroplane. Actually we had asked Lord Tredegar – we knew there were pigeon parachutes because the Army Pigeon Service had been arranging these pigeon flights for us and in the Scottish region the pigeons there had been dropped by parachute, so we knew there were such things and we were asking Lord Tredegar about it.

Q   Dropped in Scotland? A. Yes; it was in the Scottish Command that it was done.

Q   They were dropped in Scotland, do you mean? A. Yes. It was in connection with these flights that the Army Pigeon Service had so kindly arranged for the Guides.

Q   Did you see how the message is carried on the pigeon? A. Yes, we had previously, of course, been attaching ourselves in connection with these same flights. We had the little containers and were putting messages on them ourselves.

Q   What colour containers had you used for your messages? A. We had used red ones.

Q   What colour was the message container for the pigeon that you were shown in Wing House? A. I think there were two or three different colours. I know there was a green one.

Q   Was anything said about that? A. I think Lord Tredegar explained that that had a different significance.

Q   Did he say what the significance was? A. I think he mentioned one was military and   one was civilian. I believe there was another one, but I am not quite certain what it was.

Q   Was anything said about not repeating what was mentioned?
A.   No.

Cross-examined by Sir Walter Monckton

Q   He did happen to say something about it being confidential, did not he? A. I am afraid I do not remember it being said, no.

Q   You knew a bit already. The Girl Guides had been co-operating with the Army Pigeon Service in relation to Wings for Victory, had they? A. Not Wings for Victory. It was in connection with the Baden-Powell Memorial Fund. The Army Pigeon Service had been extremely kind in making arrangements for us for the pigeons to bring messages to the Chief in London.

Q   In the Scottish Command were the pigeons that were dropped carried in containers? A. Yes. I was not there myself but I understand that the Scottish Command arranged that the pigeons should come to the people waiting to send them and let them off and they arranged for aeroplanes to bring the pigeons and drop them by parachute.

Q   These messages which were to go to Lady Baden-Powell on the roof of Wing House were carried in containers? A. I imagine the pigeons would be taken out of the containers and the message would be put on and the pigeons would be sent off.

Q   That was happening in Scottish Command in connection with this very demonstration? A. It was on the same day that we had it all over other parts of the country.

Q   Were you waiting on the roof? A. I was.

Q   Was it a misty afternoon? A. Extremely foggy; not only on this day we are speaking about – it happened twice. It was on the 25th February that the messages were carried. It was a thick fog and we wanted to take photographs of the pigeons arriving and we were unable to do so owing to the fog. They very kindly arranged for us to have a retake on another day and it was the other day.

Q   I must not press you too much for your secrets, but did the birds all arrive all right?   A. Certainly not at the time we were there. Some of them came in.

Q   Some were released from nearby, were not they, to make a good show of it? A. Yes, there were some, but I do not think the ones nearby did arrive actually. The distant ones turned up.

Q   Did you happen to notice, when Lord Tredegar was pointing at the map, whether he used this instrument to point with? A. I would not say. He pointed with something but I am afraid I do not know what. He might have been pointing with his hand. I am afraid I do no know.

Lt.-Col. PARKES: No re-examination

A MEMBER OF THE COURT: I am not quite clear whether as a result of the interview you had that afternoon you then attached any particular significance to the green coloured message container, and, if so, what it was. A. I really did not, no.

Q   You would not say that because it was green there was anything more to it than that? A. No, I would not say that I would afterwards.

Q   You were not told specifically? A. That I would not say. I think they did mention what the containers were, what they were used for.

Q   But not so definitely that you could now tell? A. I am afraid it is my memory. I am afraid I did not take it in in detail enough on the occasion and I could not make any certain statement about it.

The PRESIDENT: But you have a recollection that there was a good deal said about these coloured containers? A. There certainly was something said about it; the actual significance of the different colours, I think was mentioned.

Q   You do not remember the significance? A. May I say that the first time I was questioned about this I doubt very much whether I should have remembered but naturally since I have been asked I have talked to Miss Isherwood, who has a very much better memory than I have, and I may remember new things which I should not have remembered then. Therefore it would hardly be fair to say so.

Q   Your general recollection is that during the course of that demonstration a good deal was said about the use of coloured containers?

A. Not a good deal, just simply that they were mentioned, that there were different colours. I think the use of the different colours was mentioned but they were not enlarged open.

Q   You cannot remember what it was. A. No.

The JUDGE ADVOCATE: Did you use any green ones in Lady Baden-Powell's demonstration? A. No, I do not think so. The ones I saw come in here were all red ones.

SIR WALTER MONCKTON: May I ask one question on that? I did understand you to say that your recollection was that the distinction made to you was that the red ones were civilian and the green ones army. A. I said that one was civilian and one army but I really did not know which was which.

(The witness withdraws)

Miss HELEN MARGARET ISHERWOOD is called in and having been duly sworn is examined by Lt.-Col. PARKES as follows:-

Q   Is your name Helen Margaret Isherwood? A. Yes.

Q   Are you a Registration Secretary at Girl Guide Headquarters? A. Yes.

Q   On the afternoon of the 15th March we have heard that you and Miss McIntyre and two A.T.S. officers were present with the accused officer in his office at Wing House. Do you remember being in the room. A. That is so.

Q   Did you notice a map on the wall? A. Yes, there was.

Q   Did Lord Tredegar say anything about it? A. Yes, he did.

Q   Tell the court what he said, so far as you can recall it? A. Lord Tredegar said he wanted to show us something on the map. He then pointed to a place there.

Q   What place was it? Would it help you if you saw the map? A. I understood as a result of interrogation afterwards that it was the Zuyder Zee.

Q   I am asking you what you can recall seeing. If you can remember –

A.   May I explain the position? I am certain I could recognise the place on the map but I did not realise the name of the place until I tried to identify it afterwards.

Q   Let us try and put ourselves, as far as we can, in the same position as that afternoon. Here is the map. Perhaps you will for the moment, play the role of Lord Tredegar and show the court what it was he did and what he said. A. I understand that that was the place where there was something that was acting against shipping and that as a result of a pigeon being dropped at another place, which I thought was about there within 35 hours some action was taken by which the danger was removed.

Q   Did he say what the danger was? A. That I cannot remember.

Q   Will you point once more to the second place to which you say he pointed?   A. I thought it was about there.

Q   How close to the map did he point? A. I thought he actually pointed to it.

Q   Did he say anything else about the incident? A. I understood that a large amount of shipping had been saved in consequence and that congratulations were sent to the Army Pigeon Service.

Q   We have heard that a little later on a pigeon, a container and a parachute were brought in; is that right? A. Yes.

Q   What was done with them? A. We were shown how the pigeon fitted into the container.

Q   Did you see any container for carrying messages at all? A. Yes, we saw a green container.

Q   Was anything said about that? A. Only that there were different coloured containers used.

Q   Was there any indication of what colour was used for what? A. Yes, I believe there was.

Q   Can you remember what it was; what indication was given about that? A. No, I am afraid I cannot remember.

Q   <u>Cross-examined by Sir Walter Monckton</u>

Q   I gather from you that he pointed to two spots in order (1) to say there was something here, and (2) to say that this was where the pigeons were dropped? A. Yes, as I remember it I think he did.

Q   Do you say that he touched on them both? A. Yes, I think he did.

Q   Can you tell me whether he did it with this instrument; did he have something like this skewer in his hand with which he touched them? A. I would not like to say so.

Q   You do not know either way? A. I would not be certain either way.

Q   You had had a conversation, I take it, which led up to this point about the pigeon and the area that you have mentioned. Had you had a conversation about pigeons in general, that you remember? A. Except that the whole reason for us being there was pigeons.

Q   Did you discuss the courage of the bird? A. Not on that particular occasion, I think.

Q I wonder if you recollect his saying how the pigeon would fly through anything. A. No, I would not like to say that.

Q Do you remember asking him whether there was anything outstanding about the performance of pigeons which he could recollect in this war? A. No, I cannot remember that.

Q Out of the blue he started pointing to the map and saying "This is what happened" – or do not you remember? A. That was the start, as far as I can remember, when we arrived in the room

The **JUDGE ADVOCATE**: I have not quite got this clearly. You say he pointed to two separate places on the map? A. Yes.

Q One you put rather north of the other? A. Yes.

Q What did you gather was supposed to have happened at the northernmost point?

Q I gathered that the northernmost point was where the danger lay and the second point was where the pigeon was dropped.

Q You think that on the northernmost point that he pointed to there was something which was causing trouble to this country? A. Yes.

Q And that the pigeon was dropped at a place to the south of it? A. Yes.

Q He then went on to say that action was taken in 33 hours? A. Within 33 hours.

Q Action where? A. At the northerly point.

Q The spot where you thought the danger was? A. Yes.

Q Your recollection is that that is more or less what opened the conversation about pigeons downstairs? A. Yes.

A **MEMBER OF THE COURT**: Were you aware before you went out from the office at this time that we were in the habit of dropping pigeons in that way over enemy occupied countries? A. Yes.

Q   You knew it? A. I did

(The witness withdraws)

Subaltern J.A. MACKENZIE is called and having been duly sworn is examined by Lt.-Col. Parkes as follows:-

Q   Are you Subaltern J. A. Mackenzie, A.T.S. and are you a Staff Subaltern at Headquarters Signals 1A, Carrier Pigeon Service, at the War Office? A. Yes.

Q   Were you present on the afternoon of the 15th March in the accused's office when Miss McIntyre and Miss Isherwood were there? A. Yes.

Q   Will you tell the court what happened? A. The first thing that happened was that Major Tredegar invited Miss McIntyre and Miss Isherwood over to a map he had on his wall behind him and he pointed to the jutting out point of the Zuyder Zee.

Q   Look at this map. Will you show the court where it was that he pointed? A. I am not certain. I think it was there.

Q   What did he say about it? A. He said that news had been carried from that point to this country of a radio location station and a heavy concentration of enemy troops.

Q   Anything else about it? A. He said that there was news our bombers had thoroughly bombed the position.

Q   How did he point? Had he anything in his hand? A. I am perfectly convinced it was a pointer.

Q   Was it like that one which is produced by Sir Walter Monckton now?

A.   I think so. I would not swear to it.

Q   How close did the point of the pointer get to the map? A. It touched it.

Q   Then what happened? A. I think I left the room after that.

174

Q How long were you away? **A. About ten minutes, I should say.**

Q When you came back, what was happening? **A. There was a sergeant in the room and he had a parachute and he was describing its method of attachment to the container for dropping pigeons on the other side.**

Q Did you see a message container? **A. Yes.**

Q What colour was it? **A. Green**

Q Was anything said about message containers or their colours? **A. I think there was something but I would not swear to it. I was standing on the other side of the room.**

Q <u>Cross-examined by Sir Walter Monckton</u>

Q Had you seen this demonstration you have just described before? **A. Often.**

Q Had you seen it before Major Tredegar's time? **A. No.**

Q Had you seen it in the presence of Col Cullinan? **A. Yes.**

Q You say you have seen it quite often? **A. Very often**

Q And in the presence of Col. Cullinan on several occasions? **A. The circumstances in which I would see it would be when they were actually testing the containers, which were sometimes not satisfactory – not strong enough. They were in our office, the office I shared with the Staff Captain who deals with equipment. Col. Cullinan may have been there but I would not be called in by Col. Cullinan.**

Q Was Capt. Kleyn in the office next to Major Tredegar? **A. Yes.**

Q You worked with Capt. Kleyn? **No I worked with the Staff Captain.**

175

Q   You had seen this demonstration done before when they were testing containers or something of that sort? A. Yes it would be a recognised demonstration.

Q   You had seen the thing shown? A. Yes.

Q   Had you seen it shown from time to time in Major Tredegar's room to officers or people who came in. A. No.

Q   You were never in there when that happened? A. No.

Q   Did you happen to notice that he said "Let's show them the act"? Did you hear the word, "act"? A   I did not hear anything about it.

Q   There must have been some other conversation in relation to pigeons when these   two ladies were there. Was there some discussion about the courage of the birds? A. Yes, it was a sort of general discussion.

Q   Saying that it was a brave bird and would fly through anything? A. How capable and   dependable it was .

Q   Was it in relation to that that someone asked whether there had been any outstanding feats in this war, something heroic? A. I do not recollect that.

Q   But you remember a general conversation about their courage? A. Yes. I was not taking much notice, because I have heard the praises of the bird sung so often before.

Q   That would be quite natural. They were sung on this occasion? A. Yes.

Q   Did you know of this thing yourself before, this thing you have been pointing to? A. Not at all.

Q   Did you notice how many points were pointed out by Lord Tredegar – one, two or three? A. There was only the one point to my knowledge and then he placed his hand on the other side.

Q   When you were first asked was your recollection that he put his finger on? A. Yes, I thought of that afterwards because I was

176

almost certain that it was a pointer afterwards because it was such a high map that he could not do it.

The JUDGE ADVOCATE: Was there anything on the map at all when you were looking at it? A. There were various studs, sort of buttons.

Q   Can you take the studs off? A. Quite easily.

Q   They were stuck into the map; is that what you mean? A. Yes.

Q   Can you tell us whether there was anything at all on this particular piece of land that jutted out, any mark on that? A. I could not say. I am very short sighted.

Q   I suppose you have seen this map on many occasions? A. Yes.

Q   You often go into Lord Tredegar's room, I suppose? A. Yes.

Q   When you talk about these numerous demonstrations, do you mean where they are testing the thing in the ordinary way, or are members of the outside public there?

A.   No; they are just for our benefit, to see that they are satisfactory. We deal with the equipment side of it.

Q   It is really a test to see whether they are satisfactory containers? A. Yes, to see that the whole outfit is satisfactory. They are actually stacked in my office.

Q   Everybody present there knows what should be done and they are just seeing whether it will work all right; is that what you are trying to say?

A.   Yes. As soon as a new container comes in – we are always changing the type – we would automatically attach a parachute to see how suitable it was going to be.

Q   Who is "we"; you and who else? A. The Staff Captain who shares an office with me. He deals with the equipment.

Q   Only you two? A. And any of the other officers who were present.

Q   This was a demonstration with two Girl Guides present, was not it?

A.   Yes.

Q   And you and another Subaltern? A. Yes.

Q   And the accused himself? A. Yes.

Q   Taking place in his room? A. Yes.

Q   That is all that were present till the sergeant brought the bird in? A. Quite.

(The witness withdraws)

No. 1746777 L/sgt. A. R. DONACHY is called I and having been duly sworn is examined by Lt-Col Parkes as follows:-

Q   You are No 1746777 L/Sgt. A.R. Donachy, Royal Corps of Signals?

A.   Yes.

Q   You are a sergeant loftman at the Special Section, Carrier Pigeon, at Wing House? A. Yes.

Q   On an occasion about the middle of March were you called into Lord Tredegar's office one afternoon when there were some ladies there? A. Yes.

Q   The witnesses who have just given evidence? A. Yes, the two Girl Guide Leaders.

Q   What were you told to do – anything? A. I was told to show the ladies how the bird was put in the container, etc.

Q   Who told you that? A. Lord Tredegar.

Q   Did you do so? A. Yes.

Q   Was anything said to them about the secrecy or otherwise of this matter? A. When I put the bird in the container Lord Tredegar went to his cabinet, which was on the right, and got out a (left blank)

Q   I want to know whether he said anything about this matter. A. Not at that stage.

Q   Later on did he? A. Yes.

Q   What was it that he said? A. He said "I am going to show you something now which you must not" (left blank)

Q   I want to get it quite clear. What was before that; what immediately followed his saying that? A. When I put the bird in the container?

Q   When he said "I am going to show you something". A. He went to his steel cabinet.

Q   Any warning that he gave them was in regard to something else and nothing to do with the showing of the pigeon; is that right? A. Yes.

Q   Did they see a message container? A. Yes.

Q   Was anything said about message containers? A. No.

Q   What colour container was it? A. A green one – two green ones actually.

Cross-examined by Sir Walter Monckton

Q   Had you done this before – shown these containers and pigeons to other people? A. On one previous occasion.

Q   Who to? A. To two officers.

Q   British? A. Yes.

Q   Who were they? A. The two officers who were here this morning.

Q   Major Cassidy and Major Carruthers? A. Yes.

Q   About how long were you working under Lord Tredegar? A. From the time that he took over.

Q   In November 1942? A. Yes.

Q   Did you on any occasion explain this container and the parachute to any American officers? A. No.

Q   That was not done in your presence? A. No.

Q   Was it ever done by you in the presence of the C.S.O.? A. Not to any officers at all or anybody.

Q   Not as far as you were concerned? A. No.

Q   He might have done it? A. He may have done it.

Q   Supposing he did do it, would you have known about it? A. No.

A MEMBER OF THE COURT: Would you be the only N.C.O. who would carry out his demonstration or a demonstration of this sort in Major Tredegar's office? A. The only other one would be Sgt. Sutton.

Q   He might have done it? A. He may have done it.

Q   Suggesting he did do it, would you have known about it? A. No.

(The witness withdraws

Capt. J.K. Kleyn is called in and having been duly sworn is examined by Lt.-Col, Parkes as follows:-

Q   You are Capt J. K. Kleyn, Intelligence Corps? A. Yes.

Q   Are you an Intelligence Officer attached to the Special Section, Carrier Pigeon, Royal Corps of Signals? A. Yes.

Q   Are you responsible for the operational side of the work of the section? A. Yes.

Q   For that purpose are you under the direction of MI 14 at the War Office? A. Yes.

The JUDGE ADVOCATE: Who is his C.O.?

Lt.-Col. PARKES: Do you know who your commanding officer is? I suppose it is Lord Tredegar in so far as you are attached there; is that right? A. Yes.

Q   For operational purposes you say you were under MI 14? A. Yes

Q   Look at those two operational log books (handed).Were they kept by you? A. Yes.

The JUDGE ADVOCATE: Why do we have to have these?

Lt.-Col. PARKES: I want to ask him some questions about them.

THE JUDGE ADVOCATE: Do you think it is necessary?

Lt.-Col. PARKES: I want to prove that in fact these messages were received, that the information with regard to what was charged was true, and that the accused had access to it. (To the witness). Were those books in your care? A. Yes.

Q   Towards the end of December of last year did you pass them into the possession of Lord Tredegar? A. Yes.

Q   Is there any record in that book kept by you of any carrier pigeon message having been received from persons in Holland in regard to a radio location station? A. Yes.

Q   Can you tell the court the dates? A. One was in June; the other November.

Q   In June of 1942? A. Yes.

Q   And then in November 1942? A. Yes.

Q   What part of Holland did the message purport to come from and what part was recorded in the book? A. They came from north-west of the Zuyder Zee.

SIR WALTER MONCKTON: Can he show us where it is in the book? A. Here.

The JUDGE ADVOCATE: On what principle is he working now? Is he supposed to be refreshing his memory or putting in a book?

Lt-Col. PARKES: These are documents which are proved to have been in the possession of the accused. It is said he has disclosed information to which he had access. I am therefore showing the court the information to which he got access.

THE JUDGE ADVOCATE: You are only putting them in to show what was in the book?

Lt.-Col. PARKES: Yes. That is the June one you draw attention to?

A.   Yes

Q   That is the second one? A. Yes.

(Log books marked J.1 and J.2 respectively, signed by the president and attached to the proceedings.)

Q   The second of those messages did you in fact yourself receive? A. Yes.

Cross-examined by Sir Walter Monckton

Q   There is nothing in these records, is there, to indicate what action was taken?   A. No.

Q   From a mere looking at those books the accused would not have discovered, if it was the fact, that there was a bombing of the place concerned? A. No.

Q   Either within a stated number of hours or at all? A. No.

Q   Did you in fact know whether there was or there was not? A. No.

Q   You were the Intelligence operational side? A. Yes.

Q   In that capacity you worked under Major Melland, did you not? A. Yes.

Q   He was the intelligence officer to whom you were responsible? A. Yes.

Q   The operational side was not under Major Tredegar? A. No.

Q   It was his job to produce the pigeons? A. Yes.

Q   Your job was to direct their use? A. Yes

Q   You were not in any sense responsible to Major Tredegar? A. On the operational side?

Q   Yes. A . No.

Q   Had you any other work except the operational side? A. No.

Q   The decoding of anything coming in, if it required decoding, would be done by you, and the translation would be done by you and your staff? A. Yes.

A MEMBER OF THE COURT: You say that you handed these records over to the accused at a certain time. You said at such and such a date you handed these log books over to the accused? A. Yes.

Q   How did that come about if he was not concerned in any way with the operational side? A. Lord Tredegar asked me for the books.

The JUDGE ADVOCATE: That is what is puzzling me. That is why I asked who was your C.O. That is very confidential information, is not it? A. Yes.

Q   Do I understand that the accused just asked you for those and you handed them over? A. Yes. I did not hand them over straight away; I asked advice.

Q   When you handed them over you had sought advice, had you? A. Yes.

SIR WALTER MONCKTON: May I ask a question on that? It would be right to say, would it not, that at this time you knew that if Major Tredegar came to you with a request it was something he was directed to bring to you by his C.S.O.? A. Yes

Q   It is not necessary to go into it, but relations were not good between you and Major Tredegar at that time? A. I am not aware of that.

Q   At any rate you know that if he came to you, although you were in the next office, he would only come to you if he was directed so to do by the C.S.O? I believe that is so. I believe Lord Tredegar asked as to the instructions of the C.S.O.

Q   To the best of your knowledge and belief, on this occasion was he coming to you on the instructions of the C.S.O? A. Yes.

Q   That is your belief? A. That is my belief.

<u>The witness withdraws</u>

<u>Major B. Melland</u> is called in, and, having been duly sworn, is examined by Lt.-Col. PARKES as follows:

Q   Major B. Melland, Intelligence Corps, are you a general staff officer, second grade, at MI 14 at the War Office? A. I am.

Q   Are you responsible under the Director of Military Intelligence for directing the use of carrier pigeons by the Special Section (Carrier Pigeon Service)? A. I am.

Q   So far as the War Office use of them is concerned? A. Yes.

Q   And also for the distribution within the War Office of intelligence received by that means? A. Yes.

Q   Will you tell the Court very shortly the nature of the operational work of the Special Section on the Continent? A. These pigeons are sent over to areas the particulars of which are given by me to the pigeon service. They are sent over to those areas with a questionnaire, the answers to which may or may not be supplied by persons who are friendly to us, and possible also by actual agents of ours. The information then comes back and it is translated. The translation is sent to me, and I am responsible for the distribution of that information in the War Office and also to G.H.Q. Home Forces.

Q   Are the places on the Continent where the pigeons are dropped secret? A. Yes.

Q   And the places from which the pigeons come back? A. That is secret information.

Q   To what extent are the names of countries where these operations are carried on secret? A. That depends on the size of the area. It is obviously less secret in the case of a smaller country like Holland. It would be even more secret in the case of an area within a country, and most secret in the case of actual localities.

Q   What about Denmark? Have these operations been carried out much over Denmark? A. On one occasion.

Q   So far as you know did the accused officer have any authority to communicate any information of the kind to which I have just referred to Herbert Edward Keys or the members of his group? A. No.

Q   Is it true that a radio location station north-west of the Zuyder Zee was located by means of carrier pigeon message? A. Yes.

Q   When? A. On two occasions, in June last and in November last.

Q   Is that fact secret? A. Yes.

Q   What about the containers and the parachutes used by the Special Section? What degree of secrecy attaches to them in your judgement? A. We are certain that the enemy is in possession of specimens of these containers and parachutes, but we have no evidence as far as I know that the method of release of the container and the parachute is known to the enemy, that is to say the method of release from the aircraft.

185

Q   There is evidence that the accused officer told two Girl Guide Leaders that the green message containers were used in connection with pigeons bringing back information from occupied territory; is that secret or not? A. I would regard that definitely as information which is not to be published. I think it is fair to argue that if any maliciously minded person knew that these green containers contained urgent operational information he might withhold that information from us or even possibly communicate it to treacherously minded persons.

Cross-examined by SIR WALTER MONCKTON

Q   You say it is fair to argue that. There is nothing, is there, to prevent anybody who picks up a pigeon which has a green container attached to it from opening it by just unscrewing the top, or however it is opened? A. No.

Q   So that anybody who picks up has access to the message? A. Has physical access to the message.

Q   He can get hold of it? A. Yes.

Q   If he knows the language in which it is couched can he read it? A. Yes.

Q   I suppose some are in French, some in Dutch and some may be in English? A. Yes.

Q   One of the hazards which is necessary in these operations is that either before it starts on its homeward journey or on its homeward journey some mishap may occur to the pigeon? A. Yes.

Q   It may fall into the hands in enemy-occupied territory of those who are not well disposed to us? A. Yes.

Q   Including the enemy? A. The actual bird and the container?

Q   Yes? A. But not necessarily the message.

186

Q   It depends if one is in at the time? A. As soon as one has been put in and the bird released the chances are that that particular bird will reach this country.

Q   Do none take messages out from this country? A. Not for the purpose I am connected with.

Q   They do take messages? A. I believe on certain occasions they do.

Q   We will eliminate for our purpose the stage until the bird is going to be released on its homeward journey. If it is coming across enemy-occupied territory it does not always come unscathed? I do not mean that somebody is going to shoot it down but that might happen? A. It might happen.

Q   It might fly into wires? A. Yes.
Q   When it gets over this country there are still further mishaps which may occur? A. If the bird were exhausted it might conceivably not reach its loft.

Q   Or it might fly into wire? A. Yes.

Q   It is right to say, if you look through those records, that a very large proportion of the birds that go out on these operations do not come back? A. That is so.

Q   You have no manner of doubt, have you, that the enemy have these containers? A. No doubt.

Q   And the parachute? A. And the parachute.

Q   What you doubt is whether the enemy know how the container, the bird and the parachute leave the machine? A. Yes.

Q   That is the secret which has got still to be kept? A. Yes.

Q   So far as the message contained in the container on its return journey is concerned we may say these two things, say we not; first, that if in the hazards of the flight the bird comes down, the message is there for anyone who picks it up? A. Yes.

Q   Unless that person has been told that green is more interesting than red, he is as likely to open green as red? A. Yes.

Q   Unless it is generally known that green is particularly interesting there is nothing to make someone open the green one? A. In preference to the red?

Q   Yes? A. No.

Q   There are occasions, are there not, when messages have been picked up; you know that? A. Yes.

Q   Was there not one in November 1942 of which you know? A. I would not like to say offhand.

Q   Let me remind you. Did it turn out there was a German maid in some loft and she   opened and said, "I have got a message here from a pigeon; shall I read it"? A. I heard of that incident. I do not know whether that was picked up in the way that you suggest.

Q   It was not meant to get into the hands of the German maid? A. I think it was meant to go to that particular loft.

Q   That was one of the birds that got back? A. Yes.

Q   What percentage of the birds that go out get back? A. A very low percentage. I should say by and large over the last eighteen months something in the region of 18 per cent got back.

Q   The release of the bird from the aircraft is something which will not be given away by anything said about green containers or the localities where the birds are dropped? A. No, that particular technical aspect certainly would not.

Q   You are not anxious about the distinction between the green and the red, are you? A. I am to a certain extent, because I would not like too many people to know that the green container contains urgent information.

Q   One wants to deal with realities. You do not suggest that an ill-disposed person would have hesitated to open a red container, even if he knew the green might be more interesting, if a red container came his way?

A. I think he would be more disposed to go to the green.

Q Would not he open either in any event? A. Probably.

Q Is the only thing you are worried about the messages, whether the messages are going to be interrupted because someone may open them? A. I personally am worried about that.

Q Do you think there is really much in it? Do you think that somebody who gets one of these messages is likely, because of the disclosure of the green being different from the red, to make any difference in the hasted with which he sends it on? A. Yes

Q Does not it depend on whether he is well or ill disposed? A. Yes.

Q If he is well disposed he will want to get the urgent message more quickly to the authorities? A. Yes, but the converse also applies.

Q If he is ill disposed he will stop it anyway. The ill disposed person will not be sending on to you the green or the red, will he? A. On the whole not, I should say.

Q Why on earth should he? If he is ill disposed is not his whole object to prevent information getting to us which we might have? A. He might substitute another message.

Q Would not he do that in the case of the red as well as the green? A. It depends on the nature of the message in the red, and I am not sufficiently well acquainted with that.

Q If he wants to do some harm should not he take the opportunity of putting in false messages anyhow? A. Because messages in the green containers are written in Flemish or in French or in Dutch or even in Danish. It might often be considerably more difficult to substitute a false message than it would in the case of a red one, which I take it is only used in this country.

Q   Let us ask you about localities. It follows from what you have said that the enemy know we drop pigeons in various parts of enemy-occupied territory? A. Yes.

Q   Of course, they already know some places where they have been dropped and apprehended? A. Yes.

Q   And even that map, the scale of which is 1/500,000, leaves a considerable margin of error to the observer if it is well studded with points, does it not? A. Yes.

Q   Have you been in Major Tredegar's office? A. Not in his personal office.

Q   Have you been in the C.S.O.'s office? A. Yes.

Q   There is a map in that room, is there not? A. I believe there is.

Q   Have you noticed that on it there are also pins in enemy-occupied territory and England? A. No, I have not.

Q   You have not observed that? A. It is not my duty to study his map.

Q   You did not happen to notice that there were lines and pins and things on that map? A. Not in his C.O.'s room, no.

Q   If it was so, anybody who went into the office would have an opportunity to observe it? A. If it were so, yes.

Q   Would you conceive it to be your duty to give directions to prevent such a map being   exposed in Major Tredegar's office? A. If it were within my duty which it certainly is not, I would say Yes.

Q   You had an officer attached to Major Tredegar and occupying the next office? A. Yes.

Q   Did he ever report to you that a map of this sort was hanging up which was giving   away some information? A. Only in connection with the immediate circumstances of this charge.

Q   The map, we know, had been there before then? A. That I do not know.

Q   At any rate, he never reported it to you? A. He did not.

Q   Are you saying to the Court that Major Tredegar un-warned by Captain Kleyn, ought to have refrained from having a map 1/500,000 on his wall with pin points in it? A. I do not consider that it was within Major Tredegar's function in that office to have a map of that kind on his wall.

Q   Do you think it was in the function of Captain Kleyn to tell you if it was there and it ought not to have been there? A. He did in point of fact tell me.

Q   On the 15th March, or after the 15th March? A. Before.

Q   When did he tell you? A. That I am afraid I cannot remember exactly.

Q   Can you tell me within a month? A. It was certainly in the month of March.

Q   Before or after the 15th? A. Before.

Q   What steps did you take to see that the danger was immediately stopped? A. I made a record of it.

Q   Why did not you see to it that it was taken down? A. Because I did not consider it part of my duty.

Q   Do you think it was part of Captain Kleyn's duty to take that map down? A. No.

Q   Do you think Major Tredegar might have been warned that there was something wrong with having such a map there? A. It is conceivable.

Q   Is it right? You seem to hesitate. You and those officers under you were the people who were responsible for the operational and intelligence side? A. For the   intelligence side.

Q   And the operational side? A. To the extent that we requested pigeons to be sent to certain places.

Q   Directed them to sent, I understand? A. Directed.

Q   You were responsible for that. It was you in MI 14. who would naturally be careful to see that valuable information was not being recklessly given to people outside? A. I think I should say this: at no time was it made clear to me that this particular map had all the details which have since come out in this case in it.

Q   You mean pin-points of the places where birds might have been dropped? A. Yes.

Q   What would you have thought the pin points would indicate to anybody who went into that room? A. I think the map might conceivably contain general indications as to the areas in which we were operating.

Q   The pin points? A. Not necessarily.

Q   What do you think they represent? A. I had not actually associated the pin points with the statement which has come to my attention.

Q   When it first came to your attention in what form did it come? A. I understood that there was a map hanging in Lord Tredegar's office which showed roughly the areas in which these pigeons were operating.

Q   You say it showed roughly the areas. When that was said to you, you did not imagine it was a map of the Low Countries and Brittany? A.   No.

Q   You thought there was some indication on the map of where operations were taking place? A. Yes, it struck me at the time as unnecessary for this map with this information on to be in Lord Tredegar's office.

Q   Security is something with which you are particularly concerned. Did you think that the map indicated an operational area? A. I have said I thought that the map conceivably contained information of the points   at   which pigeons were to be released.

Q   In what form were the indications? A. That I do not know.

Q   Did you ask? A. I did not.

Q   What were you told? A. That opportunity had not been given to Captain Kleyn to study the map in detail.

Q   Do you really mean to say that Captain Kleyn in the next office was   unaware whether this map showed pin points, this map in the next room? A. I understood that he hardly ever went in there.

Q   Let us dissociate what we may feel from what we may know. You   have one of your officers in the next room. Is it beyond the capacity   of the Department to ascertain in what way these indications to   which you object were shown on a map? Do you mean to say you   could not find out?   A. Well, I grant you that, but things moved very   rapidly. It was a comparatively short time before this case arose that I   first heard about the map, and it was when I heard about the disclosures in connection with this map that I took steps to make a   report on the subject.

Q   May I assume that at any rate you did not regard it as particularly   dangerous that there should be in this room a map which showed   some indications of the areas in which pigeons might be dropped? A.   That is true.

Q   You did not? A. No.

Q   What you now tell me is that you would be anxious to avoid any   precise indication? A. Any disclosure.

Q   When you say "any disclosure" let me take an instance. If somebody   points to a spot and says; "There was a radio location station there   and it was smashed as a result of a pigeon bringing back   information", that is what you want to avoid? A. Yes.

Q   You are not seeking to put on the Court the suggestion that some indication of the areas is in itself a grave dereliction? A. No.

LT. COL. PARKES: No questions.

THE JUDGE ADVOCATE: Could a pigeon coming from abroad ever properly have a red container on it? A. So far as I know, no.

Q   If I understand the scheme at all, it would always be a green one? A.   Yes.

Q   Does not it work out both ways? If people realise a message is important are not they more likely to bring it to you quickly? Speed is important? A. It is very important.

Q   Does not it work out that way? If anybody did know the green was important he would be more likely to bring it along quicker than a red one, if he was a decent person? A. Yes.

(The witness withdraws)

Major E. WALKER is called in, and, having been duly sworn, is examined by Lt. Col. PARKES as follows:

Q   Major E. Walker, the Queen's Bays, are you Security Officer, London District? A. Yes.

Q   On the 6th April were you present when the accused officer came before Brigadier Nalder, Deputy Director of Signals? A. I was.

Q   Did Brigadier Nalder direct the statements by Subalterns Harvey and Mackenzie and by Miss McIntrye and Miss Isherwood and Captain Kleyn to be read? A. Yes.

Q   Was that done? A. Yes.

Q   Was the Accused asked whether he wished to make a statement? A.   Yes

Q   Was he warned and did he say he did wish to make a statement? A.   Yes.

Q Did he then make a statement which you took down and which
he signed in your presence? A. Yes.

Q Is that the statement that he made? (Handed) A. Yes.

Lt. Col. PARKES: I have already read the relevant portions of
that. (Statement marked "A", signed by the President and
attached to the proceedings.)

SIR WALTER MONCKTON: No questions.

(The witness withdraws)

Lt. Col. PARKES: That is the case for the Prosecution.

(At 13.45 hours the Court is closed.)

(At 15.00 hours the court re-opens)

The Accused is again brought before the Court

THE JUDGE ADVOCATE: Lord Tredegar, I am not going to waste
any time by explaining to you what your rights are about giving
evidence. You are defended by eminent counsel and naturally they
will have considered that aspect of the case and will have advised you
what they think you ought to do. I will just put the formal questions.
Do you apply to give evidence yourself as a witness on oath?

THE ACCUSED: No.

THE JUDGE ADVOCATE: Do you intend to call any other
witnesses in your defence?

THE ACCUSED: One, Colonel Sir Russell Wilkinson. [517]

THE JUDGE ADVOCATE: Is he a witness as to character only?

SIR WALTER MONCKTON: Character and health.

Lt. Col. PARKES: I shall not take any point on that.

THE JUDGE ADVOCATE: He does not want to make any statement on oath?

SIR WALTER MONCKTON: He prefers that what is to be said shall be said through me.

Lt. Col. PARKES: I understand that Sir Walter is calling no evidence save a medical witness. In those circumstances I do not wish to address the court.

THE JUDGE ADVOCATE: Sir Walter, will you make your address now? You can call the witness later on.

SIR WALTER MONCKTON: May it please the court. My learned friend (I suppose I may still call him that although I now see him in uniform) opened this case with conspicuous fairness as one would have expected. The first thing to which I would desire to draw attention is the clear distinction through his speech between a charge which involves anything suggesting that the accused was actuated by a desire to act otherwise than in accordance with his duty as an officer and a charge involving an allegation of an error of judgement. The two things could not be more distinct. When one has the honour and responsibility of defending an officer before his peers it is of the most importance that one should address oneself to what it is one has to contend with. I have not here to contend with any charge involving the integrity of Major Tredegar. No suggestion casting any moral obloquy upon him has been made or could be made upon the evidence which has now been heard to the full before the court. I have to deal (and I will deal with them as faithfully and as frankly as I can) with charges which involve him in having committed an error of judgement.

I am sure the court will have observed as the witnesses came to the witness chair and gave their evidence one by one that what one was seeking to do was to shred off (if one may be given permission to use that expression) what really mattered from what really did not matter. Nobody who has had any experience, professional or otherwise, in the duty of withholding information of value to the enemy will ever be likely to fall into the error of not thinking that that is an important consideration. It is equally important that one should bear in mind, when balancing any particular charges that you are not seeking under any of the Acts, which I must come to in a moment, to prevent any information which has no value being dissociated in this country. What you are seeking to deal with is something looked at by and large and broadly, namely the necessity of withholding information which really is of value to the enemy.

I want to come straight down to what I have to deal with. Of course, if someone through an error of judgement were guilty of giving away information about future operations, that would indeed be a grave error of judgement and one to be looked at very carefully. On the other hand, you may get a case in which you may say to yourselves: "It looks as if that has some of the attributes of secrecy about it", and yet when you come to examine it there is really nothing which is of value to the enemy which would be given away if the information were broadcast.

As I hope to show you when I come to this particular case, there is a great deal with which I have to deal in this case which involves the second class, where there really is no secrecy, where what is suggested against Lord Tredegar is that he has been giving wider dissemination to something which was patently, when the evidence is examined, already known on both sides of the Channel.

Before I come to the specific charges let me deal with what one of the witnesses says (and I think rightly) he described as his "act", that is the production of the pigeon, the container, the instructions and the green message container. All that at first sight, until it is examined and until the witnesses are examined, looks as if it has about it all the elements of a secret operation. But what are the facts? It is perfectly patent that those two young ladies who were here from the Girl Guides remembered very little, but there were two things which between them they knew. They knew all about the dropping of pigeons by parachute. One of them knew how it had been done by Girl Guides in Scotland under authority. The other of them knew that pigeons were dropped by parachute in enemy occupied territory. What sort of secrecy surrounds that? Take the operation of dropping pigeons by parachute. It is perfectly plain that it is done, as one would assume. Pigeons, as we all know, have been used since before the World War and if you are going to make use of them for the purpose of conveying messages and you want the messages to come from enemy occupied territory, why should not you drop them by parachute over there just as they are dropped by parachute in Scotland for a less warlike purpose? It is quite obvious that it is something known by those children and which would be perfectly well known to the enemy.

What about the container? At one stage there seemed to be a suggestion that some breach of secrecy would be involved in the disclosure of there having been red and green containers, the green may be, being used for army messages – I do not know. The witness did not seem to know which was which, but I assume myself that the green container is used for carrying army messages for the special service to which Lord Tredegar belonged, whereas the red is used for more peaceful pursuits. But what does it come to? All we do know is that every pigeon that is dropped in enemy occupied territory, if it is used for the return journey, will have a container, not in any way sealed, out of which the first picker-up of the bird can take the message. What does it matter in those circumstances whether the container is red or green? Either the person who picks the bird up is a well disposed person, in which case if he did think that the green was more important than the red he would be all the more eager to get it where it ought to be, or he is an ill disposed person, and does anyone suppose that it really is within the realms of reason that an ill disposed person, getting hold of a container, whatever its colour, which contains a message will not take it out and do the worst he can with it, whether it is to substitute another and let the bird go , or to try and make use of the one he has got? When you analyse it and frankly face up to it I suggest that what Major Welland was finally driven to say was completely right, namely, that there is nothing secret about dropping pigeons by parachute, there is nothing secret about the colour of the container, and there is nothing secret about anything to do with it except the release from the aeroplane which, he says, is something which is not known. That, however, is quite irrelevant for the purpose of this case because nobody suggests that at any stage by any means anybody has been made aware of the method by which the pigeon is released from the aeroplane.

Once you have got rid of the idea of the impropriety of saying anything about the dropping of a pigeon by means of a parachute, the use of a container and the description of the colour of the container, you have got rid of a great deal of what would otherwise be calculated to clog our understanding of the requirements of secrecy as applied to this case.

What we have to face are three charges. I have dealt with one in advance and I will deal with them in turn in a moment. I have dealt with the one which really suggests that there was something wrong in the use of what was called the "act".

Now I want to say a word about another matter which also might, as I suggest, hinder one's complete appreciation of the case which ought to be considered on behalf of the accused here. That is in relation to the map. I observe that nobody has had the temerity to frame the second charge under the Official Secrets Act. A marked distinction is drawn between the second charge and the other two. It really would have been going some distance to have said that the gravity of the case merited the introduction of the Official Secrets Act in regard to charge number two.

Charge number two is that concerning Major Cassidy about which he and Major Carruthers gave evidence before you. It is that the accused on the 3rd February 1943 when officer commanding Special Section improperly informed Major Cassidy, M.C. Royal Army Medical Corps, who was then visiting his office, that certain pins then affixed to a map of part of North West Europe on the wall of the said office indicated localities connected with operations involving the dropping of carrier pigeons by parachute in enemy occupied territory. I do suggest to the court that no such charge has been made out on the evidence which has been given to you. What is there in it? There was a map. You will remember the evidence of Major Carruthers. He had been half a dozen times into the accused's office and on each occasion there was the map on the wall behind his desk. Everybody knew, including Major Carruthers and Major Cassidy when he went in on this occasion, that Major Tredegar was in charge of the Special Section dealing with pigeons. There he was sitting in his office with a map behind him about which no one had complained, a map with pins stuck into it of this country and the other side of the channel. As the witnesses agreed, it does not require a lot of ingenuity to think that obviously that map deals with pigeons. It is either the places they start from or come back to in this country and the same on the other side, or something of the kind. If you examine the evidence which has been given by Major Cassidy and Major Curruthers neither of them says that the pin pointing was in any way explained to them by the accused. There is no suggestion that he said: "Look here; that pin means this or that pin means that or this system of pins means this, that, or the other" – nothing of the kind. All that is really said is that there he sat with a map behind him.

I do ask the court to take into consideration that in the room next to Major Tredegar was Captain Kleyn, an officer serving under Major

Welland who was in charge of the operational and intelligence side of this type of work. Do you suppose that over all this period Captain Kleyn if he had thought there was something in the way of secrets being given away by the presence of that map, would have allowed it to stand there without a word to his own chief or a word to Major Tredegar who was next door? Yet that is what happened. It is not without significance that at some stage in March before the events which constitute the background of the third charge, attention was drawn to that map, but if it really were something which had behind it any seriousness at all, would it have been left where it was? Would Captain Kleyn have been content for a map with those pins on it, meaning that everybody who saw the map would assume it meant, namely, that it was something to do with pigeon operations, to remain there without one word to Major Tredegar and without one word to his senior officer, Major Welland? When he does, what happens? Major Welland does not even know what were the indications which were upon that map at that time to show that pigeon operations were concerned with particular localities. If there had been any seriousness in it, when it was brought to the attention of MI 14 that map would not have stayed there the time it did; it would have been taken down. You would not have had this hesitation about what was wrong with the map when Major Welland was charged about it. May be you would have found that there were other maps of a similar kind in the C.S.O's office.

But whether that be so or not, the charge is not that he had a map in his office; the charge is that he improperly informed Major Cassidy that certain pins then affixed to a map of part of North West Europe on the wall of the office indicated localities connected with operations etc. There is not one word of evidence in support of that charge at all – not one. Neither Major Cassidy nor Major Carruthers, who were called before you, has attempted to say that one word in explanation of the pin points was given. In my submission the whole background, the whole substance of that charge falls to the ground. If the charge had been that it was improper to have had a map there with pins on it at all, there would have been all those things to say which I have touched on and have not thought it right to weary you with by going into them. But that is not the charge. The charge is that he explained it. There is no evidence in support of it and I confidentially ask the court to say that that charge is not supported and cannot be allowed to stand.

I add one point as I pass from it, and that is this. The events of which complaint is made occurred on the 3rd February. The 3rd February and 8th April; in between the two falls the subject matter of the second charge, but nothing happened. Nobody reported this matter. It was there next door to Captain Kleyn from February, when Major Cassidy saw it. Nobody reported it. Neither Major Cassidy nor Major Carruthers thought: "Here is something which is being given away; we must report it". None of the Intelligence officers attached to Major Tredegar's headquarters reported it. You do not hear a word about until this other matter comes up on the 15th March. Then it looks as if there was a bit of a search back to see whether something which had escaped attention before might not be added to the charge relating to the 15th March, upon which charge alone Major Tredegar at the outset was asked to furnish an explanation.

The first thing that is added, or one of the things that is added, is the events of the 3rd February, about which in March he had not been asked for an explanation at all. One other thing that is added carries you further back still; it carries you back to the 4th January 1943, two months or more before the events in March which brought some of these matters to a head.

May I say a word or two about the first charge? Members of the court will bear with me if I draw attention to the passage read by my learned friend this morning from the Official Secrets Act of 1911. There is no question but that that Act is calculated to deal with serious offences. The first section (which I will not read to you) provides penalties for spying. That is what is in my mind – treachery and spying. The second section deals with the wrongful communication of information and is the one here in question. The passage was read to you: "If any person having in his possession information which he has obtained or to which he has access owing to his position as a person who holds or has held office under His Majesty communicates the information to any person other than a person to whom he is authorised to communicate it or a person to whom it is in the interest of the State his duty to communicate it, that person shall be guilty of a misdemeanour."

There is one more thing about this Act to which I wish to draw attention. If one is in a civil court (not a military court I mean) there is a section which prevents a prosecution under this Act without the consent of the Attorney General. It is section 8 of the Act and it is very familiar to the learned Judge Advocate. I draw attention to that for this purpose: one does not lightly embark upon a prosecution under this Act: one does not lightly record a conviction under this Act, the Official Secrets Act of 1911. If you want to do it in a civil court you have got to get the consent of the Attorney General before you can get going.

It is with a charge under that very serious Act that I was faced in relation to the events of January 1943. I can summarise the matter to you because the evidence is well within your recollection. It is what I call the Keys episode. There are some things unchallenged about it. Mr. Keys was a man who had under his charge, as pigeon supply officer, some twenty five pigeon breeders or fanciers, or whatever they are called, who were collecting pigeons to be used through Lord Tredegar under the operational direction of Captain Kleyn and his superiors. There was, as the evidence has shown you, considerable requirement of persuasion to encourage Mr, Keys and his group to continue with his work. In the course of his duty and for the purpose of his duty, Major Tredegar was detailed by the C.S.O. to go down and try to persuade them to carry on with their valuable work in the interest of the State. It is interesting; to observe that for that purpose he required a summary as he thought of certain operations which had previously taken place in relation to enemy occupied territory.

I want to say a word or two about that summary. You will remember that Sergeant Sutton (who is the one witness in this matter) gave evidence to the effect that he did understand that when Major Tredegar wanted the log books from which the summary was to be prepared he had been instructed by the C.S O to get them. In the same way Captain Kleyn, when I asked him about this, eventually told me that he also had understood that these instructions were started by the C.S.O.

Just remember the circumstances. He was being detailed to go down on the instructions of his C.S.O. to persuade the suppliers or breeders to continue their work. For that purpose he wished to persuade them that what they had done in the past was worthwhile. You will see that those suppliers, on the admitted evidence knew a great deal. You cannot have pigeons coming back to your loft without having some idea of what has happened to them. You have bred them; you have supplied them. You know that they are being dropped much better than those Girl Guides would know. You know that they are being dropped in enemy occupied territory in the hope that they will bring back messages. You cannot do that work for a considerable period of time without having some idea of what they do. If you have any knowledge of you know that there is a range within which they can work, and it will occur to you that they will probably be used in the Low Countries and parts of France, which would obviously be within that range. You are not giving any information to pigeon fanciers or breeders if you tell them, "Well that is exactly where some of the operations did take place". Two things happen; either your bird comes back or it does not. If you have sent out a number of birds and a few come back you may see the messages. If you do see the messages you will have a very good idea where they have come from. At any rate you have got some idea of the range within which they must have worked.

All the information which was in the logbook and which was passed on to the pigeon fanciers was really this: they got a clearer idea than they would otherwise have had of the places to which their pigeons had been sent and from which they had come back. They had a rough idea before; they would have known perfectly well it was Holland or Brittany or something of that sort and they may have known a good deal more if they occasionally undid the messages when the birds came back.

There you are. That was the information which he added for the purpose of encouraging them to continue. Is there any doubt about that? I should have thought that it was more likely that men whose birds were being used in this way would be encouraged if they thought their birds had done some good work in the past or that their work had been useful in the past. I do not ask the court to do it here and now, but if they find it possible to spare the time to I ask them to compare the log books with the instructions, a good deal is in the log books (which would have been very interesting but which perhaps it would not have been necessary to tell these suppliers) which is not carried into the summary. All the summary gives you is the number of birds that went – they know that, the number of birds that got back – they would know that seeing it was to their lofts that the birds would come back; and then in most cases the country and in some cases – I think it is some six out of thirty-eight in the list I saw – identification of the place from which they came. If the court bears in mind what I have said about information of value to the enemy which is the foundation of secrecy they may think that if you are telling these pigeon supply people whose co-operation you are trying to secure and who must know a great deal already "In the past" it has nothing to do with future operations – "we have from time to time dropped pigeons in an area more precisely defined than you knew before and they have brought back messages in a certain case", you may find that you are greatly encouraged then. But are you really helping the enemy? When I asked the witness what percentage of these birds got back you will observe he said it was 18 percent. What happened to the other 82 percent? I suppose the vast majority got into enemy occupied territory and never got out of it. They got into the hands of people who I suppose are still likely to be in a majority of those territories who would find it either desirable or convenient to hand over the birds and anything they have got with them to the occupying authorities. At any rate, we may safely assume – I think Major Welland assumed it – that the Germans not only know a great deal about our methods, but they have got a good many of the containers and the birds. Therefore, you are not giving them much information if you say: "In the past among the vast variety of operations which we have undertaken, some of them have been in those particular localities."

Mind you, this is not a man who got up at Ipswich at a public meeting and said: "Look here, I am now going to broadcast information which many of you have not got". He was speaking to men he wanted to work for him and who had been working for him. He was telling them a great deal that they already knew and a very little bit that they did not. I ask the court to bear that in mind and to say that it is to no such case as that that the Official Secrets Act is meant to apply. The court may well think that this is a case in which the persons to whom he communicated what he did communicate were persons to whom it was in the interest of the State his duty to communicate it. I am not saying that he had specific instructions; it had been left to his discretion; he had been given some instructions as a result of which the summary was prepared. I am saying it is very hard to say in those circumstances that he has been guilty of that grave crime.

You remember the evidence about the case; it is only Sutton.(sic) The summary is prepared on the Saturday or Sunday and the meeting is held on the Monday, a meeting confined to these particular people. They get that degree of information and the thing is over. He makes a report to his commanding officer as, of course, he has to, coming back from that sort of thing. Nothing is heard of those events until after the matter which forms the subject of the third charge and then like the second charge it is added. I leave it confidently to this court to determine that that charge has not been made out.

I have done what I can as shortly as I can with regard to those two charges, because I want to come as soon as I can to the third charge. Strip this case of everything else and I have something which I must meet there frankly and fully. Admit, as you must admit; that everybody who matters knew – it was public property – that pigeons were dropped by parachute and that the enemy have got these containers. The messages that came back you cannot assume are in any sense secret. Any man who picks up a pigeon that has fallen by the way will get them, he will be ill disposed or well disposed. Then it will be said to me: "Yes, but there is a third charge that on the 15th March having in his possession information as to carrier pigeon operations in enemy occupied territory to which he had access owing to his position as a person holding office under His Majesty unlawfully communicated the same to two Girl Guides who were not persons to whom he was authorised to communicate it".

The way in which the case was put was really twofold. First of all there is what I call the "act" and that I have sufficiently dealt with. There is, as I submit, nothing in that. Secondly, there is the communication to those two girls of existence at some date of a radio station location station at some place, information as to which had been brought to this country by pigeon. I apprehend that that is really what I have to meet in this case.

Let us get this clear. It is sought to say that he had access to this information owing to his position – I suppose from the log book. You will, I am sure, look at the log book but you will not find – and the prosecution have not found – any identification of the spot. What we are told is this: there is in June of 1942 and there is again in November of 1942, a message which came back from Holland in relation to a radio location station. If you look you will not find that the information which was passed on to those Girl Guides can have been information which came from that source. If the prosecution with their resources cannot put their finger on those two and say one of them was June and the other November and he must have been talking about June, well I cannot.

You will also remember that I asked those who produced those documents whether they could say that in the log books from which their information came there was also contained information about the action taken, and there was not. There is not a shadow of a suggestion in those books that as a result of this message coming back some bombers were sent out which laid bare the area, or attempted to lay bare the area in which this radio location station was.

The information which he is supposed to have given to these two Girl Guides is, first of all: "There is the spot" and, secondly, "This is what happened about it". It is said he got that from a privileged source. He certainly did not get the second half from there. If it is sought to be said: "You got this information from the log book" well, I say that is not made out.

What did he pass on? I want to come to the substance of the matter. You heard those girls – I hope you will think they were treated with courtesy – asked to give their account of what they had seen and heard. When you are considering this case I am sure you will fell it is important to see into what category of case it comes. Is this a case in which you have deliberately by which I mean carefully collating and preparing what you have got to say – passed on to unauthorised persons information which they were meant to pick up as information. That is not this case. I do not think one could get more complete certainty than I have in saying that whatever else one may think about this no information was leaked out in a way that could have caused damage anywhere as a result of what happened on the 15th March. You will recollect how it all happened. Some event required publishing for and by the Girl Guides. He took them to the roof and these two girls were brought down. There was a conversation at which the two subalterns in the A. T. S. and the two Girl Guides were present. What a strange series of stories we get when we look to see if some concrete clear information of use to someone was passed on. The two girls who alone are alleged to have got it, Miss McIntrye and Miss Isherwood, certainly did not pick up anything such as has been suggested. Miss Isherwood when she went to show you on the map the point which was indicated to her, thought there were two points. She pointed to two places and said both of them were pointed out. One was the place where the radio location station was and the other was the place from which the message came back. No other person of the four gave any indication of there being more than one point pointed out. You may also remember that I was anxious to ascertain, in order to see how clear the story was in their recollections, how the pointing out was done. They pointed to different spots miles apart on the ground, but at any rate they got between them some unsecure hold upon the spot that was really meant. One of them says two points and others say one. They are not in the same locality, they are in the same part of the map, they are somewhere in the Hook of Holland, yes. I asked them one after another: "Did he point it out with his finger", because they all said when their evidence was taken that he put his finger very near the mark and one of them said he put his finger right on it. The first three today had no recollection of the use of anything but his finger, but the fourth, Subaltern Mackenzie remembered that what he had used was what I had been suggesting to the others he had used, namely this instrument or something very like it. It was interesting to see how she reached that conclusion. She said: "I thought at first he used his finger then I thought it out. He needed that pointer because he could not have reached the place on the map he wanted to point to". That is what we call reconstruction; she had thought out what it must have been and as she thought it out she reached a conclusion which was the right conclusion. So imprecise was the recollection of the others that not one of three of them had the smallest recollection of that event.

I suggest that that is only one example. In itself it is not of any great importance; it is only one example of the fact that as the result of this conversation no clear impression of any sort or any kind was formed in the minds of these girl guides. I cannot carry my recollection to the exact language which they used, but I think you will have no doubt that they did not get into their minds the words "radio location" at all. That is the thing which it is said I have given away; I have given away the fact that there was a radio location station, about which information was obtained by pigeon. Neither of the persons to whom that information is alleged to have been imparted remembers the words "radio location station", or "enemy concentration", or anything of that kind. What they say is they think there was something said about a danger to shipping, or a danger to lives, that a pigeon came along and that as a result of the message lies or shipping were saved. One of them recollects something about congratulations as a result.

I ask you to bear this in mind. When one is saying that somebody has been guilty of this grave crime it is important to see what impression was left on the minds of those to whom it is alleged he has improperly passed on the information. My suggestion to you is that you can reach no other conclusion but that in fact no impression of any clarity, certainly none which contained in it the core of what is suggested against the accused remained.

I have not attempted to deal with all the dissimilarities between their stories, though they are important as indicating a lack of precision. I think one of them spoke about four and a half hours, and another spoke about thirty hours; those are only instances of inconsistencies between the stories, which are important, not as suggesting that the story is made up – nobody has suggested that, and if I wanted to suggest it I should know how to – but as showing that when these people tax their recollections perfectly honestly, as I am sure they did, they are unable to give you any picture involved which involves the suggestion that information was actually conveyed to their minds. There are the facts of that case. No doubt it may be said that it was very wrong to mention radio location.

Let me just say this. Do you remember one other thing I put to some of these witnesses? I can say frankly and honestly it was in order to see how the conversation arose. It was not until the very last one of the four once that she recollected the conversation which I was putting. She recollected that it did arise; it was not a case of a man suddenly saying "Here is a radio location station, you might like to know we bombed it after a message brought by a pigeon informed us of its whereabouts". Not a bit; there had been a general conversation about pigeons, about the courage of the bird and its habits, in the course of which the accused had said, from his great knowledge of ornithology, that they were very brave birds, that they would fly through almost anything and so on. Then in an unguarded moment no instance is taken out of this war.

It is not suggested here that the accused is a person who had been warned of the necessity of secrecy in relation to operation. Operations, as regards direction, were wholly out of his hands, and were in the hands of MI 14. It is not suggested he had been told he had got to be particularly careful about this, that or the other. Yet it will be said that it was in an unguarded moment that he was guilty of an error of judgement in passing on information about this spot, however little in the result, by the mercy of God, it matters, because what did not enter their could not have been passed on by them. When you are dealing with this, and considering the quality of it, you should bear in mind in favour of the accused that even if it was wrong to give away the location of this particular place from which the message came, it was information which could not have gone any further, because it was not passed up by those to whom it was addressed.

I am not going to keep you much longer. I began by drawing a distinction between cases in which integrity was involved, and cases in which there was an error of judgement. It is not the most attractive part of an advocate's job that he may have to say something in front of a client which he would very much like not to say, but I have my duty to do so, and I am going to do it. If you did come to the conclusion in relation to the last charge that there had been an error of judgement, and that the charge had not been made out, then I should ask you to bear in mind what I am going to say now about the judgement and balance of this accused officer. He does not have the advantages which some of us have, though he has some which we have not. I shall call before you a doctor who has known him for 30 years, and who has been his physician for 12 years. He has an unhappy background, a background to his own life and to the lives of those about his, singularly likely to affect the balance of his judgement and his mind, singularly likely to lead him into an error of judgement in an unguarded moment such as I have been describing to you.

He was a child in an unhappy home where his father and his mother were ill-assorted. His mother, as the doctor will be able to tell you, was suffering from what laymen know as a divided personality. His parents had one daughter of whose balance I cannot speak now, except to say that certainly she was not balanced, and met her end largely due to that. He himself was, not unnaturally, a somewhat spoilt child. He was given his hand and allowed to run riot, and he lived an irregular life. As a result he was warned from time to time by this doctor that the balance of his health and of his mind might well be affected. I do not think he ever passed a medical board for service in the army, and he was during a large portion of his service extremely unwell. From May 1942 until November 1942, when he took charge of this unit, he was on sick leave, marked "D". I do not know exactly that involves in this war, but he got back to "C" at a later stage. From November onwards he was away for considerable periods on sick leave or on privilege leave. At the very moment when these events into which we are now enquiring came along, he was in a singularly ill-equipped position to deal with them. As is what I told you in relation to his balance, his judgement and his mind were not enough, his domestic life was crashing round him in circumstances of misery and anxiety, and is still doing so. During this period his marriage was breaking up. I need to say no more than that it is breaking up in circumstances which would worry any man.

I have tried frankly to face these charges. I have tried to say what can be said on behalf of the accused in relation to the distinction between an error of judgement and an act which was deliberately wrong. If it were necessary, I could show you high testimonials from the Generals who commanded in chief in Western command, testimonials to the integrity of the accused. Perhaps you will take it from me, but if you desire it I will hand in a letter from General Sir Robert Gordon-Finlayson, and another from General Sir James Marshall-Cornwall, who had opportunities of seeing him and judging him for themselves. However, his integrity is not challenged.

When I come to deal with the other side of the picture, the error of judgement and the lack of balance, if you come to the conclusion that there is something here which needs to be excused I ask you to find the excuse in what I have laid before you and will prove by evidence. If you do take that view, I ask you to remember this: it is none too easy for a man in the position of the accused to live the life which is put upon him by his position in the part of the world in which he has to move about from time to time in a public capacity. I ask you, taking the distinction which I have laid down between attacks on integrity and attacks on judgement, to say that the right and proper way of dealing with such a case as this is one which will not inflict disgrace where disgrace ought not to rest, and will not prevent somebody who has a great deal of opportunity of service in the public interest form wearing the King's uniform. It may be you will think that from a task such as the one he has been trying to carry out, in which there is a great call upon judgement and commonsense and balance, he may be unfit, but I would ask you at the same time to realise that it would be too much to say that there are no tasks which he can perform and which he could be called upon to perform which would involve his wearing the King's uniform.

When you have heard the evidence of the doctor – I cannot ask you to take it all from me – I ask you to approach this case as one in which, since it is not a deliberate act, but a slip in an unguarded moment – if you feel that on one of these charges there must be a penalty, I ask you not to make it unnecessarily rigorous. There are courses which are open which you know better than I, and it would be improper and impertinent for me to suggest them, but it is right that I should draw attention to the difficulties which have been in his path, and which may have made it harder for him than for somebody else to exercise a sensible and plain judgement.

I ask you to say, in the light of all that I have said about these offences, and about him, that here is a case which does not need to be visited with a disgraceful punishment. If there has been an error he must suffer a warning about it, but it should not be something which will disgrace a person who might do great service to the State, for he has qualities of which the doctor will speak, though they say not the qualities of balance, discretion and judgement.

I would like to supplement what I have said by calling the doctor, who knows him, in order that you may have the advantage of evidence in the place of mere observation on my part.

Lt. Col. SIR RUSSELL FACEY WILKINSON is called in and having been duly sworn is examined by Sir Walter Monckton as follows:

Q   I think your full name is Sir Russell Facey Wilkinson? A. Yes.

Q   You are a Lieutenant-Colonel in the R.A.M.C.? A. Yes.

Q   I need not ask you your professional qualifications except to say in general terms you are a fully qualified medical practitioner? A. Yes.

Q   I think you have known the accused, Major Lord Tredegar, since about 1912?A. I have been acquainted with him since then,

Q   How long have you been his doctor? A. Since 1931 or 1932.

Q   In October of 1942 – which happens to be about the month before the   events which put him in command of this unit – he had been ill for   some time? A. He had had an accident to his right arm [and   disability to his knee.].

Q   Were you minded to send him up to Ruthin? A. Yes, to a clinic in North Wales.

Q   Who looks after that? A. Sir Edmund Spriggs.[518]

Q   Did you think that in the circumstances of the case you ought to send a report about him with him? A. Yes; one always does.

Q Have you a copy of it with you to refresh your memory? A. Yes. It was principally, of course, about the disability to his knee for which he wanted treatment, but at the same time one always sends a sort of resume of his past history and so on.

Q Does it begin by setting out something about his background?
  A. Yes. It is dated 3rd October 1942. I have known him since 1912. He has been my patient since 1930. Psychasthenia on his mother's side, who is of schizoid temperament.

Q Does that mean divided personality? A. Yes. "Very intelligent, artistic, and erudite. Dramatises himself and his surroundings and prefers fiction to fact. Has been repeatedly warned of the risk of mental or physical breakdown. In short, he would be more at home in Papal Palace or Doges Court in the 15th century than in our times."

Q That report was written at that time for no purpose but to let them know your view about his stability? A. Exactly. I felt that as I was responsible for introducing what was a stranger to them into their community it was only fair that I should give them a line.

Q Did you get a report on his return? A. One always does in the ordinary course. In the report, under the heading "central nervous system" they said "odd mentality with pride in the unusual".

Q In your judgement is he a fit person to be in military service where any sort of secret work is concerned? A. Frankly, I was very surprised to hear that he had been accepted for service in the Army. When I was asked to make a statement for a War Office Medical Board in 1942 I described his known condition and medical history and so on and ended by saying "I was very surprised that this officer has been accepted for service in the Forces and he tells us that no medical examination preceded his commission".

Q From your knowledge of him, do you regard him as physically using that word in the widest sense – fit to continue in military service? A. I do not.

Lt. Col. PARKES: No questions.

SIR WALTER MONCKTON: There is one other thing I might mention. If it will be of any assistance to the court, there is the medical officer from Chelsea Barracks here, who has seen him very recently and for a short period. He would do no more than confirm the judgement you have just heard. It probably would not assist you.

SUMMING-UP

THE JUDGE ADVOCATE: May it please the court. Lord Tredegar holds a commission in His Majesty's Forces and in November 1942 he was in command of this special unit at Wing House dealing with pigeons. You have not heard a great deal about Lord Tredegar but you have heard from a medical man called for the defence what kind of man he is from the point of view of mental stability and from the point of view of being able to form a sure and safe judgment. I am not going to refer to that again because it would not be kind to repeat that before Lord Tredegar, who is listening to what I have to say. You will consider that aspect of the case. It is entirely for you to say what use you will make of that evidence in arriving at your findings on these charges. If you think it goes more to mitigation than to a defence, then you will be able to deal with it accordingly.

The prosecution here are alleging – and it is for them to establish beyond reasonable doubt the guilt of the accused – that on three occasions this officer said things which he should not have said and that by doing so he was guilty of an offence against the Army Act, in one case under section 40 and in two cases under section 41.

I think you know that it is not for the accused to come here and prove that he is innocent. It would not be right or proper for you to say; "We cannot accept the case for the defence here because the accused has not given evidence". He is entitled to give evidence or not as he likes – that is his right – and you will not, of course, make too much of that.

I would remind you that if you have a reasonable doubt on any of these charges it is your duty to acquit the accused. I would also remind you that if after hearing all the evidence you were to be in the state of thinking that here there were three weak charges preferred against this officer it would not be right to support one by the other and to say "Three weak charges at any rate make one sound one".

You must consider separately each charge and the evidence which relates to that particular charge; you must deal with each one separately and not reinforce one by another.

I think you will be satisfied that in this case you have not had any witness who has come here to tell you any lies but that all the witnesses have come to try and help you by giving you the truth. That, however, does not absolve you from considering whether they have made some genuine mistakes or may have misunderstood what was being said at any particular time.

The first charge is laid under section 2 of the Official Secrets Act 1911. It is quite clear that Mr. Keys down in Ipswich was concerned with the provision of pigeons and that he had some 25 other persons to assist this. It seems to be the case that those men were perhaps losing a little enthusiasm for their work and on this particular day Lord Tredegar, not unnaturally, was going down there to try and induce them to keep on with their good work. Before going he provided himself with certain information. The evidence before you is the evidence of one of the witnesses, Sgt. Sutton. It is not disputed that Sutton made out this document which is before the court, that Lord Tredegar took it down to Ipswich and there addressed this meeting of Mr. Keys and 25 others.

It is for you to decide whether you agree, but the prosecution say that he committed an offence against the Official Secrets Act by divulging the contents of that document to Mr. Keys and those 25 other persons. It is quite clear that the motive actuating Lord Tredegar was an excellent one, but what is said about it is that although he wanted to achieve a certain result – and a laudable result – in the doing of it he should have used his discretion and not divulged what were really State secrets or information which the State would not like passed on to these particular people in those circumstances.

I think we would all agree that it was right and proper for Lord Tredegar to tell these people what was happening to their birds. What the prosecution complain of is that he gave them the information which is set out in the last column of that document. It is only your view that matters, but it is suggested that it was wrong and a breach of the Official Secrets Act to tell these people – true it was in an hotel and they were people with a common bond – that those pigeons had been dropped in some of those places. Exception apparently is particularly taken to the use of such words as "Amiens" and so on. According to the witness, the wider and bigger the area the less important it is. I am not going to labour that; that is before you. I think the real issue is: was the accused committing an offence in disclosing the information contained in that last column?

You appreciate that the Official Secrets Act used certain language which you will have to consider. Are you satisfied that this information was in the possession of Lord Tredegar by reason of holding His Majesty's commission? Having heard how he got it (there is no suggestion that he got it improperly) from these log books, I think you will be satisfied that he does come within that part of the Official Secrets Act. Did he then communicate it to Mr. Keys and some 25 other civilians present in the hotel? You have got evidence of that. Was it an unlawful communication? That is for you to decide in all the circumstances.

On this particular charge the prosecution have got to prove that these people were persons to whom he was not authorised to communicate it or that they were not persons to whom it was in the interests of the State his duty to communicate it. Learned counsel has told you that he does not suggest that the accused could say here that he was authorised to give that information to those people but he does ask you – and asks you most earnestly – to consider whether in all the circumstances that information (the disclosure of which is put at the highest as an error of judgement on the part of Lord Tredegar) was information which it was not in the interest of the State his duty to communicate to those particular people.

I cannot assist you very much on that charge. You have been addressed most eloquently by learned counsel. The ingredients of the charge are very simple. They are set out in the Manual of Military Law and when you come to deal with this particular charge I will invite you to read them as they are set out on p. 896 of that book. There is very little more that I can say on the first charge. What was said is not in dispute. The defence urge most eloquently that you should say that in all the circumstances that very serious charge under the Official Secrets Act has not been made out.

We come now to the second charge, which is laid under section 40 of the Army Act. That charge – I took a note of what the learned prosecutor said in opening – appears to be a charge that the accused was setting a bad example as to security matters. Even if he did, Gentlemen, it if for you to decide whether it amounts to conduct prejudicial both to good order and military discipline in all the circumstance.

We have to go to the 3rd February, in London, when this interview took place between the three people concerned, Lord Tredegar, Major Cassidy and Major Carruthers. I want to remind you that on this particular charge you are not being asked to say anything about what was disclosed in the way of a demonstration. The charge is a specific one; it is that the accused was telling Major Cassidy of the R.A.M.C. (who was not concerned with pigeons so far as military operations were concerned) that certain pins then affixed to a map of part of north-west Europe on the wall of his office indicated localities connected with operations involving the dropping of carrier pigeons by parachute in enemy occupied territory.

Before you can convict the accused on that charge you must have some satisfactory evidence to establish that that was said by Lord Tredegar to Major Cassidy. We have not heard Lord Tredegar's version but we have heard Major Cassidy and Major Carruthers. Major Carruthers was a sick man and I think it quite fair to say what he told you was of no use whatsoever to the case for the prosecution. I do not propose to deal with him because in my view (and I think it is a fair view) he did not carry the prosecution any way at all.

Therefore in dealing with the second charge you are really left with the evidence of Major Cassidy – with Major Cassidy's recollection. In this case, in case there is some dispute about it, I think I ought to refer to what somebody said "Let's show him the secret stuff".

That is rather a slang expression and the defence suggest that Major Cassidy has got it wrong and that the kind of phrase that Lord Tredegar would have used would have been "Lets show him the act". That is not of much importance except that the defence are really attacking Major Cassidy's recollection and suggesting that Lord Tredegar never said anything of the kind.

Major Cassidy said that an N.C.O. was sent for and brought in a pigeon, a container, a parachute and a bag of rations and showed him how they all worked. There was a map on the wall (the very large map which you have seen) and there were a number of pins in it on both sides of the channel – in England and on the other side. Major Cassidy said that the accused told him that the pins marked points where pigeons were pin-pointed. That apparently was all that was said and what exactly it seems is for you to decide. A member of the court asked Major Cassidy what he thought it meant.

It is upon that phrase – I do not think anybody suggests anything more was said – that the prosecution are framing the second charge. It is entirely for you to say, but learned counsel has argued and argued strongly, that in regard to the second charge the evidence of Major Cassidy is not sufficient to substantiate the charge at all. He went further than that and said that even if that were so, you have to approach this matter in a commonsense way. Here was a map which had been hanging up there for a long time. If it was pin-pointed in the way suggested and a man of ordinary intelligence went into that office, knowing that that office was there to deal with the provision of pigeons, he would be making a reasonable assumption if he assumed that the pins were there to indicate that pigeons had been dropped at those posts or thereabouts. Therefore learned counsel asks you to say that there is not sufficient substance in this incident to amount to an offence under section 40 of the Army Act.

I now come to the third charge. I think Sir Walter Monckton has made it quite clear that at any rate from his point of view he rather distinguishes between the first and second charges and the third charge. He invites you to say that there is perhaps more substance in the third charge than there is in the other two but he by no means pleads guilty to that charge. Therefore it is your duty to examine the evidence and to see whether the charge has been made out.

You will remember that this incident took place on the 15th March after there had been on the roof some demonstration to do with pigeons with which Lady Baden-Powell had been concerned. There is no dispute that in Lord Tredegar's office there were assembled himself and these four women you have seen. As I understand it, the last charge is that the accused was giving information wrongly to those two Girl Guides. No complaint is made as regards the two subalterns because presumably the prosecution took the view that they were concerned with this pigeon procedure. The case for the prosecution (and the case which they have to establish beyond all reasonable doubt) is that Lord Tredegar was unlawfully communicating to Miss McIntrye and Miss Isherwood information to which he had access owing to his position as a person holding office under His Majesty relating to carrier pigeons operations in enemy occupied territory.

I will deal shortly with the evidence in a moment, but the suggestions against Lord Tredegar seem to be of three kinds; (1) that he demonstrated the way in which pigeons were put in the containers; (2) that he mentioned something which was secret about the distinction between green and red containers; and (3) that he made some specific remarks about a particular place on the map which he pointed out to these women.

I am not going to take up your time in dealing with the demonstration; you have heard a good deal about it. Perhaps you will think it will be sufficient to say that in the particular circumstances of these Girl Guides there was no offence committed by the accused. However, that is a matter for you to consider.

We spent a little time in trying to follow what the witnesses were talking about and what points they were trying to make in regard to this green container. I daresay you have been left just as puzzled about it as I am. Probably you will take the view that at any rate so far as that is concerned the accused has not done anything which brings him within the Official Secrets Act.

Then we come to the point to which learned counsel addressed himself, and that is the question of this point on the map. You will remember that Subaltern Harvey was the first witness. She had been working with the accused. She said she came into the room and the first thing that attracted her attention was that the accused was saying something about radio location and enemy concentrations and that he pointed to a place on the map on the wall. She was invited to point it out here and I understand from the learned prosecutor that she pointed to a spot north-west of the Zuyder Zee. She went on to say that the accused said that news of it had been brought to this country by a pigeon and that a very short time afterward – she thought about 4 and a half hours – we had bombed that point and flattened it out.

That is really the serious allegation which is made against the accused on the third charge. Do you think that the accused said that or something like it? It is for you to decide whether that girl's recollection is right or not, but the prosecution sat that at any rate even if he mentioned it before Subaltern Harvey he had no right to tell it to the two Girl Guides. They say that the accused must have had access to that information by reason of holding his commission, that the Girl Guides were certainly not people to whom he should have passed it on and that it was not in the interests of the State his duty to communicate it.

I will take Subaltern MacKenzie next. She said she did hear some conversation about pigeons, that then the two Girl Guides were taken over to the map, that the accused pointed out a point on the Zuyder Zee and said that news had been carried from that point to this country of a radio location station and a heavy concentration of enemy troops and that in four and a half hours our bombers had thoroughly bombed it. Then she left the room. That was her recollection of what was said.

Then you had the version of Miss McIntrye. She said there was some reference to the map and that the accused pointed to an area on the map in the top right hand corner. She said he mentioned that a pigeon had been dropped there and owing to that, action had been taken resulting in many lives and tons of shipping being saved. That was her version of it. It was not very specific, but that was all she remembered about it.

The other witness was Miss Isherwood. She was the one who spoke to the accused having pointed out two places on the map, one to the north of the other. She told you that he said that some action had been taken against some danger to shipping and that some 33 hours after the action had been taken the danger was removed and a large amount of shipping was saved in consequence.

I do not propose to weary you by going further into their evidence because you have heard it very recently. That it shortly the effect of what those girls had to say.

You will remember that Viscount Tredegar (who I am sure you will think was very frank in the statement he made which was written down and which is before the court) has given you his version of what happened as regards this particular incident. He said in that statement: "I did point out to the Girl Guide Leaders a point north-west of the Zuyder Zee. I remember telling them that at the point which I indicated on the map there had been an important enemy radio location station, information as to which had been brought back by pigeon and that as a result within a very short time the RAF laid it flat. This information was given to me by Col. Cullinan, who also told me that he had been congratulated by superior authority, which information I also passed on the Girl Guide Leaders". That is of course not on oath, but it is a frank statement which has been put before you as the accused's version of what was said then. Having regard to that testimony of the accused and the four girl's the prosecution are asking you to say that that information was passed on to them and that it amounts to a breach of section 2 of the Official Secrets Act, as amended by the Act of 1920.

There is very little more than I can say to you about that aspect of the case. Are you satisfied that the accused did that? Are you satisfied that he had access to that information? He said he got it from Col Cullinan. The prosecution have rather suggested he might have got it from the log book but with that the defence do not agree. You have then to ask yourselves: was he authorised to communicate that to the Girl Guides, or alternatively, was it in the interests of the State his duty to communicate it? So far as the law is concerned, the same points arise there as on the first charge.

There is very little more that I can say in this case. Indeed, there really is very little for a judge-advocate to do in a case of this kind. The issues are quite simple and quite straightforward.

Now, Sir I am going to ask you to close the court and consider whether the prosecution have made out their case on any of these charges. If they have satisfied you that the evidence is of such a weighty kind that if you had to act upon it in some matter which affected your own business or your own life you would do so, then you are entitled to convict. On the other hand, if you say "No, if this were a decision I had to make which affected me I would not for one moment act upon this evidence", then you should that same very fair test to Lord Tredegar in dealing with these charges.

THE PRESIDENT: The court is closed for consideration of finding.

> At 16.30 hours the court is closed.
> At 16.50 hours the court re-opens.
> The accused is again brought before the court.

The JUDGE ADVOCATE: I am directed by the court to announce the following finding.

The court find that the accused Temporary Major (War Substantive Captain) The Viscount Tredegar, Royal Corps of Signals, attached

Holding Battalion, Scots Guards, is not guilty of the second charge. The findings of the court on the first and third charges, being subject to confirmation, will be promulgated later.

Lt. H. W. DODS is duly sworn and examined as follows:

The JUDGE ADVOCATE: You are Lt. H. W. Dods, Holding Battalion, Scots Guards? A: Yes.

Q   Have you any evidence to produce as to the character and particulars of service of the accused. A. I produce A.P.B. 296 relating to the accused.

(A.P.B 296 marked "L" signed by the president and attached to the proceedings).

Q   Is the accused the person named in the statement we are going to   read? A: Yes.

The JUDGE ADVOATE: Will you listen to this, Lord Tredegar? If I read out anything you do not think is right you can turn to your counsel and get it put right. (A.P.B. 296 is read).

The JUDGE ADVOCATE: I see the form says: "The accused holds in the army the rank of War Substantive Lieutenant (Acting Major) dated 28.5.42 and in his corps the rank of War Substantive Lieutenant (Acting Major) dated 28.5.42. I have been calling him Temporary Major, War Subaltern Captain. What are you, Lord Tredegar?

The ACCUSED: A Captain.

The JUDGE ADVOCATE: You are a War Substantive Captain?

The ACCUSED: Yes.

The WITNESS: He is down on his 199A as War Substantive Lieutenant, Acting Major.

The PRESIDENT: What is the date of his appointment as acting Major?

A: 28.5.42

221

The PRESIDENT: He is a temporary Major after three months. Therefore he became a War Substantive Captain. A. That is not recorded on here.

The JUDGE ADVOCATE: When do you say you were a War Substantive Captain, Lord Tredegar?

The ACCUSED: I did not know until this case came up. Then I saw what I was. I was made a Major in November.

Lt.-Col. PARKES: As he was clearly appointed acting Major in November he ought to have been promoted Temporary Major three months after that. Therefore he must be a War Substantive Captain.

The JUDGE ADVOCATE: Well, Sir, I do not know what punishment you are going to award, but if you decide to give him forfeiture of seniority it must be in some rank he actually holds. Why did you put in the charge sheet "War Substantive Captain", Col. Parkes?

Lt.-Col. PARKES; As he had been promoted acting Major in November it followed that he would be a War Substantive Captain three months later on his being made temporary Major. All that has happened is that the records of the unit are not up to date.

The JUDGE ADVOCATE: Well Sir, I propose you treat him as what he has pleaded to, that is to say temporary Major, War Substantive Captain.

THE PRESIDENT: From my military knowledge I know that after three months he becomes a temporary Major and a War Substantive Captain.

The JUDGE ADVOCATE: That satisfies you, does it, Lord Tredegar?

The ACCUSED: That is correct; yes.

Cross-examined by SIR WALTER MONCKTON

Q   He is in fact Honorary Colonel of some regiment, is he not, A. There is nothing about that on his record.

Lt.-Col. PARKES: He is certainly shown in the Army list as Honorary Colonel of at least two Territorial regiments.

SIR WALTER MONCKTON: It is the Royal Engineers, Territorial Army; the Rifle Brigade (Prince Consort's Own), and the 1st Battalion, the Monmouthshire Regiment, Territorial Army.

The JUDGE ADVOCATE: If you want to add anything about his record the court will hear anything you want to say.

SIR WALTER MONCKTON: I do not want to add anything. I just wanted to draw attention to that matter.

The PRESIDENT: The court is closed for the consideration of the sentence. The sentence to be awarded by the court, being subject to confirmation, will not be announced, but will be promulgated later and the proceedings in open court are accordingly terminated.

The Verdict and Sentence

Temporary Major, War Substantive Captain The Viscount Tredegar was found Not Guilty on Charge 2 and Guilty of Charges 1 and 3.

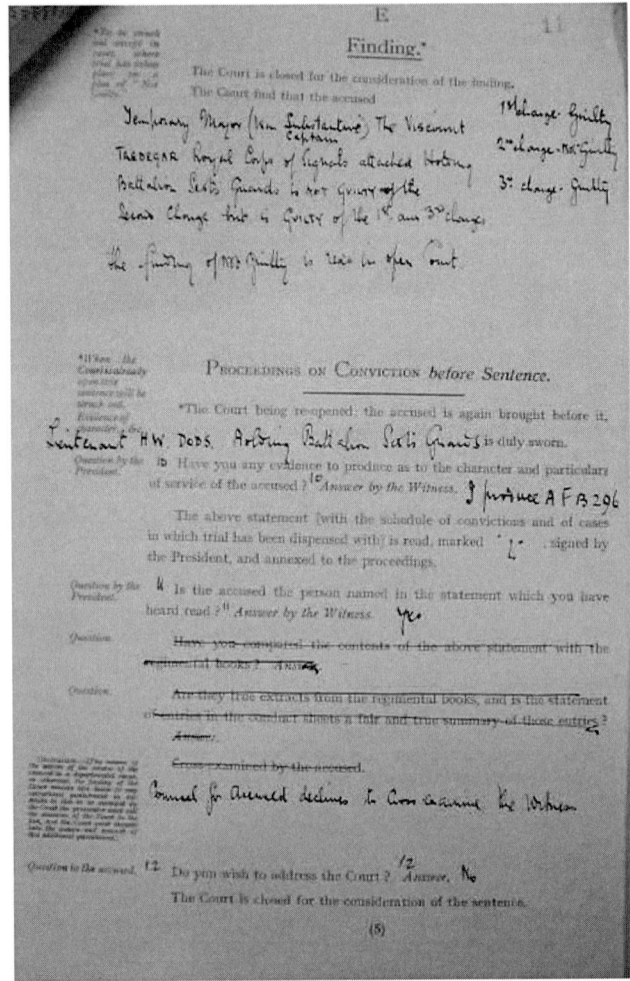

He was severely reprimanded.

Sentence.

The Court sentence the accused *Temporary Major (War Substantive Captain) The Viscount TREDEGAR, Royal Corps of Signals attached Holding Battalion Scots Guards to be Severely reprimanded.*

Signed at CHELSEA, this nineteenth day of April 1943.

Littlestone. Colonel.
President
G.C.M.

C. Stirling
Judge Advocate

Confirmed

Signed at Leconfield House, Curzon Street London W.1. His 24th day of April 1943.

Arthur Smith
Lieutenant General
Commanding London District.

Promulgated and intimate taken at Chelsea Barracks, S.W.1, this 26th day of april, 1943.

J.E.M. Bland

225

The many titles listed in this Section can be used as a basis for bibliography in which to delve further into the life and times of Evan Morgan, The last Viscount Tredegar.

[1] Von Stutterheim Kurt. *The two Germanys*. Sidgwick & Jackson. (1939)

[2] Cartland, Barbara. *We Danced All Night.* Arrow Books (1973)

[3] Made in 2003, written and directed by Stephen Fry – based on Evelyn Waugh's novel *Vile Bodies.*

[4] Taylor, D J. *Bright Young People The Rise and Fall of a Generation 1918-1940.* Vintage Books (2007). p205 " *onlooker participants such as Hon. Evan Morgan"*… who " *had been at large in London Society before the Great War..*"

[5] Graves, Robert. *The Long Weekend – A Social History of Great Britain 1918-1939.* Faber London (1940).

[6] See Rose Francis Sir. *Saying life. The Memoirs of Sir Francis Rose.* Cassell. (1961).

[7] Ibid.

[8] http://www.history.com/topics/roaring-twenties

[9] The fictional works of 1920s writers Aldous Huxley (1894-1963) and Ronald Firbank (1886-1926), remain popular, with several of their respective books (e.g Huxley's *Brave New World* and Firbank's *Vainglory*) enjoying a cult following. In 1921 Huxley based the character of Ivor Lombard in first book *Crome Yellow,* [which is a glorious caricature of the inhabitants and visitors of Garsington Manor, (where Evan first met Huxley)] on the Hon. Evan Morgan. In 1923 Firbank recreated Evan as the Hon. Eddy Monteith in a biting satire of sex and religion *The Flower Beneath the Foot.* But these novels are among the lesser known works of the authors. The books can be downloaded for free from Internet Archive. http://archive.org/

[10] According to Welsh Biography Online The family claims " *descent from CADIFOR FAWR , lord of Cil-sant , who died in 1089 . His third son, Bledri , who died in 1120 , was on good terms with the Norman conquerors, who may have granted him lands in Monmouthshire , because he appears, along with other residents of that district, as a witness to a grant of the church of Bassaleg to Glastonbury in the early 12th century..*" A baronetcy was given in 1792 by King George III to Charles Gould (who changed his name to his wife's surname of Morgan, in order to continue the family that had failed on the male line.) The Barony of Tredegar is of more recent creation, from 1859. The Viscounty stems from 1926. Godfrey, the second Lord Tredegar (1831-1913) was a Viscount in his own right (created 1905) but he died without issue, so that Viscountcy lapsed.

[11] Bedford, Sybille. *Aldous Huxley: 1894-1939.* Chatto and Windus (1973).

[12] Ibid. Evan first befriended Huxley during the First World War when they were both guests [in Huxley's case long term] at Garsington Manor, home of the socialite and hostess Lady Ottoline Morrell.

[13] *The Daily Gleaner*, 7 January 1939. (NB *The Daily Gleaner* is the chief newspaper of the Island of Jamaica where Evan often visited.)

[14] Ibid. Cribbing from Cecil Roberts' *The Bright Twenties.* Hodder & Stoughton

(1974).

[15] Tredegar House, Newport, NP10 8YW is now in the hands of the National Trust – they took a 50 year lease on the building from 2012.

[16] Ettie, Lady Desborough (1867-1952). See Davenport-Hines, Richard. *Ettie : The Intimate Life and Dauntless Spirit of Lady Desborough.* Weidenfeld & Nicolson (2008) p332. refers to " Evan Tredegar (whom she [Ettie] thought *quite mad..)"*

[17] Virginia Woolf (1882-1941). *The Diary of Virginia Woolf* edited by Bell, Anne Oliver] Volume One 1915-1919. A Harvest Book Harcourt Inc (1977). Entry for Monday 19 November, 1917 p.79 " *But he [Evan] was as innocent as a chicken & so foolish that it didn't seem to matter."*

[18] Alan Pryce-Jones (1908-2000). See Pryce-Jones, Alan *The bonus of laughter,* Hamilton (1987).

[19] Evan's Death Certificate details are shown in the image included on this page.

[20] Lois was a daughter of Humphrey Napier Sturt, 2nd Baron Alington (1859-1919) and Lady Feodorowna Yorke (who died in 1934) with a family seat of Crichel, Dorset.

[21] Powell, Anthony. *Messengers of Day* Holt, Rinehart and Winston (1978)

[22] King George V commanded this rescue to save her Russian relatives. The story of *HMS Marlborough* is revealed in Welch, Frances. *The Russian Court at Sea.* Short Books (2011). In addition to Olga, her father Prince Serge Dolgorouky, (1872-1933) an equerry to the Romanovs was also saved as well as her cousin Princess Sofka (later Skipwith).

[23] Olga Tredegar [Olga Sergeivna] Viscountess (nee Princess Olga Sergeivna Dolgorouky) Born 13 May 1914 died 19 January 1998 peacefully at the Princess Elizabeth Hospital Cremated at Le Foulon Chapel, Guernsey, CI.

[24] See *The Times* 25 January 1957 and 21 June 1957 for sales at Sotheby's and Christie's respectively. by John Morgan, by then 6th Lord Tredegar. These included his late father's possessions. On 20 July 1954 *Messrs Knight, Frank and Rutley* also offered Honeywood House, Rowhook, Dorking with 172 acres for sale. This was Evan's last home and belonged to his mother.

[25] Letters of Olga, Viscountess Tredegar in files at Tredegar House.

[26] The poet and Evan's Oxford friend, Robert Nichols was offered £100 by Evan to write his biography in the 1930s. In the 1970s several people attempted Evan's biography. *The Times* of 8 June, 1972, contains one appeal:
" VISCOUNT TREDEGAR 13/7/93 to 27/4/49. Biographer needs information, anecdotes, photographs, documents, letters of Evan Morgan, 2nd Viscount. Please write in confidence to Gibson, BM/1567, London W.C.1."
Several members of the curatorial staff at Tredegar House in the 1970s including David Beevers and David Freeman had an interest in writing Evan's life. Today, Paul Busby, is poised to publish his work *"Only Evan : The eccentric life of Lord Tredegar"* which was expected as far back as 2009. This is supplemented by his recent announcement of another book called *" The Peculiar Career of Lord Tredegar"* in April 2013.

[27] " *The Peculiar Career of Lord Tredegar"* due in April 2013 from Paul Busby is to be based on many previously unpublished letters written by Evan and those of his second wife, Princess Olga Dolgoruky.

[28] The vast Tredegar-Morgan family Archive, Estate and legal documents is held by the National Library of Wales, Aberystwyth. The catalogue can be gleaned on the National Library's website. http://www.llgc.org.uk/index.php?id=introduction0

A small collection of curatorial papers is retained at Tredegar House itself. Access was granted to these papers by the former Curator, Emily Price – with much thanks to her and to Newport City Council. An important book (now sadly out of print) is recommended to anyone interested in the history of the Estate. See Philips, Roger. *Tredegar: The history of an agricultural estate 1300-1956*. Self Publishing Association (1990).

[29] H Montgomery Hyde (1907-1989) Barrister and Biographer. Hyde lost his (Belfast) seat as an Ulster Unionist in Parliament after campaigning in favour of reform of the law relating to homosexuality. Evan is described as *"a [wealthy] homosexual"* in Hyde's *The Love That Dared not Speak its Name* (Little, Brown) (1970). p.200. See also The Other Love, by H Montgomery Hyde Mayflower Books (1972)

[30] Jenkins, Roy. *Twelve Cities : A Personal Memoir*. Pan (2004)

[31] This is how Evan described Bali (quote from *The Daily Mirror* 13 March 1939).

[32] Donald Friend, (1915-1989) Australian artist and sometime resident of Bali. See Friend, Donald, National Library of Australia. (2006) *The Diaries of Donald Friend : 1967-1999 p.70*. See also p.24 *"there were many scandalous anecdotes [from the 1930s] about one Tuan Raja ' who is remembered by many Balinese who had a house on the beach ..The dimensions of his cock, and many of his doings have become folklore. Tuan Raja was Evan Morgan (Lord Tredegar) ...."*

[33] A handwritten note in the Tredegar House file on Evan (based on interviews with those who knew him) declares *" Evan in Thailand – fancied that type."*

[34] Ruperra Castle (now a ruin),close to the villages of Draethen and Rudry in a triangle between Caerphilly, Newport and Cardiff. http://www.ruperra.org.uk/ and http://www.ruperratrust.co.uk/ The Castle was built in 1626 by Sir Thomas Morgan in the Jacobean style. It was historically the home of the heir to the Morgan family's lands and titles.

[35] Sir Compton Mackenzie (1883-1972). Writer, historian and ardent Scot.

[36] Mackenzie, C, Sir *My Life and Times*. Chatto & Windus (1963).

[37] *The Times*, 28 April 1949.

[38] See Quennell, Peter. *Customs and Characters. Contemporary Portraits*. Weidenfeld and Nicolson (1982). Quennell identifies *" three generous dilettantes.. Napier [Naps] Alington, Evan Trdegar and Gerald Berners..."* Naps and Berners were close to Evan in his life and adventures.

[39] The Sexual Offences Act 1967 decriminalised homosexual acts in private between two men, both of whom had to have attained the age of 21. The Act applied only to England and Wales and did not cover the Merchant Navy or the Armed Forces. Homosexuality was decriminalised in Scotland by the Criminal Justice (Scotland) Act 1980 and in Northern Ireland by the Homosexual Offences (Northern Ireland) Order 1982.

[40] *South Wales Argus*, 28 April 1949.

[41] Henry Maxwell's letter (dated 9 February 1979) to David Beevers, the former Assistant Curator of Tredegar House casts some doubt on whether Evan actually met Arbuckle. See Tredegar House files.

[42] Ibid.

[43] Frederic George Morgan (1873-1954).

[44] (Frederic Charles) John Morgan (1908-1962). Married a divorcee with two daughters. As Evan's estate was unravelled by the tax authorities, John sold up everything that was his own personal inheritance. Tredegar House became St Joseph's Convent School until it was taken over by Newport Borough Council (and reopened as a tourist attraction) in the 1970s. Today (2012) the house is leased to the National Trust for 50 years.

[45] *Hull Daily Mail*, 5 January 1950.

[46] National Archives Kew files IR 40/9713 and IR 40/11982.

[47] Compromise settlements were reached with the authorities by and on behalf of Olga, Viscountess Tredegar and Mrs Emily Sutherland, Evan's former secretary, who each had contractual allowances paid from out of the Tredegar Estate.

[48] This was Monsignor Augustin Fernand Leynaud (1865-1953). Appointed Archbishop of Algiers in 1917. An expert archaeologist. Evan was frequently North Africa 1918-9 on account of his health and for sex.

[49] He was Cardinal Amette, Cardinal Archbishop of Paris (1850-1920). Evan was a regular on the Paris scene travelling with his mother and later socialising with friends. Evan was also at the Paris Peace Conference in 1919.

[50] *South Wales Argus*, 28 April 1949.

[51] In his last Will and Testament Evan stated *"I desire that the Trustees of the said Abbey [of Buckfast] shall arrange for one Mass to be said each week for a period of seven years from the date of my death for the Repose of my Soul"*.

[52] Last Will and Testament of Evan Morgan dated 2 March 1948.

[53] Dom Raphael Stones, O.S.B., a monk of St. Mary's Abbey, Buckfast, Devon, who was a Chaplain with the Forces stationed in East Bengal and Burma,

[54] An Irish peer, the Earl of Carrick (a cousin of Evan's) was also an Executor of his Estate. He was in America at the time of Evan's death and was not expected to return to Britain except if essentially required. NB Several other Executors were appointed in the years that followed by the trustees of the Tredegar Settled Lands.

[55] Evan's Testamentary documents can be gleaned via the Probate and Family Division of the High Court.

[56] Henry Maxwell (1909-1996) son of William Babington Maxwell (a novelist). There are several letters written by Henry Maxwell in Evan's file at Tredegar House describing Evan and his days as Lord Tredegar .

[57] Cyril Hughes Hartmann (died 1967) *"well loved historian and writer of Stuart times."* A collection of Evan's letters to Hartmann (and other material) is held in Evan's file at Tredegar House.

[58] Sir Charles Alexander Bannerman Carnegie of Kinnaird and of Pitcarrow, 8th Baronet, 11th Earl of Southesk, 11th Baron Carnegie of Kinnaird, 11th Baron Carnegie, of Kinnaird and Leuchards, and 3rd Baron Balinhard, of Farnell in the County of Forfar, (1893-1992).

[59] Major Raymond Alexander Carnegie (1920-1999) He was the son of Commander Hon. Alexander Bannerman Carnegie and Susan Ottilia de Rodaskowski-Rivers.

[60] Evan's obituary in the Journal of the Royal Society of Arts. Volume 97 Page 437 (1949).

[61] Dart, Monty and Cross,William. *A Beautiful Nuisance: The Life and Death of the Hon. Gwyneth Ericka Morgan*. William P Cross. (2012).

[62] Hon. Frederick Courtenay Morgan (1834-1909). Soldier and MP and Squire of Ruperra Castle. Fought in the Crimean married Charlotte Anne Williamson (1841-1891) of Lawers, Perthshire.

[63] Sir James Carnegie, (1827-1905) 9th Earl of Southesk. Landowner and Poet. 1st Wife Catherine Noel (1829-1855) (daughter of 1st Earl of Gainsborough) 2nd wife Lady Susan Catherine Mary Murray (1837-1915) daughter of the 6th Earl of Dunmore. Katharine was from James'second marriage.

[64] According to John Burke's *A genealogical and heraldic History of the Commoners of Great Britain* Volume 1 *" LEWELLEN, Lord of St Clare and Gwynvaye, the county of Camarthen, who m. Aughard, daughter and co-heir of Sir Morgan Meredith, Lord of Tredegar, descended from RHYS, King of South Wales, and had two sons"*

[65] Sir (Charles) Leolin Forestier-Walker (1866-1934).

[66] Charlotte Morgan lost two children. On 20 March 1864 *"prematurely, a son, who survived his birth but a few hours"* (Source *Guardian* 30 March 1864) and On 3rd December 1871 *"prematurely, of a daughter, still born."* (Source *Guardian* 11 December 1871).

[67] Courtenay Morgan's three surviving siblings were Hon Blanche Frances Morgan (later Mrs Charles Hoare) (1859-1948); Hon Violet Morgan (later Mrs Basil St. John Mundy) (1860-1943) and Frederic George Morgan (1873-1954).

[68] See Patton, Brian. *Tales from the Canadian Rockies*. Mcclelland & Stewart Ltd (1993).

[69] See Lowndes Marie Bellec and Lowndes Susan. Diaries and letters of Marie Belloc Lowndes, 1911-1847. Chatto & Windus. (1971) p 273 [Diary entry for 22 September 1946] *" His [Evan's] mother lives in bed, in the dark."*

[70] Katharine Agnes Blanche Carnegie, Viscountess Tredegar died in London on 4th October 1949, aged 82.

[71] Courtenay was ADC to various military figures in London in the 1890's and served in the Boer War. He was invalided home from South Africa, and had a role in the training Empire troops for to take part in the Coronation of King Edward VII.

[72] See the Court Martial evidence of Sir Russell Wilkinson giving a diagnosis of Katharine's condition as *"Psychasthenia on his mother's side, who is of schizoid temperament - meaning a divided personality."*

[73] Leolin was elected an MP for Monmouth in 1918 and held the seat until his death, only a few days after his cousin, Courtenay (Lord Tredegar) in 1934. He was made a baronet in 1924.

[74] Courtenay took part in golf competitions in North Berwick in Scotland, Sandwich in Kent and in Ireland.

[75] William Sayzeland was Courtenay's valet for 34 years. His family, (who emigrated to Australia) enabled the Friends of Tredegar House to recently purchase several items given to Sayzeland and to his son Henry, who was a valet to Evan Morgan.

[76] See Monty Dart's article in Newsletter April 2012 of the Friends of Tredegar House. http://www.friends-of-tredegar-house.co.uk/. The Butler's book is held by Shropshire Archives. Document Ref 4924/11/9 and covers the period Jan 1901 to October 1905.

[77] Charles Morgan Hoare (1893-1914) Joined a Cavalry Regiment in 1902, killed in action in the great War. Frederick Mundy MC RNVR (1895-1917).

[78] Captain Raymond Juzio Paul Rodakowski, 1st Battalion Irish Guards, whose memorial is at Tyne Cot, died on 9 October 1917.

[79] The poem is reproduced in this volume.

[80] Raymond (1895-1916) and Susan (Suki) (1897-1968) were the children of Major Ernest Rodakowski-Rivers (died 1944) and Lady Dora Carnegie (1863-1952). Ernest Rodakowski-Rivers was an Austrian cavalry officer who was sometime Clerk of the famous Brooklands Motor Racing Circuit. Suki married her half-cousin, Commander Hon. Alexander Bannerman Carnegie (a son of Charles the 10th Earl of Southesk).

[81] *South Wales Argus*, 28 April 1949.

[82] Matthew Davenport Hill (1872-1958). Known as *"Piggy"*. An Eton master 1896-1927 specialising in science.

[83] Robert Penrice Lee Booker (1864-1923). Assistant Master at Eton from 1888.

[84] E-mail exchange 26 March – 7 April 2009 *"We much regret that we are unable to find any photographs of Morgan in our resources. Best wishes M.T.Phillips, Curator."*

[85] Hartmann, Cyril, Unpublished Memoirs p.166.

[86] *South Wales Argus*, 22 May 1920.

[87] In early 1914, *The Times* printed the name of Evan and other notables reaching 21 that year, including his cousin Charles, Lord Carnegie, who had a birthday in September and Hon. Gerard Sturt, the Alington heir; Evan later married Gerard's sister, Lois. Gerard died from horrific injuries sustained in the First World War.

[88] Sir Denis George William Anson, 4th Baronet (1888-1914). Eton and Oxford.

[89] Anson had recently become a baronet. On 3 July, 1914 he was celebrating with a party (with the Thomas Beecham orchestra) on board a boat in the Thames. Everyone was in high spirits (some reports suggest an orgy was full swing) as the boat sailed up towards Battersea Bridge, where Anson attempted to leap off the boat and jump back on again. He slipped and was carried away by the river. A bandsman from the orchestra also died trying to save him. An inquest returned a verdict of death by accident. Among those on board the boat were Nancy Cunard, Lady Diana Manners, Duff Cooper, Raymond Asquith and Iris Tree, all chums of Evan.

[90] Nina Hamnett (1890-1956). Welsh born writer, painter and poet. Author of the best selling reminiscences *Laughing Torso*(1932) came to know Evan in the years that followed and they were often in each other's social company in Paris and London. Evan features in the book at parties in Paris in 1920, one dinner party in Montparnasse for Evan's birthday. Another namedropper mentioned in *Laughing Torso* is Aleister Crowley, the occultist. One of Evan's early meetings with Crowley (who visited Tredegar House in 1943) took place in Paris at Nina Hamnett's instigation at the Hotel de Blois in the Rue Vavin. Crowley served up cocktails of gin, vermouth and a tincture of laudanum! Later Crowley unsuccessfully sued Nina for libel. Crowley's title of " *the wickedest man in the world*" stems (in part) from the disclosures made by Nina about his links with black magic and death rituals in a temple in Cefalu, Sicily. Nina died in a fall (and was impaled by railings) by accident or design from her flat forty feet above the ground.

[91] This is taken from the Royal Yacht Squadron History: *"World War One took its toll on the steam yachts of the Royal Yacht Squadron. In 1916 there were 90 vessels – 2 years later the number had fallen to under 60. Among the craft fitted out and cruising again is Lord Tredegar's 1571 SY Liberty. This fine steamer, originally built for the late Mr Joseph Pullitzer, of American newspaper fame was placed at the disposal of the Admiralty on August 4, 1914, the day Britain declared war on Germany. It was not long before Liberty, full equipped as a hospital ship at her owner's expense and under the command of her owner, who had been granted a commission in the Royal Naval Reserve, was in commission in the North Sea. She was in attendance on Admiral Beatty's command, and was in the first big naval scrap of the war in Heligoland Bight, and brought home many of the wounded. Liberty was for 2 years in the Mediterranean escaping all the mines and submarine traps into which so many Red Cross ships fell. She conveyed men from the Suvia Bay adventure, and later, until the armistice was signed , served the men of the Dover patrol in the frequent fights with the enemy."*

[92] Prince Arthur of Connaught (1883- 1938) A grandson of Queen Victoria, he had an army career and was later Governor General of South Africa. Married his cousin Princess Alexandra Duff (1891-1959).

[93] Evan's name is cited in the Court Circular for 4 July (see *The Times* 5 July 1914). A report of the opening of the new lock is in *The Times* for 15 July 1914.

[94] Lees- Milne. Harold Nicolson : 1930-1968. Chatto & Windas (1980)

[95] According to a correspondent, an expert on the London auction houses of the 20th century " *Queen Mary was very much into hard stones, and would go to London auction houses like Peter Sparks for crystal rabbits, agate frogs, jade crabs, amber snuff bottle, etc, which usually didn't cost much, comparing with porcelains..*".

[96] Evan apparently owned the largest piece of Jade outside of the Smithsonian Collection. His Chinese collection was housed at his London home at South Audley Street, which he occupied when Tredegar House was shut up. It was said that Queen Mary once called in on Evan to see his collection (but this did not make an entry in her diaries) (in The Royal Archives, Windsor Castle). Evan gave a lecture on 25th October 1945 at the Royal Society of Literature (under the Tredegar Memorial Lecture - which he founded in memory of his father, Courtenay) The subject was " Chinese Jade ". John Morgan, 6th Baron sold a collection of "Japanese & Chinese porcelain " at Christies on 1st December 1958.

[97] Paul Busby e-mail 10 November 2010.

[98] Cyril Hughes Hartmann, Author and Historian: a contemporary and confidante of Evan at Oxford. Hartmann (who remained a close life long friend to Evan) has left behind a detailed appreciation of him. This record in held in Evan's file in Tredgear House. The file also contains a number of typed letters to Hartmann from the years of WW1.

[99] Gwyneth was presented at the last Court of 1914, in June. The war suspended the ritual. It was said that when restarted in 1920 *"12,000 debutantes"* awaited their presentation at Court.

[100] The Chapter Entitled *"Evan"* is a typed draft which occupies pages 43-62 of a folder presented to Tredegar House by George Hughes Hartmann (Cyril's son).(with other Evan papers in Tredegar House).

[101] Lady Helena Mariota Carnegie (1865-1943. Unmarried sister of Katharine, Lady Tredegar. Nellie was known as a lady of letters and was a published Author.

[102] Hartmann, Cyril, Unpublished Memoirs. In Hartmann's obituary in *The Times* of 19th May 1967 it records *"To his beloved friend Lady Helena Carnegie he owed – during her lifetime – the encouragement and criticism which contributed so largely with the writing of his best works."*

[103] The letters are typed up in a folder (of 42 pages) (transcribed from the originals, with some notes on people mentioned (presumably by Cyril's son, George Hughes Hartmann).

[104] In one letter (written at Honeywood House on 30 December 1917) Evan says *" my actual complaint has attained such an immence [sic] that I am shortly starting for Algeria where I hope to remain these following six months."* Another (written from Algeria dated 15th June, 1918 continues " *Owing to my illness I get these grim fits of depression… and the constant attacks of fever which frequently begin at 6 in the evening causing a deadening sense of despondency to settle upon me. My lung though on the whole is better though one spot in the left apex is still active. No wine, little exercise, arsenic injections and deep breathing exercises are the order of the day…."*

[105] Sir Lancelot Carnegie (1861-1933). Old- style diplomat. Brother of Lady Katharine Tredegar

[106] For Examples See Plimpton, George : Truman Capote. Pan Macmillan (1999) *" the dowager Lady Tredegar, had built the largest bird's nest in all the world: it had taken her twenty years and can still be seen at Tredegar castle. Yes, a bird's nest. She apparently hatched nothing in it except – who knows?...EVAN? ".*

See Conway, David. Magic Without Mirrors: The Making of a Magician. Logios Printing (2011) *"Evan's mother, the former Lady Katherine Carnegie from time to time persuaded she was one [a bird] herself. When that happened, she would go out into the grounds and build a large nest of sticks and mud then install herself inside it, cooing prettily at all who chanced to stroll by…"*

See Marks, Howard Senor Nice: Straight Life from Wales to South America. Harvill Secker (2006) p47 *"She [Lady Tredegar] built bigger and bigger bird's nets in the house and ended up living in one of them.."*

[107] For a more representative picture of Katharine's bird nests (which she made as a way of helping to cope with severe arthritis in her hands) See Cecil Roberts' *The Bright Twenties*, Hodder & Stoughton (1974).

[108] Twentieth-century literary critisism Gale Research Company. (1984). p205 " *a story of Lady Tredegar, who had, says Mrs Belloc Lowndes "the unusual gift, perhaps the mania for making chaffinches' nests".*

[109] Katharine's Carnegie nephews and nieces called her *"Auntie Kats"* . She appears as such in the unpublished diaries of Charles Carnegie, 11th Earl of Southesk, held in Kinnaird Castle, Brechin.

[110] Holman-Hunt Diana: Latin among Lions : Alvaro Guevara. M Joseph. (1974) p110 *" Lady Tredegar was, in most people's opinion, as mad as a hatter and preferred making bird's nests to needlework in her leisure."*

[111] Roberts Cecil. The Bright Twenties. Hodder & Stoughton (1974).
Pryce-Jones, Alan :The Bonus of Laughter. Hamish Mamilton (1987)

[112] Huxley Aldous and Smith, Grover Cleveland. Letters of Aldous Huxley. Harper & Row (1970) " *I have been seeing a good deal of the dashing Evan Morgan recently as well as his mother, Lady Tredegar, who is a very delightful person.* "

[113] Campbell John. *If Love Were All : The Story of Frances Stevenson and David Lloyd George.* Random House (2007). Based on extract from 1919 diary whilst Frances was making ready to go to stay with Katharine at Honeywood House for a quiet weekend.

[114] Holroyd, Michael : Augustus John : The New Biography. Random House (2010) makes it clear reference to identify Katharine with the bird fetishes indulged in by Evan in describing his mother to others.. p415" *The roll-call reverberated on. Lady Tredegar, with her strange gift for climbing into tress and arranging nets in which polite birds would settle; Iris Tree, with her pink hair and poetry, 'someone quite marvellous'; Sylvia Gough, with her thin loose legs....*"

[115] Ibid.

[116] Augustus John Collection, National Library of Wales, Aberystwyth.

[117] Cawthorne, Nigel Sex Lives of the Great Artists. Prion (1998). p183 " *The list of girls went on – Sybil Hart-Davis, Iris Tree, Lady Tredegar, a famous ballerina whom John was said to have " borrowed" from her husband.*"

[118] This quote is attributed to Nancy Cunard. It first appears in Benkovitz, Miriam J. *Ronald Firbank : A biography.* Knopf. (1969)

[119] Ambrose McEvoy (1878-1927). Society painter. This painting is on display at Tredegar House, Newport, now a National Trust managed property. McEvoy also pained Lois Sturt, Evan's first wife.

[120] An Elizabethan residence with 456 acres.

[121] Lady Ottoline Morrell (1873-1938) had aristocratic links to the Cavendish-Bentinck family (the Dukes of Portland). She had many lovers and maintained a life on the grand scale at her London home in Bedford Square and at Garsington Manor . She married Philip Morrell (1870-1943), a Liberal MP.

[122] Willis, John H: *Leonard and Virginia Woolf As Publishers : The Hogarth Press, 1917-41.* Volume 32 Google E-Book.

[123] *The Diary of Virginia Woolf: 1915-1919.* Hogarth Press (1977).

[124] See Waller, Philip J, *Writers, Readers, and Reputations: literary life in Britain, 1870-1918.* Oxford University Press (2006) who quotes Woolfe p552 " *he [Evan] was most carefully prepared to be a poet and an eccentricity both by his conversation, which aimed at irresponsible brilliance and lack of reticence, and by his clothes, which must have been copied from the usual Shelley picture.*"

[125] Strachey, Lytton and Levy Paul. *The letters of Lytton Strachey.* Literary Collections. (2005)

[126] Ibid.

[127] Henry Maxwell records in a letter in the Tredegar House files dated 9 February 1979 Evan was *"Altogether a most remarkable person, who could be the soul of charm and a perfect demon alternatively"*

[128] Letter in the Tredegar House Archives from Henry Maxwell to David Beevers (Assistant Curator at Tredegar House) dated 9 February 1979.

[129] Courtenay was too busy helping the war effort to have his life disrupted by Evan's antics. Yet, he knew the boy had one talent – that was for spending money. This is evidenced from Courtenay's Private Bank Accounts – held now in

the National Library of Wales. Evan spent close on £2000 a quarter on hotels, restaurants, secretaries, tailors and travelling.

[130] Purser, Philip: *Poeted : the final quest of Edward James* : Quartet Books (1991). " *though no longer up at the university, [Evan] still haunted Oxford at the weekends, throwing fancy-dress parties at the Randolph* "

[131] Milton, Billy, (1905-1989). British entertainer.

[132] According to Evan's cousin Alan Carnegie Stewart, (born 1920) – and who lived sometime at Tredegar House, (1947-8) Evan enjoyed being nude. There was a system whereby any maid or other party who knew Evan was inside would first knock on the door. Evan if clothed) would ring a bell if/ when they were allowed to enter.

[133] Milton, Billy: *Milton's Paradise Mislaid*. Jupiter Books. (1976).

[134] Quoted by Nicholas Murray in *Aldous Huxley*. Hachette UK. (2009).

[135] Rosita Forbes (1890-1967). Travel writer and wanderer in Libya. Source See " Amos William: *The originals : who's really who in fiction.* Cape (1985). p314 " *Morgan was a Oxford/ Bloomsbury figure, remembered for his penchant for fancy-dress parties (he fancied himself as the explorer Rosita Forbes) ...*" Rosita met Evan years later on a cruise.

[136] A handwritten note in the Tredegar House file on Evan (based on interviews with people who knew Evan) refers to this as a group called the " *Black Circle*".

[137] Publications in the early 20th century included *The Occult Review* (with contributors like poet and mystic Meredith Starr) and Aleister Crowley's publication *The Equinox*.

[138] A handwritten note seen in the Tredegar House file on Evan.

[139] Edward Alexander Crowley (1875-1947), commonly known as Aleister Crowley. Besides being involved in the black magic rituals he was a drug addict. Evan first met him in Paris in the 1920s. Their paths crossed a few times and Crowley stayed at Tredegar House for a few days in 1943.

[140] See Symonds, John. The King of the Shadow Realm : Aleister Crowley, his life and magic. Duckworth. (1989). p559 includes A snippet from Crowley's diary of 20 June 1943 (when he was staying at Tredegar House) that records " *Saw Tredegar's Magick Room - far greater than I thought ....*"

[141] Interview with Alan Carnegie Stewart (born 1920) (Scotland 2009). Alan's grandmother Lady Beatrice was a half-sister to Katharine Tredegar. Alan worked as a land surveyor in the Tredegar Estate Office, Newport before and after the second world war. After the war Evan's estate manager, Captain Ware arranged accommodation for Alan's and his wife at Tredegar House, the Stewarts used the Brown Room as their sitting room. At this time (1947-8) Evan visited infrequently.

[142] Phillip Arnold Heseltine (1894-1930). Composer. DH Lawrence based the character Halliday in *Women in Love* on him. He was found dead from gas poisoning and an open verdict recorded.
http://www.peterwarlock.org/WARLOCK.HTM

[143] A photograph in the Tredegar House files (circa 1915) taken outside a London restaurant shows Evan, Warlock, Earp and Epstein.

[144] The Tredegar House files contain correspondence from author and researcher Anthony Swerling (1944-2004), an authority on the playwright Strindberg. He was enquiring into " *the Cave of the Golden Calf and the Vorticist movement* in art)" as Evan and his Mother were closely associated with it.

[145] The Club was opened in 1912 by Frida Strindberg (third wife of the playwright). The club's book/prospectus was illustrated by Wyndham Lewis. Reviews of the opening of the club were featured in *The Times* and *The Bystander*, the latter giving it a cautious welcome.

[146] A story from Nina Hamnett in her book *Laughing Torso* (1932) refers to Evan dressing up as a sailor. p163 " *Evan Morgan…arrived back from Marseilles; he was dressed in black and looked very smart. He said, " How do you like my clothes?" I said, " How smart!" He said, " Oh, no, a sailors' shop in Marseilles."*

[147] In 1935 a case arose at Bow Street Police Court of Robert Gregory, a former groom to Courtenay Morgan, Evan's father. Gregory had tried to sell a pair of onyx and diamond cuff links he found on clothing left to him after Courtenay's death. Fearing disclosure by Gregory of family tales Evan intervened sending a solicitor to defend the man and to declare that " *Gregory had no intention of committing any theft. Not only did Lord Tredegar intend to continue him in service, but the servant's hall would be glad to see him back."* See *The Times* 6 and 16 September 1935.

[148] Evan's godson Desmond Leslie mentions this in his memories of Tredegar House, attributing the story to Emily Sutherland, Evan's private secretary.

[149] The Cafe Royal was established in 1865 by a Parisian wine merchant and was to the Bohemians of the 19th century a French gastronomic oasis in the midst of Victorian London. It was a frequent place for Evan to entertain and dine in the years before, during and after the Grest War.

[150] Phillips, Neville. *The Stage Struck Me!* Troubador Publishing Ltd (2008) p178 *"In the 1920's and 30's the Fitzroy Tavern in Charlotte Street was the centre of bohemian London and many of the Bloomsbury painters and writers regularly met there. It had a slightly raffish atmosphere which they found to their liking."*

[151] Leonard [Woolf (1880-1969)] [husband of Virginia] formed the "*17 Club*" which took its name from the events of the 1917 February Revolution in Russia….He hoped the "*Club*" might prove a setting for exchanges of ideas among kindred spirits.." Virginia Woolf records in her diaries about Evan being discussed there by Aldous Huxley and a lady friend. See Woolf Diaries 9 March, 1918 *"They were discussing Evan Morgan & his affairs of the heart.."* [This almost certainly refers to Evan's proposal of marriage to Frances Stevenson – Secretary/ mistress and later wife of David Lloyd George] .

[152] See *The Times*, 4th July 1914.

[153] Adrian Allinson (1890-1959). *"Painter detached from Fashions"*. See his Obituary in *The Times* 21st February 1959 and *The Times* 13th November 1971. Trained at the Slade (where his contemporaries in the intake of 1912 were Dorothy Carrington, Mark Gertler, and Stanley Spencer) and in Paris and Munich. *"In his youth Allinson ..was an athletic, bearded man, earnest in conversation.."* At the time he painted The Café Royal he was scenic designer for the Beecham Opera Company.

[154] Dorothy (Dorelia) McNeill, (1881-1969) model and common law wife of Welsh painter Augustus John (1878-1961).

[155] Paul George Konody (1872-1933). Art critic of *The Observer* and *Daily Mail.*

[156] *The Times* of 9th November, 1968 refers to the sale of this picture by Allinson , the previous day at Christies. It was purchased by Charles Forte (at the time owner of the Café Royal) for 650 gns.

[157] Alan Odle (1888-1948), artist and illustrator. In 1917 married the novelist Dorothy Richardson (1873-1957) They lived in retreat in Cornwall.

[158] Nancy Cunard (1896-1965). Poet, publisher and Negro and jazz lover.

[159] William Horace de Vere Cole (1881-1936) Society hoaxer and prankster. He is well described – with other colourful references to the Café Royal-Eiffel Tower brigade by the composer Cecil Gray in *Musical Chairs* his life and memoirs, published in 1948.

[160] Iris Tree, (1897-1968), poet, artist and model.

[161] Geghy G and Waterhouse, K. Café Royal: Ninety Years of Bohemia. Hutchinson. (1955).

[162] Percy Wyndham Lewis (1882-1957). Artist and Novelist.

[163] Robert Malise Bowyer Nichols (1893-1944). Subject of a biography by Anne and William Charlton: *Putting Poetry First: A Life of Robert Nichols 1893-1944.* Michael Russell Publishing Ltd (2003). The London socialite and Scottish clan chief Myrtle Farquharson (1897-1941) of Invercauld, (sometime Mrs Robin d'Erlanger) suggested that Robert Nicholas write Evan's biography. £100 was mentioned as a fee. Myrtle died in an air raid during the London Blitz on 11th May 1941. According to her friend Amy Stewart Fraser in her memoirs *In Memory Long.* Routledge (1977) Myrtle was distributing " *clothing to people rendered homeless in the Blitz when she was killed on duty.".*

[164] Alvaro Guevara (1894 - 1951). An artist of Chilean origin. Frequently referred to as "Chile"

[165] Arthur Annesley Ronald Firbank (1886-1926) Writer and gay icon. Although Ronald was born in London the Firbank family derived much of their wealth from the railways and as landlords in St Julians, Newport, South Wales.

[166] Nancy Cunard (daughter of the celebrated hostess and socialite Emerald Cunard) personified the mood of the iconoclastic 1920's, with Evan (whom she adored and wanted to marry) and others as fellow A-listers on the social scene. After her marriage failed (it was finally annulled in 1924) she moved to live in Paris in 1920 and spent long periods in USA, Southern France, Spain and famously visiting her cousin, Victor Cunard in Venice where she met a group of American Negros who inspired her muse and suited her sexual desires. Nancy also wrote *"free verse".*

[167] Ford, Hugh and Cunard, Nancy : Negro : An Anthology. Continuum International Publishing Group. (1996). Introduction to Cunard's original 1934 title " *Negro*" with an Introduction by Hugh Ford.

[168] Holman-Hunt, Diana. *Latin among Lions. Alvaro Guevara.* Michael Joseph. (1974).

[169] While at the Slade School, Iris Tree and Nancy Cunard formed friendships inside and outside with Wyndham Lewis and Augustus John, Alvaro "Chile" Guevara, Robert Nichols, Evan Morgan, Osbert and Sacheverell Sitwell, Edward Wyndham Tennant, and Tommy Earp. Bloomsbuy's Vanessa Bell, Duncan Grant, Dora Carrington, Roger Fry, Jacob Epstein were also regulars.

[170] Stulik merited an obituary in *The Times* on 14 November 1938. *"for 30 years his restaurant was a meeting, dining, and wining place for London Bohemians… Composers, writers and well known actors and actresses from many parts of the world met at the Eiffel.."*

[171] Leslie, Seymour . *The Jerome Connection.* John Murray (1964).

[172] A short lived art movement in Britain based on Cubism. Best reflected in the magazine Blast (published 1914 and 1915) with Wyndham Lewis as Editor.

[173] See Benkovitz, Miriam J. *More About Ronald Firbank*. Columbia University Library Columns Volumes 2406 (1974). She lists " *Cuthbert Hamilton, Ezra Pound, William Roberts, Wyndham Lewis, Frederick Etchells, Edward Wadsworth, Jessica Dismorr and Helen Saunders*" appearing in the painting. These artists contributed to a magazine called *Blast*, published during the Great War.

[174] A group of intellectuals, poets and political figures from late Victorian England which included personalities like George Curzon, Arthur Balfour, the Asquiths, the Grenfells and the Wyndhams. Many of the promising sons of the Coterie (e.g. Raymond Asquith and Julian Grenfell) were killed in action during the Great War.

[175] The help Evan (and Olga) gave to Bosie Douglas is covered is several biographies. See Hyde, Montgomery H. *Lord Alfred Douglas*. Methuen.(1984).

[176] Letters folder in Tredegar House from Evan Morgan to Cyril Hughes Hartmann.

[177] According to medical historian Virginia Berridge Lady Diana Cooper (formerly Manners) (1892-1986) " *a close friend of Iris Tree. Lady Diana doped*" *with chloroform ..and morphine..*"

[178] Berridge, Virginia. *The Origins of The English Drug "Scene" 1890-1930.* Medical History . 32 : 51-64.

[179] See Dart, Monty and Cross, William. *A Beautiful Nuisance : The Life and Death of Gwyneth Ericka Morgan*. Book Midden Publishing (2012).

[180]The New Age was edited by A R Orage = Alfred Richard Orage (1873-1934) an intellectual and follower of Nietzsche, also interested in mysticism. Evan met Orage at Lady Ottoline Morrell's house Garsington Manor near Oxford.
The New Age is available from 1909-1921 on the internet. Se Modernist Journals:
http://dl.lib.brown.edu/mjp/render.php?view=mjp_object&id=1158589415603817
Three poems by Evan have been identified. 11th March 1915 : *What of the Dead*; 16th August 1917: *The Writing on the Wall* and 28th August 1919: *Eaden, Eaden Sequentur.*

[181] ",Volume 51. (1917).

[182] *The Times* 18th June 1915 records : "*The Hon. Evan F Morgan only son of Lord and Lady Tredegar has received a Commission in the Welsh Guards and joined his regiment at Wellington Barracks last week,*"

[183] Ibid. Evan may have briefly met Rupert Brooke (1887-1915) whether at Garsington or in Oxford itself, just before the latter's posting to Greece, where he died of blood poisoning, off the island of Skyros before taking part in the fighting. Evan's first appearance at Garsington may have been later than 1915. One of the timelines in Evan's file in Tredegar House states "*October 7, 1917 – [Evan] signs in the Garsington visitors book.*" However the biography of Kathleen Mansfield by Anthony Alpers, The Viking Press (1980) Chronology p410 shows that Evan was at Garsington "*16-17 July, 1916 with Mansfield, David Garnett, Lytton Strachey and many others..*"

[184] Evan's books of poetry include *Fragments* (1916), *Gold and Ochre* (1917), *A Sequence of Seven Sonnets* (1920), *At Dawn and other poems, profane and religious* (1924), *The Eel and Other poems* (1926) and *The City of Canals* (1929).

He also wrote *In Pace,* in 1925, as a tribute to his dead sister, Gwyneth. Many of the poems are given dates and the places where they were written, with the text.
[185] The Letters of Wyndham Lewis. Taylor & Francis The reference to *"Pound"* is to the American poet Ezra Pound (1885-1972).
[186]   Smith, Barry [Ed] Frederick Delius and Peter Warlock : *A Friendship Revealed.* Oxford University Press (2000). Writing from Honeywood House, Oakwood Hill
(Evan's mother's home) on 28th March, 1915, Philip Hestletine (aka Peter Warlock) records in a letter to the composer [his hero] Frederick Delius " *I was suddenly called upon yesterday to escourt [sic] down here a friend who is on the point of a nervous breakdown. He is suffering from acute mental strain and has lately had several lapses of memory, which make it quite unsafe for him to go about alone"*
[187] Letters folder in Tredegar House from Evan Morgan to Cyril Hughes Hartmann. Letter dated [by Censor] 26th February 1916 from Honeywood House . Evan reported in the same letter that *"Oxford has cast me off, rightly punished me for my behaviour towards it when there…."* He also adds that " *I still paint a little, and write poems to various magazines.."*
[188] John Moorhead Byres Moir (1853-1928). MD CM Edinburgh and London.
[189] Augustus John Collection, National Library of Wales, Aberystwyth.
[190] Letters folder in Tredegar House from Evan Morgan to Cyril Hughes Hartmann
[191] Ibid.
[192] Augustus John Collection, National Library of Wales, Aberystwyth. Mocking Evan's birthday parties became the norm. In 1917 Dora Carringtron wrote to Mark Gertler [two of Evan's acquaintances at Garsington] *"How I loved your letters, they did so please me, especially the description of Evan (Morgan's) party. I was glad not to go. Just to have that description from you."*
[193] John completed two pictures of Katharine (whom he described in a letter as *"a trying subject, but will pay up"*) *"Woman in the green coat"* (which is in Tredegar House, Newport) and " *Woman in a black velvet hat* " (at Kinnaird Castle, Brechin)
[194] Augustus John Collection, National Library of Wales..
[195] Source Evan's file in Tredegar House. The gist of this is in a letter from Evan to Cyril Hartmann dated 7 February 1918 when Evan was staying at the Hotel Villa Olivage, La Redoute, Algiers receiving a course of arsenic injections… " *Algiers is to me an enchanting city, full of mystery and romance, but my poor health forbids great inroads being made into its more occult regions, the Arab quarter – the Kasbah…."* He adds about his journey to North Africa (by way of Paris where he must have picked up Foreign Office documents to take to the British Embassy/ Consulate in Algeria) " *…The boat I was to have taken to this spot also – thank God the F.O. bag from Paris caused me to go by an earlier one…"*
[196] General Robert Nivelle (1856-1924). A prominent commander at Verdun, appointed later (December 1916) Commander in Chief of the French army. But his actions caused the deaths of 130,000 people and lead to widespread mutiny. He was virtually banished to North Africa.
[197] War losses by the Morgans and Carnegies and off-shoots was large. Among those who fell were these cousins of Evan:
Lt Charles Morgan Hoare 15th The King's Hussars killed 24th August 1914

Captain George Walter Thomas Lindsay killed 26th June 1917
Captain Raymond Juzio Paul Rodakawski Irish Guards killed 9th October 1917
Lt Frederick Mundy MC RNVR killed 26th October 1917
Lt Archibald Thurston Thomas Lindsay killed 26th March 1918
Captain Claud Frederick Thomas Lindsay killed 3st March 1918

[198] Hodge was described by a contemporary as *"fat, rampaging and most patriotic Tory working man"*. He later wrote his memoirs *"Workman's Cottage to Windsor Castle"* but makes no mention of Evan probably as Hodge moved to the Ministry of Pensions in August 1917 never having set eyes on the underling as he was frequently on sick leave.

[199] The fox hunting man Sassoon, an officer and a holder of the Military Cross was determined to be heard over the greater madness about the war. He had refused to fight on, but instead of facing a likely Court Martial and possible firing squad, the War Office wanted Sassoon's campaign against the war (which it was said was encouraged by pacifists whom it was said were exploiting Sassoon) totally muffled. These so called friends of Sassoon were also asking awkward questions in Parliament about a statement made by Sassoon *"Finished with the War: A Soldier's Declaration"* Graves eventually help calm things and persuaded Sassoon to go to Craiglockhart Hospital, near Edinburgh for treatment for shell shock. According to Max Egremont, one biographer of Sassoon (see *Siegfried Sassoon* Pan Macmillan (2006)) Graves suggested " *that Morgan should encourage the War Office not to take disciplinary action [against Sassoon] and to offer a bland response in Parliament."*

[200] On Monday 20th January 1919, *The Times* announced the first day of the Allies meeting at the Paris Peace Conference. Evan had obtained a job working for George A Riddell…. (later Lord Riddell) in Paris on the staff of the Foreign Press Bureau.

[201] Bodley, Ronald Victor Courtenay. *Indiscretions of a Young Man*. H Shaylor. (1931)

[202] List of Etonians Who Fought in the Great War MCMXIV- MCMXIX. This book can be downloaded from the Internet Archive web site. The list was compiled by E L Vaughan and Graily Hewitt and contains details of the 5650 Etonians who served in WW1 ; 1999 honours; 1157 killed; 1467 wounded.

[203] Frances Stevenson (1888-1972) was the mistress, personal secretary, confidante and second wife of David Lloyd George (1863-1945), British Prime Minister 1916-1922.

[204] Letter held in the Frances Stevenson Collection by the Parliamentary Archives

[205] Ibid.

[206] Diary of Frances Stevenson for 22nd July 1919 (Held in Parliamentary Archives)

[207] Evan's "affairs of the heart " are noted by Virginia Woolf in her diary for 9th March 1918 " *We had tea at the 17 Club. One room was crowded, & silent; at the end of the other Aldous Huxley & a young woman in grey velvet held what should have been a private conversation… They were discussing Evan Morgan & his affairs of the heart"*. Evan's marriage proposal to Stevenson is also commented upon by Augustus John.

[208] Hotels on the South coast of England like *The Knowle* were the haunt of titled dowagers and rich invalids during the First World War who because of the

conflict were unable to seek refuge and improvement in the South of France. *The Kwowle's* advertisements featured in the press made claims about it being *"high, grandest position on the South Coast , very sheltered, with sea views, good cuisine, wines and attendance, with rooms furnished by Maple & Co. "*.

"Sidmouth, with its striking red cliffs was always a select Regency resort, its railway, opened in 1874, was situated a mile from the esplanade to deter the riff-raff""

[209] Poem entitled *Hexameters.* Sidmouth October 25th, 1917.

[210] Letter in Parliamentary Archives from Evan (at Northgate House, Rottingdean, Sussex) to Frances Stevenson. In Stevenson's own typed notes she records *"The Hon Evan Morgan ..aspires to a position of literary adviser to the Government held under the Asquith regime by Mr E Marsh"* [i.e. Sir Edward Marsh (1872-1953) Private secretary to a number of cabinet Ministers and arts patron, sponsor of Rupert Brooke and Siegfried Sassoon . A homosexual and also a friend of Evan]

[211] One history of The Knowle (See Notes and Queries 5 Feb 1921) says : " *Later on, at any rate, the aviaries and the small collection of" animals and the .sub-tropical plants were well known.."*

[212] Letter in Parliamentary Archives from Evan (at Knowle Hotel, Sidmouth 27th October 1917) to Frances Stevenson.

[213] Letter in Parliamentary Archives from Evan (at Northgate House, Rottingdean, Sussex) to Frances Stevenson.

[214] *The Times*, 2nd March 1918.

[215] The Parliamentary Archives (aka Portcullis Archives) holds copies of at least four telegrams sent by Evan to Frances as *"Miss Stevenson -Private Secretary Prime Minister - 10 Downing Street – London. "*

[216] The late American writer Gore Vidal refers to aspects of Evan's later life in a book on Truman Capote by George Plimpton. He covers the proud possession by Evan of a huge diplomatic dossier bag. *"Evan had a papal passport and a big attache case with the Tredegar coat of arms, more elaborate than the Queen of England's."* NB One of Evan's document bags is in the Tredegar House Collection.

[217] *The Times*,3rd March 1918.

[218] Huxley Aldous. *Letters of Aldous Huxley* Edited by Grover Cleveland Smith Harper & Row (1970).

[219] Stevenson Frances. *The Years That Are Past*. Hutchinson. (1967).

[220] Sir Osmond Thomas Grattan Esmonde (1896-1936) An Irish politician.

[221] A letter dated 25th June 1917 in Evan's file in Tredegar House shows Evan replied to Cyril Hartmann " *..let us turn to other topics, Esmond(e) ......for instance..What you have written to me, about his feelings for myself, quite naturally pleases, and in so far as he is concerned your intelligence on the matter shall be kept hidden from him."* However this relationship progressed, Evan and Esmonde did see each other regularly. There are photographs of Evan, Esmonde and a young Lois Sturt together in the Lady Ottoline Morrell's albums in the National Portrait gallery website.

[222] Benkovitz, Miriam J. *More About Ronald Firbank*. Columbia University Library Columns Volumes 2406 (1974).

[223] Introduction to *Vainglory* by Richard Canning.

[224] This account of Firbank by Evan (and Nina Hamnett and Duncan Grant) was prepared at the request of the ballet critic Richard (Dicky) Buckle (1916-2001) who was collecting material for a book on Firbank. See Buckle, Richard : *The Most Upsetting Woman*. Collins(*1981*). See also Benkovitz Miriam J. *A Bibliography of Ronald Firbank*. Rupert Hart-Davis (1963).

[225] Shakespeare Nicholas. *Bruce Chatwin : A Biography*. Nan A Talese (1999).

[226] Benkovitz Miriam. Ronald Firbank. A biography. Knopf (1969)

[227] Ibid.

[228] Ibid.

[229] Benkovitz Miriam J. *A Bibliography of Ronald Firbank*. Rupert Hart-Davis (1963)

[230] Ibid.

[231] Ibid.

[232] Horder Mervyn. *Ronald Firbank: Memoirs and Critques*. Duckworth. (1977)

[233] Ifan Kyrle Fletcher, (1905-1969) author, theatre and dance historian.

[234] Fletcher, Ifan Kyrle. *Ronald Firbank*. A Memoir (1930)

[235] Some interesting comments are to be found on this in Quennell. Peter . *The Wanton Chase. An autobiography from 1939*. Collins. 1980. pages 120-3 which also includes a very good description of the characters who frequented the Eiffel Tower restaurant.

[236] In a letter to Richard Buckle in 1941 (an extract of which appears in Miriam Benkovitz's *Bibliography of Ronald Firbank*) Evan claims that he was being considered for the post of *"equerry to Lord Aberdeen, then [1921] Viceroy of Ireland"*. [In fact Lord Aberdeen was Viceroy only until 1915].

[237] In Godfrey, Rupert [Ed]. *Letters from a Prince. Edward, Prince of Wales to Mrs Freda Dudley Ward, March 1918 – January 1921*. Little, Brown & Company (1998) the company is described by HRH as *"the huge, boring"* house party in Cardiff.

[238] Lois's time as a flirt *" behaving disgustingly with the King of Spain"* [is recorded by Frances Stevenson in *If Love Were All*] Other contemporaries including Lady Diana Duff Cooper cite her [see *A Durable Fire*) as linked to taking part in *" an orgy that would have made Nero and Caligula turn in their graves with envy"* and as Prince Edward's lover and enjoying a fling with his brother Prince George, the bisexual Duke of Kent, the fourth son of King George V who was killed in 1942. Royal Biographer Sarah Bradford makes a direct link between Lois and Prince George *" interested in women; among his* [Prince George's] *mistresses were the black singer Florence Mills and a string of society girls, notably Lois Sturt and Poppy Baring. ..."* [Biography of Queen Elizabeth (1994).]

[239] Murray, Nicholas. *Aldous Huxley*. Hachette UK (2009).

[240] In a letter dated 22nd August 1919 in the Tredegar House files from Evan (writing from 48 Grosvenor Street) to Cyril Hartmann, Evan says " *..the rumours you have heard about my travels are in each and every way correct. It was first suggested that I go to Switzerland into a sanatorium, but after a consultation with two eminent London physicians it was decided it would be better for me to go to Colorado, on which ranch I propose spending the whole of this winter.."*

[241] Rev Charles Williamson was the only son of Evan's great aunt Selina Morgan and Colonel David Williamson of Lawers, Perthshire. He was a contemporary and life long friend of courtier Reginald Brett, (2nd Viscount Esher). Chat (his

name at Eton) became a Catholic priest and later lived for many years in a homosexual relationship, in exile in Italy. On his father's death he joined his mother in Scotland and was a parish priest for many years there until his death in 1943.

[242] Huxley suffered blindness in his mid-teens and was a manic depressive, a condition only later controlled by experimenting with narcotics. But he later went on to read English Literature at Oxford. He became a highly successful writer and guru.

[243] Huxley uplifted Ottoline Morrell's personality and mannerisms for the character of Mrs Bidlake in his book *Point Counter Point*. Ottoline could and did hit back at those who made fun of her. Of Huxley, she said he was always " *lacking in the imagination of the heart".*

[244] Huxley also worked sometime as a land labourer at Garsington. He was declared medically unfit to serve in the military. He met his wife (a Belguin refugee) Maria Nys during this time, notwithstanding that Huxley then and later had an infatuation for Nancy Cunard.

[245] Huxley, Aldous. *Letters of Aldous Huxley* Edited by Grover Cleveland Smith Harper & Row (1970).

[246] Ibid.

[247] Raffel, Burton :Possum and Ole Ez in the public eye: contemporaries and peers on TS Eliot and Ezra Pound, 1892-1972. Archon Books. (1985). p.7 " *I [Huxley] was whisked to lunch with Lady Tredegar.....*"

[248] Huxley, Aldous. *Letters of Aldous Huxley*. Harper & Row (1970)

[249] Ibid.

[250] This remark is attributed to the Aga Khan by Cyril Connolly in Horizon: a review of literature and art . Volumes 7-8 page 412 (1943).

[251] *South Wales Argus*, 22 May 1920.

[252] Ibid.

[253] See *Daily Mail* 19th May 1920. NB A letter in the correspondence file at Tredegar House between Evan and Cyril Hartmann make this clear.

[254] See *The Daily Mirror* 30th May 1929.

[255] Ibid.

[256] Attendants to the Pope "*known as Papal Chamberlains (Cameriere di spada e cappa). Many were from families that had long served the Papal Court over the course of several centuries, while others were appointed as a high honour, one of the highest the Papacy conferred on Catholic laymen (often prominent politicians or wealthy philanthropists)."*

[257] Pope Benedict was Pope 1914-1922 ; Pope Pius XI was Pope 1922-1939.

[258] *South Wales Argus*, 28th April 1949.

[259] Monty Dart and Will Cross visited The Vatican Secret Archives, in Rome on 11 May 2009. They were guests of Father Marcel Chappin, the Vice Prefect of the Archives. Father Chappin's staff provided copies of the various historical documents in the Archives relating to Evan Morgan's application for Papal Chamberlain.

[260] Catherine Mann (1896 -1959), the Marchioness of Queensbury, was an artist as well as costume designer. Her picture of Evan in Papal costume is in Tredegar House. Gossip (by Andrew Barrow) reports [circa 1923] *"The Machioness of Queensbury was driving herself to Rome in a two-seater sports car. During the*

journey, the car lost its horn and left mudguard and the Marchioness, a former Gaiety Girl, ran out of money and had to live on buns."

[261] E-mail from Father Marcel Chappin, to Will Cross, 2009.

[262] Viscount Campden was Arthur Edward Joseph Noel, later 4th Earl of Gainsborough (1884-1927); Mr W Kerr was Captain William Walter Raleigh Kerr (1863-1942)[The Kerr family are related to Marquis' of Lothians]. *"Mr Johnson"* must be Mgr H J T Johnson (1890-1958), latterly Chaplain to Roman Catholics at Women's colleges at Cambridge.

[263] Copy of this document is held by Monty Dart and Will Cross, provided by Father Marcel Chappin. Later in 1923 Evan arranged for Vatican passes for his cousin Charles Carnegie and his new wife, Princess Maud to see the treasures of the Vatican during the part of their honeymoon they spent in Rome. A copy of the passes was seen by Monty Dart and Will Cross at Kinnard Castle, Brechin, the home of the Carnegie family.

[264] Cardinal Gasquet was Francis Aidan, (1846-1929). He was created a Cardinal in 1914. He was also Archivist of the Vatican Secret Archives, and Librarian of the Vatican Library. During the visit to the Vatican Secret Archives Father Chappin acknowledged that Gasquet was one of his predecessors. A check of the records to see if Cardinal Gasquet's diaries were held, found nothing. During the visit to Rome by Monty and Will, the Cardinal's Palace was visited at 38 Piazza Sanata Maria in Trastevere / Palazzodi San Callisto.

[265] Sir John Randolph Leslie, 3rd Baronet (1885- 1971) Known as Shane. Irish born diplomat and writer. The family home is Castle Monaghan. Related to Winston Churchill through his mother. Evan spent time at Castle Monaghan. It was one of the sanctuaries he chose to retreat to during his last illness. Shane's second son Desmond (1921-2001) was Evan's godson. Desmond's memories of Evan and Tredegar House are held in a file at Tredegar House.

[266] Leslie, Shane: *Gasquet : A memoir.* Burns Oates (1953) Extract is from page 259.

[267] Ibid.

[268] Leslie, Shane. *Long Shadows.* Murray (1966).

[269] Beda College was founded in 1852 to form older men, often convert clergymen, for Catholic priesthood. *"First situated in 67, Via San Niccolo da Tolentino near the Piazza Barberini and then from 1960 a new College was built on land near St Pauls: Outside the Walls."* Address : Pontificio Collegio Beda Viale San Paolo, 18 00146 Roma – ITALIA.

[270] Horace K Mann (1859-1928) A Londoner. Rector of Beda College from 1917 onwards. Priest and Historian. Ordained in 1886, taught for several years at Saint Cuthbert's Grammar School, Newcastle-on-Tyne, and was headmaster from 1890 till 1917. From there became Rector at Beda.

[271] Paul Busby on BBC Radio Wales.

[272] E-mail from SO to Will Cross 2010

[273] Boyle, Andrew : *Poor, dear Brendan: the quest for Brendan Bracken.* Hutchinson (1974).

[274] Randall Sir Alec. *Vatican Assignment.* Heinemann (1956)

[275] The present Rector of Beda College did not see Will Cross and Monty Dart at the visit, but his female secretary (an American with an Italian family background with whom Will had exchanged various e-mails ahead of going to Rome) was charming and accompanied Will and Monty on a (pre-planned)

tour of the premises, including some diversions into the Chapel, classrooms, refectory, with a quick shunt into the gardens and a clear indication that there was no point in us looking for any further information about Evan's time at Beda.

[276] Boyle, Andrew : *Poor, dear Brendan: the quest for Brendan Bracken*. Hutchinson (1974).

[277] Held by the National Library of Wales, Aberystwyth. Augustus John Papers.

[278] Cecil Roberts (1892-1976) Author and Journalist. See in particular *The Bright Twenties*, Hodder & Stoughton (1974) (third volume of autobiography) which has an extended narrative on how Roberts first met Evan and contains a long biographical sketch on him (Highly Recommended). Also fourth volume of Roberts' life story, *Sunshine and Shadow*, which covers 1930-1946.

[279] http://carrietomko.blogspot.co.uk/2008/09/birth-control-commission-turning-point_30.html See the works of Randy Engel including a series of books entitled *The Rite of Sodomy*.

[280] *Some Aspects of Mysticism in Verse* was delivered at the Royal Society of Literature on 28th November 1928 and *John Donne – Lover and Priest* was delivered at the Royal Society of Literature on 29th October 1935. He also delivered the first Tredegar Memorial Lecture on Donne at the Royal Society of Literature on 29th January 1936.

[281] Culled from various Irish Newspapers November 1930 notably *The Irish Times*.

[282] Ibid.

[283] Father Marcel Chappin, Vice Prefect of the Vatican Secret Archives doubted this would have ever happened, in particular as Evan was not even confirmed as a chamberlain until after Pius was Pope.

[284] Ibid.

[285] Ibid. Charles Henry Bewley (1888-1969) (Irish Minister to Holy See 1929, later Berlin. He died in Rome where he became exiled).

[286] See Gogarty, Oliver St John. *The Renvyle letters: Gogarty family correspondence, 1939-1957.* Daletta Press. (2000).

[287] Leonard Alfred George Strong (1896-1958).

[288] Strong, L A G. *Green Memory*. Methuen & Co Ltd London (1961).

[289] Ibid.

[290] Alfred Noyes (1880-1958) Poet, best known for his ballad *The Highwayman*.

[291] Beaton, Cecil, and Richard Buckle *: Self portrait with friends : the selected diaries of Cecil Beaton, 1926-1974.* Times Books (1979).

[292] Letter dated 26 October 1922nd from Evan at 48 Grosvenor Street, London to William Bridgeman. See the *Bridgeman Papers* in Shropshire Archives Ref 4629/1/1922/141/1

[293] Lloyd George held a dinner in Wales, at which Evan was present in December 1922. Lloyd George was Prime Minister from 7th December 1916 until 22nd October 1922 – therefore this is after he resigned - because of a knighthoods and peerages scandal. Had Lloyd George continued in power Evan might have been one of the people for whom he had things planned, despite Evan and his family being Tories and Unionists.

[294] Augustus John Collection, National Library of Wales, Aberystwyth.

[295] Brian Howard (1905-1958) , a homosexual, poet, and socialite,

[296] Lancaster, Marie-Jaqueline Brian Howard : *Portrait of a Failure*. Timewell Press (2005). Howard was a consumptive who drank heavily, had a short fuse and committed suicide.

[297] Hartmann, Cecil. Unpublished Memoirs p.177.

[298] See Boulestin, Marcel. *Ease and Endurance*. Home & Van Thal Ltd (1948).

[299] Lady Gladys Mary Juliet Duff (nee Lowther) (1881-1965). Daughter of the 4th Earl of Lonsdale, married Sir Robert Duff, who was killed at Mons in the Great War. Lady Juliet was a notable Society figure. Friend of Cecil Beaton. One text says she " *lunched, dined and travelled with her wide circle of friends and acquaintances ….* "

[300] Sidney Fairbairn, (1892-1943) cricketer. Guards officer awarded the Military Cross died on active service in Second World War.

[301] Fielding, Daphne :*Emerald and Nancy : Lady Cunard and her daughter*. Eyre & Spottiswode (1968). Another version of this is in Anne Chisholm's biography of Nancy published by Penguin (1981). p61.

[302] One of these affairs was when Nancy fell madly in love with a soldier Captain Peter Broughton-Adderley (1891-1918) whom she met through Sidney Fairbairn. She was inconsolable at Peter's death in action a few weeks before the Armistace.

[303] The papers are held in National Archives, Kew under J77/2141/7055. Wife's petition for divorce in 1924.

[304] Between 1820 and 1832 buildings were erected around what became Tredegar Square, Bow. A pub here is named after the firs Lord Tredegar, a square and a street named Morgan Street. A nursing training college (Tredegar House) was also opened as a part of the London Hospital.

[305] Augustus John Collection, National Library of Wales, Aberystwyth.

[306] Rose Hoare (daughter of Charles & Hon. Blanche Hoare) (Mrs G Clayton) died 1st April 1927 in a car accident. *"Well known in Society and in sporting world and lived in a flat in Queen St Mayfair.) "*

[307] Fothergill John. *An Inkeeper's Diary*. Penguin Books edition (1931).p 136.

[308] Fothergill John. *An Inkeeper's Diary*. Penguin Books edition (1931). p.244.

[309] See *Daily Express*, 25th October 1927.

[310] *The Times* Circular from the 1920s and 1930s records Evan in the company of several personalities in literary fields (eg staying with Somerset Maugham), giving talks and poetry reading (eg with Shane Leslie, Harold Nicholson) including some broadcasting on radio of his poetry.

[311] See *The Times* 19 February, 16th, 19th, and 30th March and 4th April 1928.

[312] *The Times*, 4 April 1928. " *The Prince [of Wales] was given a rousing cheer before he took his seat in the middle of the front row. On one side of him were the Mayor and Mayoress of Stepney and on his other the Hon Evan Morgan and Hon Lois Sturt".*

[313] Held by the National Library of Wales, Aberystwyth. The Lois Sturt Collection includes some appointment/engagement diaries, books of verse, photographs and several hundred love letters sent 1920-5 by Reggie Pembroke, 15th Earl of Pembroke and Montgomery.

[314] Lois started to carve a name for herself during 1921 and 1922 in Carillon de Minuit, Le - a film directed by Jacques de Baroncelli in which Lois played a character called Laura. There was the release in April of her movie 'The Glorious Adventure' - in which Lois played Nell Gwynn, also 'Amour' – although Lois' character is un-named. She appeared that month too on 'Picture

Show' magazine – Lois Sturt on its front page cover. To crown this she also appeared on the cover of the Cinemagazine in May 1923.

[315] Lewis, Wyndham. *Blasting & Bombardiering*. University of California Press (1967).

[316] *Chasing Clues* was a sort of *"treasure-hunt"* amongst the Bright Young Things, whizzing around London and surrounds in their motor cars, often lasting all through the night. The antics were often fuelled on alcohol and drugs.

[317] In 1926 Lois knocked down and killed a pedestrian, Arthur George Lewis whilst driving in Regent Street – she was doing OMS Work. To her relief the verdict was Accidental Death.

[318] Cartland, Barbara. *We Danced All Night.* Arrow Books (1973)

[319] On 17 February 1928 The Times announced " *Forthcoming Marriages : The Hon Evan Morgan and Hon Lois Sturt. The marriage arranged between the Hon Evan Morgan, son of Viscount Tredegar CBE and Viscountess Tredegar and the Hon Lois Sturt daughter of Lady Alington will take place on April 21 at Brompton Oratory*"

[320] Ruby Miller (1889-1976). Gaiety girl. See Miller Ruby. *Believe me or not!* J Long (1933).

[321] Ibid.

[322] The ceremony for this took place in London at the Church of the Immaculate Conception, Farm Street, conducted by Father Martindale.

[323] The two best men were Count John de Salis and Henry Drummond Wolff. Count de- Salis (1891-1949) was the son of a Vatican diplomat. Irish Guardman. After Great war he became assistant attaché in Paris and in 1920 was posted in the diplomatic service to Washington. Henry Drummond Wolff (1899-1982) was a grandson of Sir Henry Drummond Wolff a founder of the Primrose League. He travelled extensively best known as a Tory politician. His death notice appears in *The Times* of 8 February 1982. Both men were to be found at Evan's Tredegar House weekends.

[324] Teeling, William. *Corridors of Frustration*. Johnson (1970)

[325] See Rose Francis Sir. *Saying life. The Memoirs of Sir Francis Rose*. Cassell. (1961).

[326] Based on remarks made to the authors by David Freeman, former curator of Tredegar House.

[327] *Lethbridge Herald*, 15 October 1929.

[328] Christabel Mary Melville MacNaghten (1890-1974). From a notable Irish family. Her obituary in *The Times* of 17 August 1974 has some wonderful nuggets " *For the unconventional her sympathy was innate. In the 1890s she horrified Nanny by smiling at Oscar Wilde from her pram*."

[329] See Aberconway, Christabel McLaren, Lady. *A wiser woman? A book of memories*. Hutchinson (1966). One story relates to Evan asking to borrow Christabel's dining room for a meeting of the Catholic Poetry Society, with guest of honour Lord Alfred Douglas. Christabel snubbed Douglas as *"he behaved abominably to Oscar Wilde..*

[330] This quote is attributed to Evan by Cyril Connolly.

[331] Like Evan, Naps was a sexual predator, an international playboy with good looks he had a taste for both sexes. He had a passionate fling with the American actress, Tallulah Bankhead and they shared male lovers. Another source says " *Naps knew all the "boys" – tinker, tailor, soldier, spy...as well the sailors and*

stewards on board the ships on crossings to New York and the Channel ship and train journeys to the South of France and Italy."

[332] In March 1928 Lois and her brother Naps (Napier Sturt, 3rd Lord Alington (1896-1940) stood as the Municipal Reform Party candidates (a local party allied to the Parliamentary Conservative Party to aim to represent the Shoreditch division of the London County Council. The Alingtons were large landowner in nearby Hoxton. On 8 March the votes were declared- Labour and Liberal were in the top two with over 5000 votes each - the votes were otherwise Lois 2776 and Naps 2725.

[333] See *Daily Express*, 9 April 1928. Evan wrote a long letter (from his London home at Queens Gate) to the Daily Express including photographs about " *atrocities committed against Roman Catholics in Mexico*" pleading for the British Press to cover the story and expose a conspiracy of silence.

[334] English Aristocrats Gather to Raise Fund for London Talmud Torahs Jewish Telegraphic Agency 9 May 1929.

[335] Ibid.

[336] Ibid.

[337] Ibid.

[338] Antony Bulwer-Lytton, Viscount Knebworth, (1903-1933) son of the Earl of Lytton. " *a dashing athletic pilot of the heroic mould*" who was killed when his plane crashed at Hendon in 1933. He contested Shoreditch in the 1929 General Election.

[339] One of the boxing centres frequented by Evan and his friend Prince Paul of Greece was the Stadium Club, Limehouse. See *Daily Mirror*, 22 April 1929.

[340] Captain Napier George Henry Sturt, (1896-1940) 3rd Baron Alington of Crichel). Known as Naps. Succeeded his elder brother Gerard, who died of war wounds in 1918. Naps was in the RAF in the Great War and serving in Egypt in the second World War when he died of pneumonia. His wife predeceased him and there was one daughter, Hon. Mary Sturt, later Mrs Toby Marten. Mary died in 2010.

[341] See Rose Francis Sir. *Saying life. The Memoirs of Sir Francis Rose*. Cassell. (1961).

[342] William Teeling (1903-1975) who was a young Irish Tory fighting an election in London's East End and later saw Evan in Germany in the 1930s reflects on this period in his Memoirs *Corridors of Frustration*. Johnson (1970). He also infers that the Morgans were the area's slum landlords. " *far and away the most active of us all was Evan Morgan who had tremendous courage in taking on the constituency of Limehouse, especially as his father, Lord Tredegar, owned most of the slum property there*."

[343] Results of voting on Stepney Limehouse (1929) C Attlee (Labour) 13872; E Morgan (Conservative) 6564; J J Addis (Liberal) 4116; W Tapsell (Communist) 245. One of Attlee's biographers records "*In Limehouse Attlee survived a four-cornered contest without great difficulty*."

[344] See *The Times*, 13 October 1931 Evan Morgan steps down as Unionist candidate for Cardiff in order to avoid a split of the National Party vote supporting Sir Ernest Bennett. Stanley Baldwin asked Evan to withdraw by letter.

[345] Letter in the Tredegar House Archives from Henry Maxwell to David Beevers (Assistant Curator at Tredegar House) dated 9 February 1979.

[346] See *The Times*, 17 August 1929 : Evan goes to Canada from Liverpool on the liner *Duchess of Bedford* for the Empire Parliamentary Association. The item says he will not return until early October.

[347] See *Daily Express*, 17 August 1929.

[348] Letter in the Tredegar House Archives from Henry Maxwell to David Beevers (Assistant Curator at Tredegar House) dated 9 February 1979.

[349] See *The Times*, Court Circular 22 February, 15 April and 9 December 1930.

[350] See Richard Shead's biography of the composer/ conductor Constant Lambert (1905-1951). Simon Publications (1973). This refers to the Peter Warlock Memorial Concert at the Wigmore Hall, London on 22 February 1931. Evan was among the financial backers, with Lambert acting at conductor.

[351] A book on Evan is announced by Paul Busby, *The Peculiar Career of Lord Tredegar*, (due April 2013). The book is expected to present evidence of Evan's secret links with Nazi Germany and with members of Hitler's inner circle.

[352] See *The Times*, Circular 8 February 1932.

[353] See *Daily Express*, 27 May 1933. There was bathing group photographs among the Lois Sturt Collection in the National Library of Wales.

[354] Edward George Boulenger (1888-1946) a British zoologist.

[355] The full quote is *"Lois Sturt and her lover, a hideous bald headed man, Capt. Fellows or Freeman?"* and comes from Carrington, Dora de Houghton and Garnett David. *Carrington : letters and extracts from her diaries.* Art. (1971)

[356] E G Boulenger was a leading curator in the Reptile House at London Zoo. Cyril Connolly observes in his memoirs about the latter that Lois was *"always accompanied by a zoological friend"*, Augustus John makes a similar remark in his memoirs . Both these men friends of Lois are listed as among the mourners at Crichel House(the Alington family home in Dorset) after Lois died . They were also beneficiaries under her Will. Freeland was left £500 and *" any personal object of mine which he may wish to select"* whilst Boulenger was given options over her residence of *Mumpumps.* Lois also left substantial items to her niece Hon. Mary Sturt (only daughter of Naps).

[357] Pryce-Jones, Alan. *The Bonus of laughter.* Hamilton (1987)

[358] Ibid.

[359] See *Daily Mirror*, Personality Parade, 16 November 1936 page 11 and 13 July, 1937, page 9.

[360] Winn, Godfrey. *The Infirm Glory.* Volume 1. Joseph (1967).

[361] Maurice Leahy: born in County Kerry, Ireland, 1900.

[362] Francis Alphonsus Bourne, Cardinal Bourne (1861-1935) Archbishop of Westminster from 1903 until his death.

[363] One possible reason the divorce proceedings were left in limbo is that Lois got cold feet about Evan contesting her charges, especially if this was going to lead to unwelcome newspaper coverage against Lois. A heavy headlined divorce case involving the dancer Tilly Losch and her husband, the homosexual artist/ poet Edward James in 1934 had precisely that effect leaving Tilly humiliated after asserting James was more interested in young men on their honeymoon than in his wife.

[364] National Archives, Kew File Ref J77/3117/5878. Appellant: The Hon. Lois Morgan. Respondent. The Hon. Evan Frederick Morgan. Wife's petition for divorce. Evan cites as co-respondents EG Boulenger and A Freeland.

[365] See Glendinning Victoria : *Vita : the life of Vita Sackville-West*. Quill (1985) p88 " *lunched at this time with Lady Tredegar in Grosvenor Square 'She did not mince matters about her husband living openly with a woman at the Ritz' "*

[366] *Daily Mirror*, 4 May 1934. Courtenay died of bronchial pneumonia at the Ritz Hotel, London (after recently travelling back from a health trip to Australia).

[367] Von Stutterheim Kurt. *The two Germanys*. Sidgwick & Jackson. (1939)

[368] Fully reported by *The Times* on 29 May 1935.

[369] A similar Bill on Spring (Gin) Traps was introduced in 1951 by Lord Elton, but it was two further years before the measure came into law as a part of the Pests Act of 1954.

[370] Some uncorroborated information suggests Evan or the Estate Manager (acting for Evan) may have discontinued other utility supplies to some tenants.

[371] The Advert for sale included this " *Ruperra Castle near the coast between Cardiff and Newport was restored in 1780, and it has been residentially modernised. The trustees of the Tredegar Settled Estates have instructed Ms Knight, Frank and Rutley to sell it with 870 acres or over 3,000 acres according to buyer's wishes.*"

[372] Pat Jones-Jenkins has published several books (as Pat Moseley) about Ruperra's history. This work has been undertaken from interviews and diaries including *Ruperra Castle War and Flames 1939-46* and (with Chris Jones-Jenkins) *Serving Under Ruperra, 1900-1939.*

[373] Transcript of an interview with Mary Thomas by Pat Jones-Jenkins.

[374] Ibid.

[375] Ibid.

[376] Jones-Jenkins, Pat. and Jones-Jenkins, Chris. *Serving Under Ruperra. 1900-1939. Tower Printing.*

[377] Philips Roger. *Tredegar: The history of an agricultural estate 1300-1956.* Self Publishing Association (1990).

[378] Memories of Noel Stevens (1979). Letter in Tredegar House files.

[379] Ibid.

[380] Ibid.

[381] Passenger Lists : Board of Trade : *Evan Tredegar aged 41 – Southampton to New York. Giving the address Berkeley Square there were two other people giving this address - Henry Ware aged 39 'Theatrical' and Alfred Locker – Valet aged 16.* [Ware is later transformed into " Captain" Harry Ware.]

[382] According to a note in the Tredegar House files Evan " *went to Switzerland c 1937 after breakdown*".

[383] See The Robert Stradling Collection in the University of Limerick P/13, item 58 for a " *letter from Welsh landowner, Evan Morgan, Lord Tredegar, to Louis (alias Fleur), as he made his way to the Canary Islands referring to his travelling companions on board the SS Alondra as the vanguard of General O'Duffy's Greenshirts' and stating...some of these gentlemen were by no means easy in their minds respecting the adventure into Spain. They had just received orders to go, so they went. Some had thrown up a good job. One of the youngest, a certain Connolly had had to leave a £12 a week job at the Ford car place at Dagenham... Connolly was endeavouring to work himself up to a blood thirsty mood by studying*

the poems of Thomas Davis…This was a fine young fellow, far too good to be wasted on that affair…."

[384] An assertion is made that Lois's death was drug-related, including her suffering a reaction to a increasing dependence on slimming aids and other pills. Henry Maxwell says in a letter to David Beevers (in 1979) *" I don't think there was any great mystery about her [Lois'] death. She had undertaken a severe slimming course, when her heart was very weak, and as usual pushing it be excess, eating nothing at all, taking very strong drugs for reducing and living it up at the same time.."*

[385] See letter in the Tredegar Archives from Henry Maxwell to David Beevers (Assistant Curator Tredegar House) dated 9 February 1979.

[386] See *The Times*, 27 September 1937. According to David Freeman, the former Curator of Tredegar House, the rose garden at Crichel was removed in the 1960s. David is proud to have been associated to Tredegar House in its *" heyday in the 1970s…when there was over 20 full time staff"*. He organised two trips to Crichel during his time as Curator. He was on good terms with the late Hon. Mary Marten (1929-2010) (daughter of Naps Alington) and her husband Toby (died 1997).

[387] Lois' brother Naps and Captain Alex "Tim" Freeland were her joint executors. Lois left estate worth £31,861. 10s 7d.

[388] Extracted from *A Branch of the Stewarts* by Alan Stewart. 2nd Edition.

[389] Alan's first wife Margaret Guest died in 1983. He remarried in 1984, Zoe Seager, daughter of Lord Leighton of Cardiff.

[390] Interview with Alan Carnegie Stewart, 2009 (Scotland).

[391] Letter in the Tredegar House Archives from Henry Maxwell to David Beevers (Assistant Curator at Tredegar House) dated 9 February 1979.

[392] Pryce-Jones Alan. *The Bonus of Laughter*. Hamish Hamilton (1987).

[393] Ibid.

[394] Marsh Edward and Hassall, Christopher: *Ambrosia and Small Beer.* Longmans. (1964). Edward " Eddie" Marsh (1872-1953) Private secretary to Winston Churchill and patron of the arts and artists (including Rupert Brooke).

[395] Marchesa Luisa Casati (1881-1957) From *Ambrosia and Small Beer* p57-8

"…..She must be well over 70.. Her eyes, if they were ever seen, would…be neither sweet nor subtle – but this point can't be cleared up, as they are surrounded with thick black rings of coal dust, like bits of glass bordered with lead in a cathedral window. On her head is a Burning Bush of scarlet hair…"

[396] Lady Christabel Aberconway relates a story in her memoirs *A Wiser Woman* about the Marchesa. *" I remember she [Marchesa] once arrived at Tredegar Park in a taxi from London so the driver had to be given the return fare as well as what the clock registered, but this caused no surprise to the butler nor to Evan. "*

[397] Naps Alington owned several works of art on Luisa as a subject, including a painting by Augustus John and a bust by Jacob Epstein.

[398] Ryersson Scot D and Yaccarino Michael Orlando. *Infinite Variety*. Random House. (2000)

[399] Ibid.

[400] Roberts Cecil. *Sunshine and Shadow*. Hodder & Stoughton Ltd (1974)

[401] Hartmann, Cecil. Unpublished Memoirs p.181.

[402] Those featured in the newspaper picture are Major B. Corbet, Mr Mackenson, Mrs Carnegie, the Countess of Carlisle, the Marchesa Godio-de-

Godieo, Mr H.G.Wells(novelist), Viscountess Massereene and Ferrard, Mrs Richard Guinness, Mr Derek Jackson (the Oxford Don gentleman-rider, who rode his own horse, Princess Mir, in the Grand National), Mrs Alan Pryce-Jones (a daughter of the First Lord of the Admiralty), Viscount Tredegar, Mr Alan Pryce-Jones, Lord Faringdon, Captain H. Ware and Colonel Mason.

[403] Roger Philips in his wonderful book *Tredegar: The history of an agricultural estate 1300-1956.* Self Publishing Association (1990) describes Ware : " *A Devon man, Major Ware got on very well with Evan Morgan, serving him first as private secretary and then, after the war, as his full-time agricultural agent"* Philips' description of Evan as " *A single man"* with an emphasis on his frequent absence from the Estate refers to the support given by Ware to Evan in respect of local duties on the Estate *"Major Ware became a very important local figure, especially as he was the permanent resident at Tredegar House!"* [NB This is the only reference to Ware as a Major, elsewhere he is referred to as Captain Ware]

[404] Sherman Charles Austin (III): *Memoirs of Another Time.* Authorhouse (2011)

[405] Desmond Leslie (1921-2001) youngest son of Sir Shane Leslie of Castle Leslie, County Monaghan, Ireland. Renowed for punching Bernard Levin on live TV. Leslie was an RAF pilot , a writer, musician and film maker. His correspondence with David Freeman in 1992 (about Evan) is in the Tredegar House files.

[406] According to Desmond Leslie " *Two people would be sent outside [the room] where they would have to think up outrageous scenes for the rest to act 'In the Manner of the Word', by their acting, or lack of it, they would have to guess what the 'word' was. "* . Desmond adds " *I remember Evan being asked to play Norman Hartnell giving a fitting to the Queen. HG Wells played the Queen! The word was " disgustingly".*

[407] Monsignor Ronald Knox (1888-1957) Author and Catholic scholar

[408] Letter in the Tredegar House Archives from Henry Maxwell to David Beevers (Assistant Curator at Tredegar House) dated 9 February 1979.

[409] Channon, Henry, Sir. Chips : *The Diaries of Sir Henry Channon.* Weidenfeld & Nicolson (1967).

[410] Agnes Rafaelle Kennedy (died 1993). Her second husband was Edward FitzGerald 7th Duke of Leinster. She was a close friend and confidante of Princess Maud Duff, (Countess of Southesk) wife of Evan's half-cousin, Charles Carnegie, 11th Earl of Southesk.

[411] Rafaelle, Duchess of Leinster. *So Brief a Dream.* W H Allen (1973).

[412] Ibid.

[413] Ibid.

[414] Hartmann, Cyril. Unpublished Memoirs. p 177.

[415] Memories of Noel Stevens (1978). Letter in Tredegar House files.

[416] Roberts Cecil. *Sunshine and Shadow.* Hodder & Stoughton Ltd (1974)

[417] Memories of Noel Stevens (1978). Letter in Tredegar House files.

[418] Low Rosemary. *A century of parrots.* Insignis. (2006). According to Low " *Blue Boy's end was sad and swift during World War II. He crawled up a broomstick and as he reached the top it started to topple over. He took a terrible blow on the head" and died of a haemorrhage."*

[419] See Winn, Godfrey. *The Infirm Glory.* Joseph (1967).

[420] See Pryce-Jones, Alan *The bonus of laughter,* Hamilton (1987).

[421] Interview with Alan Carnegie Stewart (born 1920) (Scotland 2009).

[422] David Southesk (Present Earl of Southesk) provided this memory from his father, James Carnegie, the Duke of Fife (born 1929).

[423] See Cecil Roberts' *The Bright Twenties*, Hodder & Stoughton (1974) pages 95-104. Roberts found Evan outside the Café Royal, ill (or drunk) and took him home to Grosvenor Square and put him safely to bed.

[424] Roberts Cecil. The Bright Twenties. Hodder & Stoughton (1974).

[425] Sherman Charles Austin (III): *Memoirs of Another Time*. Authorhouse (2011)

[426] Ibid.

[427] See Rose Francis Sir. *Saying life. The Memoirs of Sir Francis Rose*. Cassell. (1961).

[428] Despite the newspaper caption declaring that the wedding of Evan and Olga was to take place on their birthdays, each of them in fact had a different birthday and neither of them was on the wedding day!!!

[429] Olga was first married to a Polish man named M Trotsky-Seniutovich.

[430] A report of one house party at Tredegar House appears in the Daily Mirror of 13 December 1937. "*Also in the party are Mrs. Myrtle Farquharson....Lady Ailwyn and Princess Olga Dolgorouky. Lady Ailwyn and Princess Olga brought their dogs...*"

[431] See Evan's tax papers in National Archives, Kew, ref IR 40/9713 and IR 40/11982. Evan paid a £500 bond to secure Dasckow's US entry.

[432] See *Daily Express*, 21 November 1938. This paper also features a photograph of Evan and Olga drinking a toast when Evan presented tennis prizes in Newport.

[433] *Dunkirk Evening Standard*, 13 March 1939. NB A copy of this photograph is in Olga's bedroom at Tredegar House.

[434] A file is held in National Archives, Kew Ref CO273/652/7 relating to an enquiry between the Governor of the Straits Settlement and the Secretary of State for the Colonies and the Metropolitan Police in London over Olga's nationality.

[435] *The Gleaner*, 30 March 1939.

[436] Taken from a record in the Tredegar House file on Olga from a letter by E D Edwards.

[437] Tredegar House Archive Files. See Princess Olga's letters (in 1979) to David Beevers, Assistant Curator at Tredegar House.

[438] Evan's cousin Chat Williamson died on 20 January followed by the death of his beloved Aunt Nellie (Lady Helena Carnegie) on 24 January 1943.

[439] *The Times* of 21 July 1943 records " *In the Divorce Court yesterday Mr Justice Henn Collins granted Viscountess Tredegar, of Whitelands House, King's Road, Chelsea, formerly Princess Olga Dolgorouky, a decree nisi of nullity of marriage on the ground of the incapacity of Viscount Tredegar. The petition was undefended.*"

[440] See handwritten (3 page note) in Evan's file held at Tredegar House.

[441] Crowley's published diaries show that he arrived at Tredegar Park at Evan's request/invitation on June 17, 1943, and stayed for just over a week. He given the Oak Room which he declares was " *the best the house*"

[442] Augustus John drew many sketches of Aleister Crowley throughout his lifetime but probably his most famous was sent to Crowley in 1946 for the front piece in Crowley's last published book *Olla, The Anthology of Sixty Years of Song*.

[443] Cornelius J. *The Fringe Datebook*. www.scribd.com

[444] Fothergill John. *An Inkeeper's Diary*. Penguin Books (1931).

[445] Conway, David. *Magic Without Mirrors: The Making of a Magician*. Logios Publishing (2011),

[446] Ibid.

[447] Crowley Diaries 20 October 1943 *"Mrs Sutherland (Lord Tredegar's Secretary) rang up and came to tea. Talked finance & my relationship with Evan"*

[448] Montgomery- Massingberd, H, Watkin D and Collie, K. *The London Ritz : a social and architectural history*. Aurum (1980).

[449] See Lewis, Jeremy. *Cyril Connolly : A Life*. Random House (2012).

[450] Richard (Dicky) Buckle (1916- 2001) is described in Howgate & Stern's David Hockney Portraits as *" the flamboyant Observer and Sunday Times ballet critic, writer and designer"*…a mutual friend with Hockney of Cecil Beaton.

[451] Buckle Richard. *The adventures of a ballet critic*. Cresset Press (1953).

[452] Olga and Henry Maxwell both cite The 2nd Marshese Conte Anthony (Tony) Mattei (born 1902) (British born, from an old Maltese family) as a long standing friend of Evan. See Archives files in Tredegar House. There is a letter from Tony Mattei [dated Feb 14 1979, Mattei was then living at Hove] reflecting on the personalities in Tredegar House and Evan's London homes over the period from mid-late 1920s onwards.

[453] This crop of artists recalled by Tony Mattei included some iconic figures in the art world. *" I also remember Christopher Wood there & Derek Hill, then very young, also Epstein & F [Frank] Dodson the sculptors.."* [Letter to David Beevers, Assistant Curator Tredegar House dated Feb 14 1979]. NB Christopher Wood (1901-1930), is included in Sebastian Faulks' vivid narrative *The Fatal Englishman* Vintage Books (1997). Derek Hill (1916-2000); Frank Dobson (1888-1963).

[454] There are ties in between several gay men on the Paris and London scene linking in Evan during the late 1920s, including Christopher Wood's close friend and playboy, Tony Gandarillas who like Evan had been painted by Ambrose McEvoy.

[455] Robert Harbinson (1928-2009). He also wrote under the name of Robin Bryans.

[456] See Costello, John. *Mask of Treachery*. Collins (1988).

[457] Harbinson, Robert. *The Protégé*. The Blackstaff Press. (1988)

[458] Tony Mattei comments in letter in Tredegar Archives *" I seem to remember …..of all people Dr Marie Stopes. Both she and Evan fancied themselves as poets.."*

[459] Evan made representations to his old friend Brendan Bracken who was at the Ministry of Information and had Churchill's ear. However Douglas had previously libelled Churchill and Bracken (whom Evan had known socially through another aristocratic eccentric, Gavin Hamilton (later the second Lord Faringdon) in Rome and Mayfair haunts in the late 1920s) couldn't help.

[460] Waugh's diaries indicate his feeling was that *"considering Milton and Wordsworth I could not agree with the judgement and that anyway I thought Marie Stopes a preposterous person to propose it."*

[461] At the time of his Courtenay's death in April 1934 Evan was with Prince Paul of Greece (off Jamaica on board the yacht of the millionaire American businessman William B Leeds Jnr, the latter's mother was a member of the Greek Royal Family.). The Prince married in 1938 and became King of Greece in 1946. Prince Paul was staying at Tredegar House with Evan in April 1935. (

Source *Irish Times* 23 April 1935). See also reference in Edward Marsh's diary extract in Christopher Hassall's *Ambrosia and Small Beer*. Longmans (1964) to Prince Paul's discovery of a bronze bust by Polycleitus in Evan's possession (bought by Evan from a German after the War) which had once been in the National Museum in Athens.

[462] See Plimpton, George : *Truman Capote.* Pan Macmillan. (1999); See Friedman Mack. *Strapped for cash : a history of American hustler culture.* Alyson Books. (2003);

[463] Plimpton, George : *Truman Capote: In Which Various Friends, Enemies, Acquaintances, and Detractors Recall His Turbulent Care.* Pan Macmillan (1999). Smith, Tyler Stoddard : *Whore Stories : A Revealing History of the World's Oldest Profession. Adams Media (2012).*

[464] Denham Fouts (1914-1948). Born Louis Denham Fouts in Jacksonville, Florida, he died in Rome on 16 December 1948. He is buried in Rome's Protestant Cemetery.

[465] Alistair Hugh Graham (1904-) According to Peerage (Graham's grandfather was a baronet) Graham was Attache to Athens between 1927 and 1929 and Cairo between 1929 and 1933. 'Graham became a diplomat and adopted a gay life overseas. Waugh disapproved and turned his back on Graham, who he believed was following a "seedy, expatriate life".'
http://www.dailymail.co.uk/news/article-1206555/Brideshead-Revisited-author-Evelyn-Waugh-homosexual-affairs-Oxford.html#ixzz29MUTTukN

[466] Rosa Lewis (1867-1952) legendary hotelier and "Madame" (the inspiration for the TV series the Duchess of Duke St) providing " *nice young clean girls*" for the English gentry and American customers.

[467] Fielding Daphne: *The Duchess of Jermyn Street : The Life and Good Times of ROSA LEWIS of the Cavendish Hotel.* Futura Publications. (1976).

[468] A quote from Evelyn Waugh: A Literary Biography By John Howard Wilson ; The Cavendish was also the home of a great many theatricals (like Michael Redgrave) Graham was well connected - with family links to the aristocracy.

[469] See Fielding Daphne: *The Duchess of Jermyn Street : The Life and Good Times of ROSA LEWIS of the Cavendish Hotel.* Futura Publications (1976) Pages 104-108 refer sympathically to Rosa's affection for both Evan and Alistair, although there is no verification of the overlap between them or their removal from the Cavendish.

[470] Those mentioned in the Tredegar House files include Geoffrey Croysdale (1919-2007) who became a Buddhist Monk, named Venerable Zenco.
http://www.purelandnotes.com/rupainaug/statuespeech_2.htm

[471] Letter in the Tredegar House Archives from Henry Maxwell to David Beevers (Assistant Curator at Tredegar House) dated 9 February 1979.

[472] See Lowndes Marie Bellec and Lowndes Susan. Diaries and letters of Marie Belloc Lowndes, 1911-1847. Chatto & Windus. (1971)p273 entry for 22 September 1946 " *He [Evan] is toying with the thought of proposing to Lady Illingworth. He has just been staying with her..*" Lady Illingworth (who died in 1986) was a member of the Wilberforce (slavery) family and a one time neighbour of Evan in Grosvenor Square. She was an immensely rich widow and second wife of a Liberal politician.

[473] Both Cecil Roberts and Alan Pryce-Jones refer in their Memoirs to Evan's abhorrence of John Morgan (1908-1962) the last Lord Tredegar. Evan referred

to John as " Pinhead". Another source confides that Pryce-Jones (to went to Eton with John) also despised John Morgan and describes him and his family *"a rather silly boy, who had a sister Avis, and a father not subject like mine to occasional silesnces, but out of rancour, silent round the clock".* NB Avis Morgan (1903-1963), she divorced her husband, Peter Gurney in 1934. Gurney died in 1950 aged 47. A note in the Tredegar House files declares " *January 22, 1947 [Evan] rejects idea of handling over some of his estate to his cousin John Morgan"*
[474] Provided with thanks to the Archivist of Portculis the Parliamentary Archives, House of Lords, London.
[475] Walter Monckton (1891-1965). Eminent Lawyer and politician. Later a Viscount.
[476] See National Archives, Kew file WO 71/1078.
[477] *South Wales Argus*, 28 April 1949.
[478] *The Times*, April 28 1949. Speaking in Jamaica in 1946 Evan said he " *was rejected for active service in 1939". [Undaunted] he joined a special branch of the Royal Corps of Signals ...until an injury to his leg forced him to be content with The Home Guards."*
[479] Rupert William Simon Allason (1951-) (uses pen name of Nigel West: author/ writer/ journalist well known for his works on MI5 and MI6).
[480] See West Nigel. *MI5 : British Security Service Operations 1909-1945*. New edition HarperCollins (1983). p.204-5 " *Apparently the old Etonian Welshman had been somewhat indiscreet after lunching with Lady Baden-Powell and actually gave her a guided tour of his office as well as describing how he was engaged in the destruction of Nazi carrier pigeons. When word leaked of Tredegar's lapse he was taken into custody at the Tower [of London] but was released soon afterwards when MI5 intervened..".*
[481] Richard Kaczynski's *Perdurabo: The Life of Aleister Crowley* (revised) Berkeley: North Atlantic Books (2010) p507 repeats West's inaccurate narrative saying " *Tredegar was....imprisoned in the Tower of London for treason because he took his date to his office and divulged details of his work; ultimately MI5 intervened to arrange his release.."* [Evan was in fact held in Chelsea Barracks awaiting his Court Martial almost certainly without being incarcerated.] Richard B Spence's *Secret Agent 666 Aleister Crowley, British Intelligence and the Occult.* Feral House. (2008), p225 equally portrays a grossly incorrect narrative of MI5 intervention and a wholly unsubstantiated twist relating to Evan summoning Crowley " *to put a curse on the officer [who was involved in reporting Evan's alleged treason]....As the story goes, the officer fell deathly ill.."*
[482] Files in National Archives, Kew detail *every* movement of Hess whilst under arrest in Britain. He was guarded at all times, although was allowed some relief outside the prison. Files consulted in the FO, AIR. DEFE and CAB range on Hess have found no reference to him meeting with Evan whilst he was held prisoner during WW2.
[483] Phil Carradice investigates Evan Morgan's possible links with Nazis and Satanism. First broadcast on 2 January 2011. BBC Radio Wales Past Master Series produced by Geoff Ballinger.
[484] Rudolph Hess (1894-1987) became Hitler's deputy, but not until 1933. Ernst Rohm (1887-1934) – was head of Hitler's SA or Brownshirts - and his deputy Edmund Heines (1897-1934) were both gay. They were executed on orders from Hitler in the " *Night of the Long Knives*" in 1934.

[485] Francis Cyril Rose (1909-1979) Right wing artist. Rose lived in Germany 1932-4. he later served in the RAF in 1940.
http://www.englandgallery.com/artist_bio.php?mainId=164

[486] See Chapter Twelve of Rose's Memoirs for his affectionate, loving portrait of Rohm. When these Memoirs were published in 1961, homosexuality was illegal in Britain, which prevented Rose from making a full disclosure of his relationship. See Rose, Francis Sir. *Saying life. The Memoirs of Sir Francis Rose.* Cassell. (1961).

[487] According to a file in National Archives on Lonsdale-Bryans (KV 2/2839) 1939- 52, he came to the attention of the security services in 1939 through pro-German comments he made in Singapore. An old Etonian short of funds, he seems to have made his way in life by associating with powerful titled sympathisers. Curiously Evan was also in Singapore in 1939 (where he married his second wife, Princess Olga) but he is not cited in the file. Lonsdale-Bryans is described as " *a dilettante playboy*" adventurer and opportunist. He wrote two books (as John Lonsdale-Bryans) about his exploits in the Second World War working he says for Britain. These books are *The Curve of Fate* and *Blind victory.*

[488] *Saying life. The Memoirs of Sir Francis Rose*. Cassell. (1961).

[489] South Wales Argus reports of the wreaths at Buckfast Abbey " *There were seven floral tributes – a beautiful spray of coloured lilies and orchids, which rested on the coffin. And those from Lady Foster Steadman, The Garth, Bassaleg; Sir Francis and Lady Rose; the Estate Office staff, Newport; H W J Powell of 27 Charles Street, London; Lady Jean Bertie of 6 Charlotte Square, Edinburgh; Colonel R C L Thomas, Chairman and members of the Old Comrades Association, First Rifle Battalion, Monmouthshire Regiment."* NB Sir Francis and Lady Rose are listed as attendees at the Requiem Mass for Evan at Farm Street Church on Saturday 7 May 1949.

[490] *Saying life. The Memoirs of Sir Francis Rose*. Cassell. (1961).

[491] Ibid.

[492] Ibid.

[493] Taken from a handwritten note in the Tredegar House file on Evan.

[494] Hartmann, Cyril, Unpublished Memoirs p.182.

[495] Note in Tredegar House file from "*Luf ex Francis Giles, Newport Rotary Club*". dated 19 December 1978.

[496] Among these friends was Cecil Roberts, who describes his impressions of Berlin and provides insider knowledge of the *Night of the Long Knives* in *Sunshine and Shadow*, the fourth volume of his Memoirs. Another lying low in Germany was the poet Robert Nichols, whose marriage was on the rocks (Evan had been a witness with Tommy Earp at the wedding in 1922). Nichols was living in Munich. Cecil Roberts also refers to Nichols in *Sunshine and Shadow* describing him as "*neurotic.*"

[497] gentlemanspy.blogspot.com/2012/10/dramatis-personae-no.html

[498] Norman Douglas by Constantine FitsGibbon Encounter, September 1974 pp23-37.

[499] Munthe Gustaf and Uexkull, Gudrun. *The Story of Axel Munthe*. John Murray (1953)

[500] Possibly named after the opera singer Adelina Patti (1843-1919) who retired to Swansea, South Wales.

[501] Evan was a friend of motor racing driver/ ace Prince Birabongse Bhanudej Bhanubandh (1914-1985), better known as Prince Bira of Siam (Thailand) The Prince (whose grandfather was King of Siam) studied art in Britain. A wonderful bronze sculpture of Evan (by Bira) (commissioned for Evan's 50th birthday, in 1943) is on display in Tredgear House, Newport. A photograph of Evan, Bira and the sculpture is in *The Prince & I : My Life with Prince Bira of Siam* by Princess Ceril Birabongse. Veloce Publishing PLC. (1998).

[502] Evan had met Munthe as far back as 1925 (he is referred to by Evan's friend Cyril Hughes Hartmann in his Memoirs as being at a gathering with Evan and Munthe in the summer of 1925). Dr Axel Martin Fredrik Munthe, (1857-1949) CVO, of Swedish birth, a fashionable doctor in Paris and Rome. A great eccentric " *possessed a genuinely healing power of sympathy*". According to his obituary in *The Times* on 12 February 1949 *"In Rome, where he lived in Keats house and had an equally large and fashionable practice, he drove through the streets in a red-wheeled Victoria drawn by a pair of splendid Hungarian horses, with a Lapland dog sitting by his side."*

[503] Munthe Gustaf and Uexkull, Gudrun. *The Story of Axel Munthe*. John Murray (1953)

[504] Ibid.

[505] http://www.loc.gov/pictures/item/2005675730/ According to Angus L Bowmar in *" As I remember , Adam: An autobiography of a festival."* Oregon Shakespearean Festival Association (1975) ..*" To demonstrate to the rest of the world the solidarity of the Axis [between Germany and Italy] [Hitler] in preparation for his own visit.. sent Hermann Goering to Italy in January 1937. In the natural course of things the General was sent to Capri for a few days of relaxation…"*

[506] In 1929 Munthe published *The Story of San Michele*. One of the best selling memoirs of all time.

[507] *The Irish Times* records at least eight visits to Ireland – mainly to Dublin during 1946-48. Augustus John records in a letter in 1948 *"Evan Morgan, at Renvyle, wants the parish priest to receive his staff into the RC church."*

[508] See National Archives of Ireland 'Office of the Secretary to the President' NA reference number: PRES 1/P 2913 Original reference number: P 2913 Description: Viscount Tredegar: personal file Date: Oct 1946-Aug 1948.

[509] Friend, Donald. *The Diaries of Donald Friend : 1967-1999.* National Library of Australia. (2006).

[510] Ibid.

[511] Ibid.

[512] Cynthia Jebb, Lady Gladwyn (1898-1990). Wife of a notable diplomat and ambassador. See Jebb Miles [Ed] *The Diaries of Cythia Gladwyn.* Constable. (1991).

[513] Marochetti died in a London hospital on 18 August 1952. He " *touched life at many points*".

[514] Quoted by Evan in the inaugural Tredegar Memorial Lecture in memory of his father) at the Royal Society of Literature on 29 January 1936.

[515] Norman Parkes of The Temple, London, Barrister-at-law- died 30 July 1949. *The Times* of 2 August 1949 said " *we announce with regret the death of Mr Norman Parkes, the well known barrister."*

[516] Sir Walter Monckton (1891-1965). GCVO, KCMG, MC, PC Advocate and politician. 1st Viscount Monckton of Brenchley.
[517] Russell Wilkinson, KCVO, MRCS, LRCP, (died 1968 aged 80). Society and Royal doctor, including to the Princess Royal (Duchess of Fife) and Prince and Princess Arthur of Connaught. See Obituary *The Times* 28 December 1968.
[518] Sir Edmund Ivens Spriggs (1871-1949). British physician and physiologist.

THANKS AND ACKNOWLEDGEMENTS

The authors graciously acknowledge the various sources and/or authors of material quoted in the text etc and their respective custodians, publishers and copyright holders. Such quotes used have been kept modest and incidental. Care has been taken *not* to exceed the spirit of the copyright principles laid down in the respective *"Permissions and Fair Dealing"* guidelines in terms of the limits under the criteria for *"the purposes of criticism or review"*. In the majority of instances - and this is reflected in the End Notes - full attribution has been made to material that has been consulted and or used. All extracts used are considered legitimate and/ or allowable under exemption or expiry provisions of UK/ EU copyright.

Besides which the book is published with no gain or profit envisaged by the authors and to extend the public knowledge of the whole life of Evan Frederic Morgan, Viscount Tredegar, and to reflect and review, and lay down with as much truth and accuracy as possible and for the essential sake of history, his life and times.

The authors wish to thank (in alphabetical order) David Beevers, David Freeman and Emily Price, formers Curators of Tredegar House, the National Trust and Newport City Council and for providing access to correspondence, photographs, images and publications referred to or reproduced herein including those in the Tredegar Archives files at Tredegar House.

Considerable thanks are also extended to the Staff at Newport City Reference Library, for their help and support and for allowing access to their files, in particular for granting access to back copies of South Wales newspapers.

Others who stand out in giving help and support and inspiration to this book are Evan's cousins Alan Carnegie Stewart (and his wife

Zoe), Jane Budgett (and her daughters) Michelle Metz (and her late husband Christopher) and Lord Southesk.

Special thanks also go to Tom Dart, Angela Evans, and Susan Woolford. The authors also wish to thank the staff at the University of Wales, Newport, the Friends of Tredegar House, Paul Busby, Goff Morgan, Steve Sully and Derw Thomas.

None of the individuals named here have had *any* part in the process to reproduce the manuscript in book form, that is entirely the authors responsibility and culpability.

Among the public records to acknowledge is the material in Crown Copyright extracted from National Archives, Kew. Thanks are due to the staff of the British Library, London. The authors acknowledge the kind permission of other UK etc repositories and collections, including the National Library of Wales, and Internet sources named in the End Notes or individuals or bodies otherwise (unintentionally) omitted.

The opinions in the text are the authors alone. Also any errors in action or implied in the text etc are the authors alone. They welcome corrections, with sources and any additional data to include in any future version of the book. They also thank Newspaper Archive.com, Abe Books, Amazon Books, Google Books, Tredegar House Archives, Somerset Archives, The British Library, including the Newspaper Library. Finally, they record considerable thanks to their spouses, family and fellow writers at NYO. Also last but not least thanks to Evan Frederic Morgan, the last Viscount Tredegar.

About the Authors

Monty Dart is a writer, archivist and researcher. She was educated in Army Schools in Hong Kong, Germany and Wales. She is a researcher for HTV and BBC Wales and BBC radio on local subjects and an authority on the Morgan woman of Tredegar House.

Monty is the author of '*Who Killed Dripping Lewis? The unsolved murder in Pontypool in 1939*' and co-author (with William Cross) of ' *A Beautiful Nuisance: The Life and Death of Hon. Gwyneth Ericka Morgan*' both these books were published by Book Midden in 2012.

William Cross (Will) is the author of many articles and booklets on Scottish history and genealogy topics. A Fellow of the Society of Antiquaries of Scotland since 1984, he is an authority on the Morgan women of Tredegar House. He is also a member of the Society of Authors. Will has written three books on the life and times of Almina, 5th Countess of Carnarvon and is co-author with Monty Dart of '*A Beautiful Nuisance : The Life and Death of Hon. Gwyneth Ericka Morgan*'. He is also author of '*Lordy! Tutankhamun's Patron As a Young Man*' a retrospective on the childhood and youth of the 5th Earl of Carnarvon.

Contact William Cross at williecross@aol.com

Other Titles From Book Midden Publishing

The Life and Secrets of Almina Carnarvon : A Candid Biography of Almina, 5th Countess of Carnarvon. 3rd Edition . ISBN 9781905914081

Lady Carnarvon's Nursing Homes: Nursing the Privileged in Wartime and Peace. ISBN 9781905914036

The Dustbin Case : Dennistoun versus Dennistoun ISBN 9781905914043

Lordy! Tutankhamun's Patron As A Young Man. ISBN 9781905914050

A Beautiful Nuisance by Monty Dart and William Cross. ISBN 9781905914104

Daphne's Story : The Long Journey from the Red Brick Building by Daphne Condon. ISBN 9781905914128

Steaming Light : by Bernard Pearson. ISBN 9781905914135

Who Killed Dripping Lewis? The unsolved murder in Pontypool in 1939. By Monty Dart. ISBN 9781905914197.

The Dancing Countess of Carnarvon: Tilly Losch & Her Husbands. By William Cross ISBN 9781905914098   [To be published 2013.]

The Five Ladies Tredegar by Monty Dart and William Cross. ISBN 9781905914203. [To be published 2013.]